solo

Women Singer-Songwriters

In Their

Own

Words

solo

Women Singer-Songwriters

In Their Own Words

Edited by
MARC WOODWORTH

Photography by
EMMA DODGE HANSON

Delta
Trade Paperbacks

A Delta Book
Published by
Dell Publishing
a division of
Bantam Doubleday Dell
Publishing Group, Inc.
1540 Broadway
New York,
New York 10036

Library of Congress Cataloging in Publication Data
Solo : women singer-songwriters in their own words / [edited] by
    Marc Woodworth and [photos by] Emma Dodge Hanson.
        p.   cm.
    ISBN 0-385-32407-3
    1. Women singers.   2. Women composers.   3. Popular
music — History and criticism.   I. Woodworth, Marc.
    ML385.S593   1998
    782.42'082 — dc21   98-9599
                                                        CIP
                                                        MN

Design concept by Kelly Hitt
Book dummy by Ellen Cipriano

Manufactured in the United States of America
Published simultaneously in Canada

September 1998

10   9   8   7   6   5   4   3

FFG

For Jenny: You bring us joy.

table of CONTENTS

INTROduction

Ani DIFRANCO

Suffused by the glaring light of a follow spot that leaves everything outside its incendiary circle in darkness, Ani DiFranco is playing to a full house comprised mostly of young women as revved up as their styles are eclectic: alternacool, hippie, punk, and every hybrid that could conceivably emerge if you crossed those disparate strains of fashion and identity. Turquoise cornrows trailing down her back, leather hip-huggers setting the fourteen-year-old girls in the front rows shrieking, this most independent of solo artists, whose passionate, genre-defying albums have sold a million and a half copies on her own label, Righteous Babe Records, never upholds a party line on anything. Yet she's delivering a verse from a song called "Not a Pretty Girl" that could be an anthem for any number of artists caught in the current women in music media blitz: "I am not an angry girl / but it seems like / I've got everyone fooled."

Reducing women artists to a category—whether "angry women" or "sensitive singer-songwriters"—is a dismissal of their wide-ranging achievements as thoughtless as the complaint which Jonatha Brooke, formerly of The Story and now on her own, has heard one too many times: there's a glut of female artists now. "There's room for all of us," she counters; "everyone has such a unique way of saying things that the question of being redundant is just a ridiculous and hateful industry concoction." A claim like that takes on the certainty of a hard fact when you consider the range represented by Ani DiFranco and Mary Chapin Carpenter, Sheryl Crow and Suzanne Vega, Dionne Farris and Jewel, Lucy Kaplansky and Cassandra Wilson, Joan Osborne and Sarah McLachlan. This book, collecting as it does the diverse ideas and stories of these gifted songwriters and performers, is proof that there is, as Jonatha Brooke would have it, plenty of room for them all. *Solo* provides the space for each artist to exercise her singular way of saying things.

Why should we assume that the experiences of Suzanne Vega, who

Sheryl CROW

grew up in East Harlem to the taunts of "You're the whitest girl I've ever seen," and those of Kate Campbell, who was raised as the daughter of a socially progressive Baptist preacher in rural Mississippi, would somehow say the same things? And the musical allegiances are all over the map as well: from Cassandra Wilson's obsession with her father's Miles Davis records to Lucy

Kaplansky's immersion in the late seventies Greenwich Village folk revival when she was still a teenager; from Sheryl Crow's apprenticeship in her college band Cashmere (think of Led Zeppelin's "Kashmir" rather than fifties sweaters) to Lucinda Williams's childhood diet of sixties rock and protest music brought into the house by her father's poetry students in New Orleans. It's this rich variety that defines these women who have so masterfully responded to their worlds with indelible takes on what it means to be human.

These artists are far more serious about their work than they are generally given credit for, however much their music is lauded, and more insightful about subjects as far-flung as politics, aesthetics, and love, both in and outside their songs, than we could know from short reviews crowded under attention-grabbing headlines. Whether it's Dionne Farris speaking about the limitations she's faced ("Being real is even more difficult for black musicians because there's less tolerance for the ones who defy the few established musical categories available to them") or Jewel reflecting on her unexpected celebrity ("Fame exists in other people's minds. I can't experience my own fame at all, but I experience it in other people's eyes when I look at them and see that they're scared"), the depth, intelligence, and self-searching expressed here

JEWEL

are the sources, in such eclectic and provocative ways, for the music itself. It's no surprise that the writers who give our own emotions and experiences shape through their songs convey such substance and insight, as if implicitly rejecting the skewed values of a pop world more likely to notice a steel brassiere than a literate turn of phrase.

And so, while there isn't anything like a consistent viewpoint that binds these artists together, they're all undeniably gifted writers who have found a way—by an often circuitous, sometimes agonizing route—to make brilliant use of their gifts. Their stories are often about that process. While the experiences recounted here were often difficult (Rosanne Cash recalls a childhood bleak as the desert landscape around her California home while Mary Lou Lord recounts the loneliness she felt as the last and late child in a large family with parents who worked opposite shifts), often the most alienating experiences have been turned to some form of redemption.

Every artist included here has served an intense apprenticeship, experiential and aesthetic, that led to an affirmation, however attenuated by dark introspection or nagging self-doubt, of what she can do. After abandoning a promising career as a singer to earn a doctorate and practice psychology, Lucy Kaplansky took years to return to her gift—writing and singing beautifully crafted and wholly original songs—with a passion made keener by her time away. Or think of what Jewel calls her midlife crisis at eighteen that left her feeling that "living hand to mouth, all our pride gone" might not be worth it. Instead of giving in to that thought, she dropped out of everything she'd known to live in her van and write songs, a risk that allowed her to locate the value of her existence.

Stories like Jewel's and Lucy Kaplansky's, however different, however singular, animate the narratives in this book. All the artists here, like Shawn Colvin, whose half-accepting, half-rueful song "The Story" asserts, "I am nobody's wife / I gave nobody life / And I seem to be nobody's daughter," have made their own way. Each of them has created a body of work that has the power to move us, to ring true, in a variety of ways. Think of any number of these unfaltering voices trying to get at the evolving complexities of the relationship between men and women or how being a woman does or doesn't define them. The artists here take on subjects as widely varied as identity politics (Dionne Farris's "Human"), low-down pleasures (Sheryl Crow's "All I Wanna Do"), the music industry (Ani DiFranco's "Blood in the Boardroom"), the state of our souls (Jewel's "Who Will Save Your Soul"), and romantic obsession (Sarah McLachlan's "Possession").

The musicians presented here in natural, introspective photographs and their own words drawn from in-depth, candid conversations don't share anything like an ethos, a single way of looking at the world or a party line. They are all, however, their own people. As Ani DiFranco ends "Not a Pretty

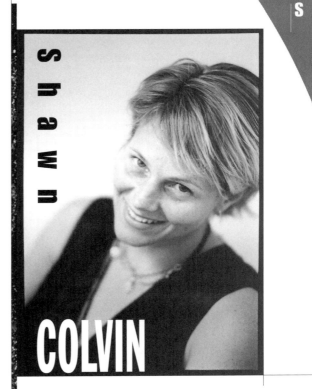

Shawn COLVIN

Girl" to a roar of nearly violent accord, her insistence that she won't be defined by anyone—"I am not a damsel in distress"; "I am not an angry girl"—makes it clear that the extraordinary ability she shares with the other artists in *Solo* to make her solitude, her singularity, a strength is an extraordinary kind of self-possession.

—Marc Woodworth

solo

Women Singer-Songwriters

In Their
Own
Words

Sarah MCLACHLAN

I'm attracted to all kinds of beauty — erotic beauty, natural beauty. I'm fascinated by the human body and psyche as well as our spirituality, which I find very sensual too. I tend to experience the world in an intuitive way. I'm drawn to the tangible, to touch, the sensation of swimming in the warm ocean, of being naked and lying near the water, nobody around for miles, the perfect freedom to do whatever you want, to make love in the sun.

Writing for me is also sensual and instinctive. That's the only way I know how to do it. Initially the process is very unconscious. Usually a song comes directly from what I'm going through or something a friend is experiencing. That's the starting point. From there I need to find a center — an image, a voice — which can bring together all the elements that particular experience brings up.

I love music and art that show a person's duality, the beauty and the ugliness each one of us has within ourselves. To be able to love both of those aspects is a real challenge. If you succeed, you find harmony. Nature is a perfect example of the harmony between the beautiful and the brutal. You turn over a pretty rock and there are worms writhing underneath. I try to write lyrics like that. "Possession" is the most obvious example: "I'll kiss you so hard, I'll take your breath away." On the surface it seems like a love song, but if you choose to look at the other side, it's actually quite violent.

Ultimately I write everything out of my own experience. It's all I can draw from that's real and tangible. I can look through other people's eyes and try to put myself in their place, try to feel what they're feeling, to be empathetic, but finally I have to bring my own experience to the writing. On one level "Possession" is about somebody else, but I'm putting myself into that voice. I'm able to do that because I've also been obsessed, if to a lesser degree.

I can only write a song if I'm able to relate on some level to the emotion it conveys. Often putting myself into a character allows me the freedom to be more ruthless. I can let my ugly side out more easily when I hide behind a persona. We all create masks for ourselves, and I've done that in songs too. We've just got to *remember* they're masks.

With the songs on *Surfacing*, I tried not to hide behind anything. If something is ugly, it's *me* being ugly rather than a character I'm speaking through. In therapy I've been learning to love even the parts of myself that aren't so nice. As a result, my writing tends to be more straightforward. Not all the lyrics have so many layers. Some of the recent songs are little rooms while in the past they've been mazes.

Writing often comes solely from my own need to work something out. It's a selfish act. People ask me what I mean by a particular line. I tell them that what I mean is only for me. When I'm asked why I wrote a particular song, some people want me to answer, "Because I broke up with my boyfriend, who treated me like shit." Sorry, I'm not going there with a person I don't know that well. My life is a soap opera for myself and my close friends—nobody else.

When I'm done writing a song, it becomes a gift to anyone who wants it. If you respond to it, it's yours. Then you have to take it into yourself and choose what you want from it. That's what's important, not what it means to me. The empathy of the spoken or sung word can be incredibly powerful if it relates something that's important to you. At some point we all need to hear our own thoughts resonating in another person's words so we can understand that each of us is not alone. If that empathy comes across on an emotional level, which is the level on which I write, then the private act of writing can make something happen beyond yourself.

So as a musician I think of a song as the generous product of selfishness, and as a human being I feel the word *selfish* gets a bad rap. If people were a little more ruthless about following their own desires, not to the point of stomping on other people to get what they want but in taking the time to figure out what they need, they'd be a hell of a lot happier. The light that comes from that kind of "selfishness" would shine, as opposed to what happens when decisions are based on what other

> **Nature is a perfect example of the harmony between the beautiful and the brutal. You turn over a pretty rock and there are worms writhing underneath.**

people want for us or what we *think* other people want for us. If you only try to please others, you're going to resent those people you're trying to please, the ones who are often closest to you. If you choose a path that you yourself want to take, then you're going to be much kinder to the people in your life.

Think about the typical patriarchal marriage of the 1950s. The husband goes out and gets a job because he has a wife and two kids. Even though he hates that job, he feels stuck because he thinks of himself primarily as a provider for his family. He starts to resent his wife and kids because he gave up what he really wanted to do, to be a poet, for example. He doesn't consider that his wife and child would be a lot happier if he had become a poet because making that choice would have allowed him to love them more. In that sense I think the value of selfishness is underestimated.

My mother loves literature and wanted to be a writer but didn't get her master's degree when she was young. Instead she dropped out to put my dad through his Ph.D. program. I wish she could have continued with her writing and literary studies, but once she decided to put my dad through school and have kids those commitments ate up all of her time and energy. For many years she was so far away from those passions that it seemed impossible for her to go back to them. Recently, though, she returned to get her master's. I think it's fantastic that she came back to what she loved.

I was the youngest and the only daughter in my family. I have two older brothers. Because I was the only girl, I wasn't allowed to do anything. There was a serious double standard operating in our household. It was okay for my brothers to run around at all hours because they were boys, but if I went out, my parents thought I would automatically be raped, of course, so I was kept under lock and key. My brothers got caught doing every stupid thing when they were adolescents, so by the time I came along my parents knew all the tricks and I couldn't get away with anything.

My mom and I were one another's best friends when I was growing up. I wasn't very popular at school, so I didn't have many close friends there, and I was practically my mother's only friend. When I was fourteen or fifteen, our relationship was complicated by my desire to become my own person. For a while my mother didn't have as much faith in my choices or my ability to take care of myself as I wanted her to have. That's probably why I'm so adamant now about focusing on trust in relationships. Learning to trust is essential to everything, whether I'm raising my dog or writing songs. The process of songwriting is very much like giving birth to and bringing up a child. You have to nurture it, then give it space and trust in it, allow it to become what it is instead of forcing it in another direction.

Originally my parents wanted all of us to go to university. They were very much into the idea that if you get

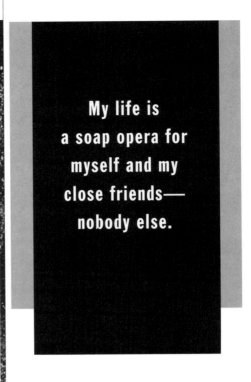

My life is a soap opera for myself and my close friends— nobody else.

your degree, you get a good job. They wanted us to do well. As children of the Depression they went through that period of losing everything, barely scraping by, so they really wanted us to have the comfort zone that came with a good job. But at the same time they very much supported my creativity, both musically and artistically. Until I was seven years old, we lived in the country, but they drove me into Halifax to take

6

classes at the art college every Saturday. Once we moved into town, I started taking music classes too. My parents really saw that my joy was in the arts, making music, drawing, entertaining. I looked at those activities as escapism then. When I sang and played, I'd get completely lost in what I was doing. During that time I was no longer this stupid, useless little ten-year-old who didn't have any friends; I was someplace else where none of that could touch me.

I spent a lot of time alone when I was a child, which I didn't mind at all. I felt an instinctual happiness when I was out by myself, lost in my own thoughts—the perfect temperament for an artist, I guess, but I certainly didn't know that then. The older I got, the more I was on the road as a

> **At some point we all need to hear our own thoughts resonating in another person's words so we can understand that each of us is not alone.**

musician, the more I lost that ability to be by myself. I was horrified to be alone because all the stuff that I hadn't been dealing with would bubble up to the surface. I couldn't allow that to happen because I always had to be somewhere or meet someone in an hour or two. I knew if I let that rage out, it would be huge. I'd be a mess. I couldn't deal with those emotions in two months, let alone two hours, so I held them in, and those hours became weeks, months, and years.

But when I was young, I loved to be by myself. I lived quite close to the ocean, and we spent every summer at our lake, so I was in the water all the time. I have strong memories of floating, being underwater, then surfacing. It was a way to shed my skin and come up fresh. Water is the element of emotion, the element I'm most comfortable in. It's another world. It's not our place. We can't breathe there, but we all came from water. *Surfacing* is such a meaty word for me. When I told a friend that I was going to use it for the name of an album, she reminded me that it was the title of a Margaret Atwood book about a woman who goes up into the woods of northern Quebec—a rich connection because that's where I go to write and record.

I don't remember having too many physical fears as a kid. We lived in a pretty good neighborhood in Halifax, very middle class, and I knew most of the kids. The city was relatively safe then, and I walked the five blocks to elementary school on my own. I was, however, terrified of adults. I thought of myself as completely separate from them. When it came to adults, I had no voice of my own. Every adult seemed like an absolute ruler to me. Now I see kids at the age I was then who are capable of saying, "Fuck you, bitch," when I try to break up a fight. I think, "I'm an adult. How can you talk to me like that? God, you have so much gall." I couldn't have imagined ever talking back to an adult, let alone saying

> When I sang and played, I'd get completely lost in what I was doing.
> I was no longer this stupid, useless little ten-year-old who didn't have any friends; I was someplace else where none of that could touch me.

something like that. I didn't like confrontation; I've always been that way. In junior high, especially, I got picked on a lot because I wanted so desperately to fit in that I stuck out like a sore thumb. I was picked on mercilessly by one girl, Laura, in particular, who was really nasty. She helped mold me into who I am. I guess I can thank her for that now.

Women talk a lot about how horrible it was for them to grow up in this culture, but I think men had it just as bad in a lot of ways. Men are raised with fathers as role models. What happens when those men are withdrawn and don't express any emotions, if they tell their sons not to be crybabies? The poor guys who have to grow up like that. We're all emotional beasts, and if you're told to deny that fact, then the wall you build up by the time you're eighteen is so high that it's very hard to break down, to achieve your capacity as a human, feeling person. So what men experience is just a different set of trials. Adolescence is the most horrendous stage to go through for everyone.

Despite my parents' academic ambitions for me, after I'd failed math enough times, they realized I wasn't going to be a scientist. It became clear that such a goal was pointless. I'd always say, "Mom, I'm going to be a musician or an artist; I don't need this." My mother would be aghast: "You're going to university, young lady. You're going to get a real job, and you're not going to be dependent on any man." To a large degree my mother raised us. My father was gone a lot, traveling, and even when he was home, he was on the periphery. My mother made it clear to me that I should not be dependent on anyone; that's one really beautiful thing she taught me. She didn't want to see me in a marriage where the husband was making all the money and had all the power and control. Her lesson has probably made me into more of a control freak than I need to be although I'm learning to let some of that go.

By high school it was clear that my passion was music. Even so, when I was in eleventh grade, my parents wouldn't let me accept a record company's offer to come to Vancouver for six weeks and test the waters as a singer and performer. My mother said, "Not a chance. You're failing math, young lady, and you're going to stay in school." After high school, though, they let me go to art college. The record company came back to offer me a five-record contract after I'd finished my first year at art school. At that point, even though I loved my classes, I couldn't turn the offer down. I knew if I didn't try it, I'd regret it for the rest of my life. I never really looked back after that.

When I left home for Vancouver at eighteen, things got better between my mother and me, in part because of the physical space between us. I came home almost a year later, still alive, looking very healthy and happy, with my first record in hand, something to show for my time away. That was a pivotal point for my mother. She could

My mother made it clear to me that I should not be dependent on anyone; that's one really beautiful thing she taught me.

breathe a sigh of relief after worrying so much that I was going to be ruined, turn into a drug addict. The only thing she knew about the music industry was what she read in the papers after some rock star OD'd. When I came back safe and sound, she was able to relax. She really liked my record and began to feel that she could let me go a little bit. She

was proud of me. It was really healthy for her to see that someone she had raised turned out well, that I wasn't a complete fuckup anyway.

More recently my relationship with my family has become even stronger. It's easy to try to blame other people for your problems. It's all too common to think that something your parents did messed you up instead of taking responsibility for yourself. Our society is based on blame to such a large degree. One of the goals of the therapy I'm in is to break this pattern of blame. I don't want to live life as a victim. Until you stop blaming other people, you can't move beyond the pain. There's an age of awareness now that's really refreshing. It seems very touchy-feely at first, but if you

> We have the capacity and ability to change our reality. Even in all the shit and tragedy of life, there are beautiful lessons if only we can see them.

learn to use a few simple tools, you can help yourself get away from all that blame. Once I saw these tools work, I understood that they were really powerful. It's as simple as thinking back to the first time you were told you were worthless, revisiting that feeling as an adult, and giving yourself emotionally what you needed then.

It's also about empathy. Look at your mother, and put yourself in her shoes. Look at her life, where she's at, what she's given up, and *be* her. How does she feel? By doing that, you can forgive a person whom you felt really messed you up in the past. If you can come to the point where you can say, "I love you for all your fucked-up-ness because it's not your fault," it sets you free. When I did this with my parents, they completely changed in my eyes. Of course they hadn't done anything differently, but I understood them differently. Because I took responsibility for myself, by saying I'm the only one who has the responsibility to change, our relationship was completely transformed. We have the capacity and ability to change our reality. Even in all the shit and tragedy of life, there are beautiful lessons if only we can see them.

I've also come out of my cocoon about feminism in the past few years. Before that, I used to say, "Oh, no, I've never seen sexism in the music industry." Since then I've

> **Putting together a tour to celebrate women is still threatening to some people. There are men who assume we're going to be up there onstage calling for women to chop off their penises.**

opened my eyes. *Fumbling Towards Ecstasy* came out around the same time as Tori Amos's *Under the Pink,* and radio stations pitted us against one another. They'd say, "We added Tori to the playlist this week, so we can't add Sarah." Why in the world would we be competing with one another in someone's mind? It's so marginalizing. Radio programmers, like other people in the industry, don't always think clearly when it comes to women. Too often they blindly follow old rules. I discovered the same thing about some promoters when I wanted Paula Cole to open for me on a tour. We got a lot of flak. They'd say, "You can't put two women on a single bill." Why not? Are we going to have catfights backstage? What are they worried about? Again, I think it was an example of not thinking about what they were saying, just following conventional wisdom. To automatically assume just because two performers are women that they're exactly the same is a good example of the sexism in the music world.

A big part of putting together the Lilith Fair Festival with all women artists was to prove this kind of thinking wrong, to show that we are not going to be marginalized. There's a beautiful abundance of women in music out there who are incredibly diverse. You can't ignore that. Most of the media and press have been great about Lilith Fair, but some still ask those marginalizing questions like "Are you worried that an all-woman bill isn't going to get the draw?" The people who ask that aren't really thinking about what they're saying. Just look who's on this bill. Put any of these people on their own tour by themselves, and they'd do just fine.

If you can't wrap your brain around this concept, just go look at how many tickets each of these artists sells by herself. Don't worry about us. We'll be just fine, thanks. So the motivation for setting up the tour was, to a degree, reactionary, a response to all these backwards attitudes, but the reasons were also selfish: I never get to see a lot of the artists I love play live; I almost never have the opportunity to sit down and talk with a musical peer who's a woman, who's gone through similar experiences. I feel very alone in the music industry as a woman. I wanted to create an opportunity for us to come together.

Despite the soundness of all those reasons, putting together a tour to celebrate women—and thereby excluding men—is still threatening to some people. There are men who assume we're going to be up there onstage calling for women to chop off their penises. Instead of being angry at that response, I try to remember that men have had just as hard a time as women in a lot of

ways. At least that's what I feel when I'm trying not to blame them for having that reaction. Look, I'm a human being. I'm also very much a woman who's becoming a feminist in many ways. Being a woman plays an important role in my work because I'm writing from that emotional point of view. A lot of what I write about comes from my experience in a world dominated by men. That's the world I grew up in. But I still think of myself as a humanist above and beyond anything else.

I knew from the time I was very young, from somewhere deep inside, that I had a calling. I knew it was an artistic calling although I didn't know at first if it was musical, theatrical, or visual. Increasingly the music I listened to expressed the things I found difficult to express. Physically and psychologically, whatever's in the combination of rhythm, tone, and words is powerful. I responded to that power early on. I always knew there was something in music that was important to me.

I was lucky that my parents appreciated music. My father, who played the guitar and banjo, taught me to play, which provided an important musical outlet. I also got something real out of his record collection: the Kingston Trio, Pete Seeger, Josh White. My father's records were a big influence, but after a certain point they weren't *killing* me,

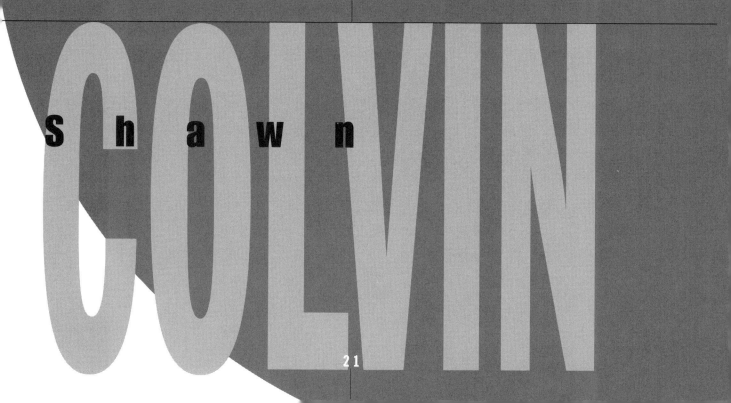

Shawn COLVIN

you know? But the Beatles *killed* me. The first record I ever bought for myself was *Meet the Beatles*. I was in fourth grade. I bought that record at the drugstore. The "woman" who sold it to me—she couldn't have been more than fifteen—took my money and said, "Play it all night." I'll never forget that. I was so embarrassed. There was something going on between me and the Beatles, something that was beyond my age. I was in *love* with these guys, like so many of us were. When we watched them on TV, I was mortified that my family knew what I was feeling but not so mortified that I wouldn't watch.

Even though I was a girl in love

I felt a violent need to be honest to the bone, and it struck me that honesty was being suppressed everywhere I looked: at school, in church, at home.

with the Beatles, I wanted to be a boy so I could *be* a Beatle too. The contradiction didn't concern me. Somehow I got hold of these Beatle boots—or the closest you could get to Beatle boots in South Dakota. If I were to look at them now, I'd probably laugh. At least they were short and black. I also had my mother's leather car coat and a pair of my brother's Levi's. Wearing those straight-legged pants, my mother's car coat, and the boots made me feel hot and very Beatlesy. I would go walking on our property—we lived out in the country—and fantasize about the Beatles, pretend to be a Beatle. I'd spend hours off alone daydreaming about all that while walking our land.

I don't think it's necessarily odd for a kid to like solitude. The recognition that you need to commune with yourself, as it were, starts really early. And if you recognize that need, the lack of solitude might make you even more sensitive to it. The natural world around water. I recently moved into a house across the street from a lake, which was always a dream I had. I

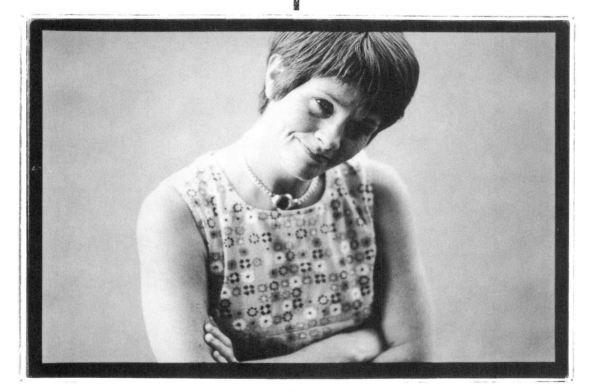

was consoling. Being on the lake, in the water, or out in the country was bliss for me. It still is. A good day for my soul is to be also found pleasure as a kid sitting alone by the record player or drawing—I really loved to draw. I liked it when everybody was out of the house. I would pretend to sing in front of the mirror with the record player going. I remember having carefree, blissful moments, but they were very hard won.

We didn't talk about artistic expression in my family. We were good, conservative midwesterners. I was expected to be a good person and a good woman in a Christian sense, which meant being polite and feminine, not making waves. From the very beginning, those qualities didn't feel natural to me. I felt a violent need to be honest to the bone, and it struck me that honesty was being suppressed everywhere I looked: at school, in church, at home. It seemed like everybody was wearing a mask.

Nevertheless, I still very much wanted my family's, especially my mother's, approval, yet—and I'm sure I'm far from alone in this—one of the uncomfortable things about growing up is knowing there's no way you're going to meet those expectations. I wish I could talk to my grandmothers about my family. They both died before I had any appreciation

of the fact that they were the parents of my parents, that they had information and were more than grandmas. I don't expect they would necessarily give me the answers I'd want, but I'd like to see things through their eyes, to look at my parents when they were young, to see my mother when she was fifteen or twenty. But it's more likely that if that wish came true, I'd end up like Emily Webb in *Our Town,* who, after she dies, begs to go back home for a day and returns only to find that life there is just too mundane. Nobody understands the importance of their lives, and she wants them to realize the enormity of everything. Instead it's like "Get the hell down to breakfast." But that's life. So, without more perspective, I can only report what I experienced. I had a lot of disdain for the value system in our family. I couldn't hide it. My big brother was the typical good child, and so I rebelled against that ideal like any good second child will do.

But I wasn't a problem child per se in terms of being wild. I just didn't belong, and I was dissatisfied. I really resented authority. I thought everyone was full of shit. I was never a juvenile delinquent out to make trouble, wreck or steal things, get bombed. None of that interested me. My father *had* been a

juvenile delinquent. He was a reformed rebel, and I probably sensed that. The adventurous things we did, or any exhibition of open-mindedness, I sensed were okay through my dad—but not very often. So I wasn't a delinquent, but I was very ornery and angry in my family. I've always thought of myself as a moral person, but what my family deemed moral I thought of as appearances. That really pissed

I was a chickenshit rather than a badass. I never wanted to be tough. I know I lack that essential ingredient of a rock and roller.

me off. I was a self-centered, pissed-off kid, and there were a lot of messed-up things about me, but the essential inability to put up with a bunch of bullshit—that never went away. I still feel that way.

Morally speaking, I don't feel that much has changed. Morality comes from empathy. I always understood that. It came naturally to me. But the values I was brought up with didn't have anything to do with that fact. Instead they were values opposed to the human condition. That seemed absurd to me. I just didn't get it. They seemed like laws out of a book, absolute rules handed down, mostly through the church, and that really drove me crazy.

School came easily enough to me so that I could get my work out of the way and devote all my energy to music and theater. I really hated school, but I was a chickenshit rather than a badass. I never wanted to be tough. I know I lack that essential ingredient of a rock and roller. I *know* I do. As a musician, it's very frustrating to grow up in the sixties and seventies and find yourself missing that ingredient. Whatever gift I was given, the essentials of rock and roll are not there in my musical talent or in my attitude. There's something else there that's really important but I was never a badass, as a kid or as a musician. That's why Joni Mitchell was so important to me. When I first heard her, I knew that here was somebody who felt one thing and then another, just like I did. That's what made sense to me: feeling all kinds of different things and analyzing the hell out of them. In Joni Mitchell's songs, for all the feeling, you never get the sense that someone's simply opening her veins and bleeding all over you because the writing is so amazing. There is something very inviting, poetic, and beautiful about her work. But her music is defined by feeling and analysis rather than a rock and roll attitude. Because of that, she was really important to me. I didn't understand Dylan until much later, when I listened to *Blood on the Tracks* and then went

crazy over his early records as well. When I was a kid, I thought of him as political, and I was too young to get it. I knew "Blowin' in the Wind" and "The Times They Are A-Changing"—I played those songs when I was learning the guitar—but they had a political edge I was afraid of.

But I was scared of everything. I was scared all the time. I was scared of pain, mental anguish, being alone, thunder, and especially dying. When I was younger, four or five, I reasoned that if I died, I was just going to get out of it. I thought, *If I die and they put me in this box, I'm just going to open the lid.* But then I thought, *Maybe you can't think when you die.* So I asked my mother, "Can you think when you die?" She just looked at me and said no. That was *not* the right answer, but that's all she said. She wasn't willing to expound, so things didn't look good for my escape from death theory. It seemed pretty bleak.

Junior high was really miserable for me. I had just started to get my footing in one town when we moved to another one. That threw me. It took me a couple years to land back on my feet, and when I did, starting about freshman year in high school, music had become hugely important to me. I was pretty good. I could do a lot with the guitar for a fourteen-year-old. That was my identity. Those were good years. The summer after my freshman year, I met a guy a year or two older than me, a wonderful person, a Christian Scientist. He was my

boyfriend for about four years. Between the two of us and some other people I knew in school, I had some of the greatest times of my life. I was part of a group of artistic, dramatic adolescents. We had a wonderful time. It was very rich for me. We were cool people. We were good to each other. We were hungry for life. We cared deeply about a lot of things and about each other, and I felt a lot during that time. It was all about my friends, and it was all about music. I take that for granted, but I think for a lot of other girls those years were more about boyfriends and drinking. I was around those kinds of people too, but I had my role, along with a few others, and it was to entertain. That's what I did. I never questioned that role and was completely secure in it.

> **Giving up that addiction was the springboard into adult thinking. I realized that everything was a choice. The world was an open book. Nothing was the same after that.**

But many years later what made me think of chucking it all and quitting music for good had a lot to do with the role I'd had since high school. What made me stop playing was probably one of the few true epiphanies I've ever come to. I didn't stop because I was disillusioned with the business or because I had been burned. I was always very lucky as a working musician. I could always get a job. I had enough people and other musicians appreciating what I was doing to feel respected. I worked hard for not a lot of money, but I never got turned down. I'd move to a town, look for work as a musician, and get it. Sometimes I didn't earn enough to pay the rent and I'd have to do something else too, but I always got to play. From the time I was fourteen years old this was my identity. Because of that, a lot of things had gone untended in my soul and in my growth as a person. There were many parts of myself that I'd neglected. The way my identity as a musician had built my ego actually became an obstacle.

How I realized that fact was very simple, really: I had a drinking problem, and I stopped drinking. There were a lot of things that had kept me going, like music, and alcohol was certainly one of them. And I'm glad, for better or worse, I made it to the point when there was no way to survive like that anymore. By giving up something you don't want to give up, it begins to sink in that you're not being made to do anything. That's what happened to me. It was very liberating to see that I was the one who'd put myself in prison. I started to recognize that I was a grown-up person and that there was nobody else responsible for how I acted. Giving up that

addiction was the springboard into adult thinking. It was the first time I'd taken responsibility for what I was doing. I found a lot of meaning in what I had to go through as a result of that process. It was very painful sometimes. I couldn't run from things in the way I was used to running from them. I had to face a lot of things that I had avoided, and because of that, I grew up. I realized that everything was a choice: the people I was with, what I was doing with my life—everything. The world was an open book. Nothing was the same after that.

But here I was, still going to my gigs, not really writing anything (I was afraid to write; I had a two-year period of writing a lot of music when I was sixteen and then just stopped), working on pop music, playing covers, not saying anything that had to do with me. I didn't feel the thrill when I stepped up to the microphone. I was just grappling to make my forty dollars without knowing why I was doing it anymore. I re-

member sitting down after one gig and feeling so sick of it. I wasn't getting anything out of playing anymore. I'd always thought of myself as a musician, but here I was going on-stage, doing the thing that used to mean the world to me, the thing that literally healed me in important ways, and I was bored. So I told myself, *You can stop playing music.* The decision to give up that role felt very right. It was really liberating because I didn't know what was going to be behind the image of myself as a performer. It was as though I said to myself, *Music is another one of your shields. Let's see what you're like when you're not hiding behind it.* Once I saw that, I could say, *Why don't you just quit it?* And I did. I just quit it. Fortunately I was old enough to realize that I had the power to make any choice but young and idealistic enough not to worry about the fact that I had to make a living somehow.

> **The first line— "as a little girl I came down to the water"—came out, and I thought, *What am I talking about?* But I knew I was talking about me.**

For about a year I lived in New York City and acted like I lived in a small town. I went to work every day and came home when I was done. My world was centered on a few important people. There was a lot going on internally, but I felt very free of expectations beyond paying the bills and—I know it sounds like a cliché—getting well. It was enough to have a little place in this world. I only paid attention to what I did, how I acted towards people, and what I thought. It was a relief to focus on those things alone. Up to that time, I had always been trying to prove something. It was such a relief just to quit working so hard to prove myself.

And then one day I asked myself what I was going to think in ten years if I didn't try music again. Answering that question was the second major epiphany of my life. I thought, *Music still moves me, I'm good at it, and I think I have something to give. I should do it.* What I realized was real and obvious. Even now it's easier to believe in the decision behind stopping than the one behind starting again. I still ask myself whether the decision to play again was intuitive, like the decision to stop. But I know it was. I often wonder what would have happened if I hadn't come back to music. I probably could have become happy and fulfilled doing something else, and perhaps the only difference would have been that I would have been stationary rather than moving around so much. Even if I

wasn't doing this, I would still be doing something that draws attention to myself, maybe teaching, where I'd be out there giving a lot of energy, performing in some way. But I think that what my character and personality require is pretty well suited to what I do.

The decision to play again was only the first stage. There was a lot to do after that. I didn't know it then, but it was only half over as far as dues paying went. But I had something new driving me on. I was able to throw out all those notions of having to write a good pop song and get rid of anything that wasn't bare-bones and genuine. I could go back to what really hit me years and years back: the honesty and directness. Forget the pop songs, forget the rock and roll. I needed to play the guitar and sing and get to people in the way that someone like Joni can. I resumed singing with that in mind.

I was trying to write with John Leventhal, who cowrote and produced a lot of *Steady On* and *A Few Small Repairs*. One day I took the music he had made, and instead of writing words to the record-quality track he'd given me, I transposed the song for acoustic guitar, disregarded his melody, and tried to sing words to it. Opening my mouth to do that for the first time was one of the most terrifying things I've ever experienced. The first line—"as a little girl I came down to the water"—came out, and I thought, *What am I talking about?* But I knew I was talking about me. It had happened the right way. I wasn't thinking, *How am I going to write about myself?* Instead the words just came out. That song became "Diamond in the Rough." I called John, said, "I know you're going to tell me this sucks," and played him the first verse. I was prepared to disregard his response because I truly thought he was going to tell me that what I'd written was really stupid or really weird, that he didn't get it. I'm so glad, looking back, that he didn't say any of those things. Instead he said, "There's something going on here. Finish the song."

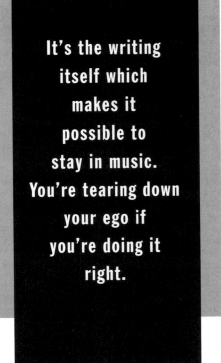

It's the writing itself which makes it possible to stay in music. You're tearing down your ego if you're doing it right.

The songs on *Steady On* were the first I'd written since I was a kid. Though albums and books aren't exactly the same, that first record was like a first novel for me. You put your whole life and experience into it. It contains some very basic and important things. After that, you can loosen up, go into more detail, and write more immediately about what's going on in your life. Still, it's always

ing for somebody to give me a ticket for pretending to be a writer. I've always been the singer. That's how I thought of myself. While singing came too easily, writing is really difficult and scary, but it's fulfilling and gives me purpose.

Part of what makes a good song is honesty. Most of the music that's vital to people is not a walk in the flowers. For me, a song has to contain writing about how things are rather than how they should be. For example, I don't consider myself a strict feminist trying to portray how things ought to look. I don't generally feel the way I would ideally like to feel, so I've got to get past the impulse to dress up reality. As a woman I feel sorry about that sometimes. I might feel apologetic, I might feel weak—all the things that it's too bad women feel given the kind of conditioning that we've had. But as a writer you've got to get past feeling bad about that fact. You have to name what's there.

Being honest, especially as a woman, encourages people to peg you as a type—

hard to write for me because of the esteem I have for great songwriters. It's a big surprise to me that I have a writer's sensibility at all. I still don't believe that one. I'm always wait-

angry or overly confessional. The "angry woman" label just expresses the limitations we place on how women are supposed to be. For a contrast, look at Dylan. There was a pissed-off guy. But we tend to see him in a more complex, more fully human way than we would an equally pissed-off woman. It's much less acceptable for women to express harsh emotions and be seen as part of the bigger picture. It's easier to view men in a way that's broader, more whole. Even though I recognize that tendency, I too fall prey to seeing things that way. If women say certain things, they are described as overly revealing, improper, or impolite. Of course women sometimes use the angry woman position for shock value too. It's a way of hitting people over the head, but commercial motivation aside, somebody's got to do it.

Even though I write very personal songs, I haven't found a situation where I've regretted what I've written. It's fine if listeners identify with my psychological development through my songs. I'm very appreciative when people tell me how they've been moved by my music, but I'm constantly moving on. I don't dwell on the songs I've written. Once I finish a song, my attitude is pretty much "That's

that." It's moving ahead that counts. My need isn't for people to know me and identify with me through the songs. My ego requires certain things, but that kind of identification isn't one of them. It's not that recognition itself isn't important to me; it is—just not in that way. In our society, certainly more now than twenty-five years ago, celebrity has become extremely important. The business of celebrity is weird. I don't consider myself a celebrity, but when I read a magazine article about my work, it's usually steeped in hype. Because I've chosen to be in this business, that's part of the world I live in. You can't ignore it. You're trying to get recognized.

And I have to confess that I'm a pop music lover from way back. If you love the Beatles you've got to appreciate a well-crafted song with commercial appeal. But, in keeping with the recognition that I don't have the essence of a rock and roller, I'm not sure that I have the essence of pop either. I don't think that writing pop songs is necessarily the best thing I do. And there's not so much a desire on my part to write a hit that will sell millions and millions of records and make me famous as there is to write a song that I think enough of, that is so good that it's unstoppable.

I've had the record company decide that certain songs of mine are going to be hits and do things to the production to make them

> It interests me when I see people who haven't been driven by fear and the need to control it. I try to imagine what that would be like.

commercial. I've allowed them to do that, but I thank God that it didn't work. I feel like I got away by the skin of my teeth. "I Don't Know Why," as it appeared on *Fat City*, was meant to be a big Whitney Houston–esque pop ballad. The way it was produced had nothing to do with the way that I write. If it had been a hit, the way it would have been perceived would have had nothing to do with me. I'm convinced of that. So I'm glad it didn't happen that way. I'll never take the chance again of letting the record company push a song that doesn't represent how I write. I think commercial calculation is most often counterproductive anyway. That was my instinctive response when they wanted to recast "I Don't Know Why" as a pop song. Letting them do it was a dubious thing. It was almost like betting against myself. But I thought I'd try it their way while crossing my fingers that it wouldn't work out. The fact that it wasn't a huge success gave me the ammunition to say, "I've done it your way, and trying to make me

into something I'm not just doesn't work with an artist like me."

In the end it's not having a hit, being recognized, or being identified with that makes this life worth pursuing. It's the writing itself which makes it possible to stay in music. You're tearing down your ego if you're doing it right. There's nothing bad about that. It's interesting to find out what works and how far you can go with that process. Having to perform the songs allows me to separate the wheat from the chaff; the words that seem essential and well written are pleasing to sing, and the work that seems pretentious, less well crafted, or less honest is more difficult to sing. I also find it hard to perform a song like "Monopoly" because it was written as a ten-minute purge. I think it's a valid song, but it's strange to go back to it because it's so journalistic. The best stuff to me is a song like "Polaroids," which has that journalistic immediacy, but it's been revised and made into a well-crafted song.

I'm lucky to be writing songs because you can get away with a lot more than you can in poetry or fiction. I'm not a studied writer. You don't have to know a lot to be a songwriter. I'm not a very well-read person. It's a character flaw. Even though books are very important to me, I don't read voraciously by anyone's standards. When it comes to reading, I wish I could be more like my friend Steuart Smith, the guitarist who often plays with me on tour. He's a real reader. He not only reads what's contemporary but he also reads and rereads classics. He'll just have to go back and reread *Heart of Darkness* because it's going to reveal something new. I have a fear of reading, or more accurately, I have a fear of sounding like a teenager talking about the books I like. I'm not contemporary or theoretical in the way I think about what I read.

The Sun Also Rises, Huckleberry Finn, and *Lonesome Dove* are important books for me. I also really respond to Sylvia Plath. *The Bell Jar* gets to me because I know exactly what

Plath's writing about. She really gets it right in that novel. Her writing, there and in the poems, is amazing. It's tough and deep, beautiful and challenging. Plath was a brilliant and studied

writer. I could never even hope to write poetry like hers. Fortunately, as a songwriter you don't have to be deeply learned. Being too literary can even be dangerous to your songwriting, but as long as you can still get to the meat of your subject, however challenging and complicated your writing is, then you're not being too smart for your work. Artists like to do drugs so much because they have the feeling that they're ripping away something that's keeping them from being pure. Sometimes purity isn't so simple. One of the marvels of good art is when someone manages to be really complex and really get it at the same time or

I'm probably disappointing to people I meet socially who have expectations about me because of my work. I'm not as dark and brooding as I ought to be.

when a song is simple but not insipid, so simple that you're just blown away. Getting there is really a mystery for artists. They try all kinds of routes: drugs, divine intervention, discipline. Sometimes it happens, and sometimes it doesn't. So even though Plath was a studied writer, she really got to the center of what she was writing about. I admire her for that.

I also like Plath and Anne Sexton because they were rock and rollers. Anne Sexton actually was a rock and roller; she had a band. Both of those writers were out of their time. They were blowing it wide open. The misery they must have felt . . . I've wanted to kill myself, and if I had come of age in their era, trying to do the kinds of things I wanted to do, I might have ended up dead too. But things were a little different for my generation. For one thing, the drugs that are available if you're a depressive are a whole lot better. If they were born a little later, I wonder if they'd still be alive. Beyond the writing itself, books like Plath's are very comforting because they make you understand you're not alone.

I do wonder sometimes what it would be like to live a less mentally anguished life. By saying that, I don't mean that I'm so sensitive and creative that I can't bear it. I'm speaking clinically. Whatever we know at this point about the physiology of addiction and depression, it does seem fair to say that you have it or you don't. When you've got it, you've got it. And I definitely have it. I always have from the time I was a kid. It interests me when I see people who haven't been driven by that kind of fear and the need to control it. I try to imagine what that would be like, what insights one would come to, what values one would hold, what kind of expectations one would have of the world and of other people. Trying to imagine that

helps me to envision a more peaceful and a more giving life as well as a less isolated one. Moving around as much as I do is stressful, tiring, and not great for relationships. I've been dwelling on that lately. I'm gone about 250 days a year. Sometimes I think that's excessive. Six months away is okay, but 250 days a year?

More often now I feel the pull of a quieter, more domestic life. At this age I think more about death, and I see that my life is as much past me as it is in front of me. That's sobering. It gives me a bit of perspective and a lot more curiosity about other people's lives. I moved to Austin, which was a good change. My sister's there. A good day is either being in the water or in the house with my sister, her husband, and my niece. To me the fact that she has her own family is the most real thing that's happened to me and my siblings. It's something that has nothing to do with us as children. One of us is now a parent, and as remedial as it might seem, I think you need to understand the value and richness of that. I

see that richness through her. My niece is extremely important to me. What I feel for her is an immediate and direct hit. The world goes out from there. She's the newest addition to the people I treasure, and it's such a great feeling to be part of her life from the very beginning. I don't know if being a parent is for me. It could still be part of my life in the future. But even if it's not, that sense of things—a domestic, quiet life with the people who are central to me—is very important. I'm passionate about the people in my life.

I guess that doesn't say very much about me. I think that artists are often less interesting in their daily lives or when they talk about themselves than people who don't have an artistic outlet. You don't get from artists what you think you want to get. Instead you get what they are. I can't envision the situation where I could sit down and really ask an artist I admire what I'd want to ask him. When I met Dylan at the Grammys, I was only introduced to him briefly. I know enough about Dylan to know the chances are slim that I could have my ideal conversation with him, so meeting him wasn't a high-stakes moment for me. Anyway, with somebody like Dylan, the answers you want are in the work. You don't really need to talk about it beyond that. Still, it's hard to separate your ideals about

a person and the reality of who that person actually is. I'm probably disappointing to people I meet socially who have expectations about me because of my work. I'm probably a bore. I'm not as dark and brooding as I ought to be. I must seem dorky. I would rather play Pictionary or light farts than be

an "interesting artist" type. I do the most absurd things. I bet people think I am just the most adolescent goofball, which is really just fine with me.

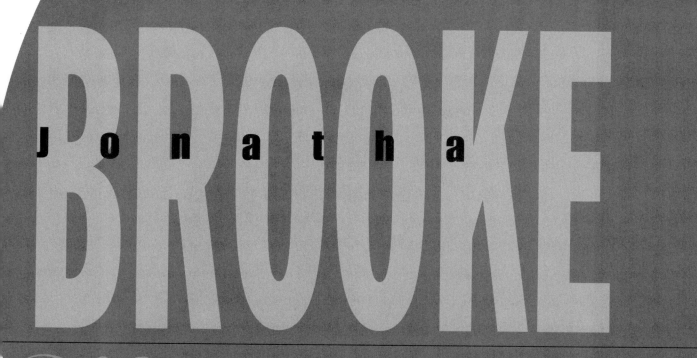

Jonatha BROOKE

My identity as a woman is absolutely central to my work. I'm a girl. That fact flavors everything, and it's a strength. Women are more gutsy at exposing themselves and getting to a deeper, more painful place—at least in public! We revel in it. We say, in effect, "I want you to see all of the dirty laundry. Here it is. Go ahead and look." We're admitting our pain and anger. I'm part of that gutsy tradition.

I'm tired of confronting the idea that having too many women on the scene at one time is redundant, the complaint that there's a glut of female artists now. I'm tired of a record company executive thinking that he can't sign another "girl artist" because he already has three on the label. What is redundant about women? As if there aren't twenty male artists on the roster. Why isn't that redundant?

Why during any hour of radio programming do you hear perhaps fifteen minutes of music by female artists? Why don't promoters want women to open for women? Why are women so freaked out about other women opening for them? It's as though there's so little space that we have to compete with one another. I don't think we should have to feel that way. All women are not saying the same thing. The notion that we are redundant is a hateful industry concoction. We believe it even though it's completely false. There's room out there for all of us. Everyone has such a unique way of saying things that the question of being redundant is ridiculous.

Also, I feel conflicted about knowing that you can get further if you're a pretty woman. You can get answers from people more easily. I'm very conscious of having to use that power. At the same time I hate the fact that I have any more of a chance than someone who's not pretty in a culturally sanctioned way. Why should that be important? The question shouldn't

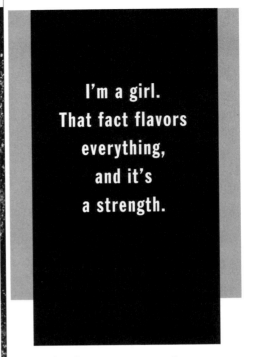

I'm a girl. That fact flavors everything, and it's a strength.

be whether a woman is pretty enough but whether the music is there or not. Look at all these hideous rock 'n' roll men. The more foul, the better in their case. Why should the standards be so different?

A number of my songs are about women and the roles they're in, the cost of being given a role. "Amelia," for example, was inspired by an amazing Sharon Olds poem, "I Go Back to May 1937." She imagines that she is standing at the gates of her parents' college as they're about to graduate: "I want to go up to them and say Stop / . . . you are going to do things / you cannot imagine you would ever do / you are going to do bad things to children / you are going to suffer in ways you never heard of / . . . but I don't do it. I want to live."

The song is also inspired by my grandmother Amelia, a woman with incredible potential who was dominated by a very strong man. I don't think she was abused, but stifled, and the fallout from that relationship of course seeps through the rest of the family. The song addresses her silence and questions the notion that long-suffering patience, kindness, and virtue are the attributes most appropriate for a woman and wife. As far as I'm concerned, that course of action goes completely unrewarded. My grandmother was a gifted pianist. She could play anything by ear in any key. She had a deep knowledge of and love for nature and birds. Her passion and talent never went further than the living room or perhaps the backyard.

Although my mother professes that she loves being a mother, that this was her real work, I think she resents in some ways that being a mother and wife was her lot, that she couldn't be granted the time and space for *other* work. My dad's job dictated where we would go and what we were doing, what she would be doing.

In subtle ways my generation of women are dealing with the fallout from the roles our mothers and grandmothers played in our families. To some degree I'm the same as they were. Part of me is incredibly accommodating and self-compromising for the good of the family or the marriage. I'll clean the house before I'll write a song — which is pathetic. How self-destructive that you would put something so meaningless before your work. Still, it happens to me every day. I'm still the one who is cheerful all the time and wants to make everything okay for my family. I feel that I'm not supposed to rock the boat. Women have a legacy of keeping things in.

But breaking that silence has its costs too. You don't necessarily win doing it that way either, something I was thinking about when writing "The Angel in the House." I had the first line—"My mother moved the furniture when she no longer moved the man / we thought nothing of it at the time"—for a year and a half before I could write the song. I asked each of my brothers what he thought of this line and whether I should use it in a song. They were both very defensive about my parents. I started to feel that I shouldn't write it. But finally I said, "Fuck this, I can at least write the song even if I don't record it." But I couldn't write it without that first line, whatever anyone thought of it.

"The Angel in the House" is about any number of women—including my mother and grandmother—but it is at the same time about me. Here I am in the same boat when I thought all along I was by myself breaking new ground. Instead of being immune to the pressures that formed their lives as women, I am plagued by the legacy, these memories and the history of my lineage. When I sing "I cannot kill the angel in the house," I mean that I can't escape this notion of femininity that makes me "clean the house" before writing a song. It still exists in me, perhaps in subtler ways than it did for my mother and grandmother, but it's still there.

Just the other day my dad came to see me perform. I could see him in the crowd. I launched into "The Angel in the House" and thought that I might not be able to sing it in front of him. I watched his face during the whole song. He would look away and then look back. I thought, *I really have to talk to him about this. I can't go through this anymore.* I did try to talk to my mother about it, but the conversation backfired to some degree. I couldn't get to the root of what I meant. I said, "There's this song I really need to talk to you about. You need to know that I wrote it in love and compassion. Your situation is universal, and there's this blurry line between fiction and reality. Pretend you're just reading poetry, Mom." That was it. We never really talked about it after that. There is always a song about my parents on each album: "No Better" on *Plumb,* "The Angel in the House" on *The Angel in the House,* "Perfect Crime" on *Grace in Gravity,* which is addressed to my father though I hope he never knew it. Maybe for the next album I'll write a nice song about them. I could call it "Oh, Dad and Mom, I Love You."

From the time that I can remember— strange, I don't remember a lot about being really young, except for ballet when I began dancing in London—I was adored by my par-

thing. I was the one who was always okay, who ignored anything bad that happened. Maybe I simply had a cheerful nature. I was an easy kid, easily pleased. I'm the youngest. I'm the only girl.

ents. That was my role: to be adored. And to be the cheerful one, the one who isn't confrontational. I will not call anyone on any-

My brothers are six and eight years older so there was a time when I felt like I was an only child. I had the run of the house and the complete attention of my parents. I never really rebelled. My rebellious phase is just happening now that I'm thirty-two. I never got into trouble or did drugs or crashed the car. I tried pot; it never affected me. I tried booze and hated it. I was more comfortable being conscious. It was a source of great pride for my parents that I came upon a vocation by myself which they could fully support. Only lately, with a certain amount of success, have I become the achiever in visible ways.

I grew up in a very religious way. Even to other believers, how I grew up seemed a radical way to live. My parents are Christian Scientists, so I have been . . . not "programmed"—that sounds like a cult word—but given a spiritual vocabulary for all the big questions, a way of thinking that will always be there whether I want it or not. Every day is a crisis in faith, one way or another. The problem of faith or not having faith is a huge part of who I am. It's a big part of why I write songs and why I try to get to that deeper place in them.

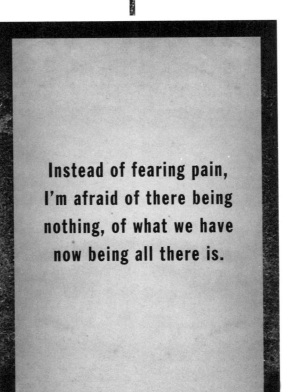

> **Instead of fearing pain, I'm afraid of there being nothing, of what we have now being all there is.**

From the time I was very young, there was a lot of metaphysical talk in my house. We were always discussing God and life as spiritual, talking about how our true identity is not evident in how we appear but in our spiritual being. These are huge things for a kid to deal with. I never got the concrete human answers that I sought to questions like: Why do we die? Where do we go when we die? Is death the end?—all the questions that are still unanswered for me. I've always wanted to know the answers to those questions. Instead I always got vague spiritual truths offered in metaphysical terms, nothing that a kid can hang on to.

These questions constitute a large part of what I think about every day. What am I going to do with the remnants of this faith? What can I do with these remnants of a childhood that in some ways was incredibly free of fear and very protected in good ways now that I'm in a place in my life where I don't want to carry myself that way any longer? We thought of ourselves as an ideal family. We were never really wanting for anything. We were never sick. I've been to a doctor only once or twice in my life. Physically we lived free of fear. We never watched medical programs on TV. I wasn't allowed to see *Love Story* because a character dies of cancer in the end. In that way we were "pro-tected," as it was called. But there are concrete issues that went unanswered and are still unanswered for me. I'm searching for those answers. I don't think Christian Science is going to provide them. I don't know yet. That's my dilemma.

I guess I stepped back gradually from "faith" although I never went fully into it. As a child you don't have much choice—you are what your parents are—but I never went into Christian Science on my own. My family is still very much practicing. It has been great for them. They live exemplary lives and are incredibly smart people. They address whatever questions they have through Christian Science, and their questions have been answered, I guess. I still imagine myself going back to church and completely falling apart because there's something so familiar and comforting about returning to the fold.

Still, Christian Science didn't answer all my questions or fears. I was scared of death as a child. It still scares me. It's still the big factor of my life. I think about it all the time.

I stopped talking about that fear with my parents after I was seven or eight because they would always say, "You're no more dead now than you'll ever be." What does that mean? It wasn't monsters and other childhood inventions that scared me; it was just plain death. I don't know why. I just assumed everyone was as afraid of death as I was.

I've met people like me who have the same cold clutch of fear that incapacitates them in the dark. You can only wait for it to pass. I'm not afraid of pain. I get my period every month. What could be worse than that? What could be more painful? I wore toe shoes for six years. I know pain. My tolerance is really high. Instead of fearing pain, I'm afraid of there being nothing, of what we have now being all there is. That pisses me off and scares me.

I was also afraid of being stupid and afraid of authority. I remember going to pick up my graded papers from the principal of the Commonwealth School—a very kindly man who taught Bible courses and American history—and bursting into tears for no real reason. I always thought I hadn't done well enough. And I hadn't. I got Bs and B–s, and even though at Commonwealth that was pretty good, it just wasn't good enough for me. Even when I went to piano lessons as a younger child, I would be in tears because I felt I didn't have the lesson down, that I hadn't done enough. I was afraid to disappoint people.

I was also a little afraid of a scary family next door, the Gibsons. I have very vivid memories of them. I was friends with Greg Gibson, who was about my age. His parents were in their sixties. I remember them as ancient smoking people. The whole house smelled of smoke. They had this bizarre, horror movie organ in their living room, which Greg would play from time to time. It gave me the creeps. I remember writing "Gibson Sucks Forever" in stones on the sand by the side of the road with my friend Sylvia Fallon. When Greg's sister Gretchen saw it, she went ballistic. She got out of her car screaming and chased us into the woods like she was going to kill us. During a sleepover at Greg's house one night, Gretchen fell in the shower, and I remember peeking around the corner and seeing lots of blood in the tub. Terrified, I ran home through the woods in the dark.

I felt really stupid at school. I was also a bit of a social misfit. No one wanted to hang out with me because I was always going to ballet class. I was totally devoted to this passion, dance. I wasn't cool or pretty. I had braces. I still feel stupid most of the time.

I went to a really high-powered high school and always felt I was in the dark, afraid to raise my hand. By the time I'd figured out what I wanted to say, my classmates

> I felt really stupid at school. I was also a bit of a social misfit. I wasn't cool or pretty. I had braces. I still feel stupid most of the time.

had moved on to something else entirely. I would get so tense and excited when I finally had something valuable to say, but by then the moment would be past.

College was a bit like that too. It seemed like the guys always offered the answers. Even if they said stupid things, they knew how to bullshit, and the professors would love it and bullshit along with them. I couldn't do that. Perhaps all the girls didn't feel that way—many seemed smart to me—but that was my experience. It wasn't until my junior or senior year in college that I found two professors who reassured me and said, in effect, "I think you're smart. I like how you think and how you write." I'd been craving that approval for so long, and I had never received it before.

In college I was most passionate about dance, food, and sex. I became a strong woman. I thought, *Fuck being a ballerina and staying skinny.* I ate a lot. I got bigger and thought, *So what?* I had this appetite for lots of stuff I had denied myself, being a ballerina. It was a phase of rebellion against myself, against my own sense of discipline, but it was still hard going to dance class when I felt fat. The jazz teacher at the University of Massachusetts, where I was taking classes, told me to lose weight, that I had a fat ass, and yet outside the studio, I felt good. Part of me liked that I had big breasts and a nice big ass. It was a confusing time, even down to my decision to go to college instead of going directly to New York to be a dancer.

A little later I started writing songs. Perhaps in songwriting I'd found something unique. Maybe I felt no one could touch me there. One of the professors who did support me was really interested in my songs. I began singing with Jennifer Kimball, and we started to perform together.

We were together, first as Jonatha and Jennifer, then as The Story, for a very long time before ending our partnership. When you start anew on your own, you're scared people are going to hate you for not doing what they first liked about your songs. It still pisses me off when people hear the new record and say, "How could you have split up? You were so special together." There are any number of folk Nazis who are angry that the music can no longer be defined simply as "an intricate and beautiful weaving of voices." For them, you are not allowed to change. We *were* special together, granted. We had an unbelievable blend of two voices that was really unique. But you have to consider two people's lives. We were miserable. There was no way to sustain that musical partnership and be happy. Happiness was more important. Jennifer and I had the balls to end it in a loving way. We had the matu-

we did this because we can still like each other.

It was really scary to decide consciously that I didn't need to follow the old formula this time. I'll always love harmony and counterpoint and saying complicated things from two places at once, but it's not something I need to do right now. I really want to focus on discovering my own voice, how to use it and how to fill the dynamic range that's now available to me. I had to learn how to sing again. I had to get all the dynamics to work solo. It was a great process to go through, to face the fact that the songs were going to be carried by my voice alone.

Being on my own gave me musical freedom. I can finally do the things that I heard in my head but was afraid to pursue because it would have meant excluding Jennifer. I knew two years ago that the songs I was writing just didn't have our name on them. I was in a frenzy about what I was going to do. I knew I couldn't make Jennifer

rity to decide that our partnership wasn't right for us anymore and we needed to be separate people. We'll both be fine. It will be really hard for a while, but we'll both be glad

happy anymore because the new songs were so much more singular. It wasn't fair to either of us. It was an incredibly terrifying realization but so freeing in the end.

Starting over by myself also meant finding a place of worth again and letting myself feel valuable, that I had more to say. The songs on *Plumb* are very much about that. I was examining Jennifer's departure, the risk it represented, the huge change it brought, and the fear of starting again. Finding a record deal and performing solo was like re-learning everything, a completely new feeling. After Jennifer left, the first time I was onstage—just me and a guitar—I could barely breathe. I felt as though I'd never been onstage before.

Being on my own has been this amazing stripping bare. I felt completely naked again. I was exploring for myself a way of being more personal, exposing more of myself. That process was both conscious and subconscious. Before this album I would shy away from that kind of

> **Starting over by myself also meant finding a place of worth again and letting myself feel valuable, that I had more to say.**

exposure. There's a lot of betrayal and a lot of loss in these songs that cut deep in me although the songs often tell about those feelings through stories of other people's situations.

Writing in voices other than my own allows me to come up with better words than I might otherwise find were I writing only out of my own experience. It's so boring to talk about yourself all the time. I'm self-conscious, always wondering who would care what goes on in my mind anyway. Maybe that's false modesty. I'm not sure. But it is more interesting for me to explore other wavelengths, other situations. Because I often delve into the dark side of things, I find writing in other voices is a useful technique. I venture out of myself, establish another perspective, and then try to find out why I'm speaking in that voice, how I connect to it personally.

I wrote "So Much Mine," for example, from a mother's perspective. I had the phrase *so much mine* in my head, and it dictated whose song it was going to be. It was clearly the older voice, the mother's voice. There were a number of other things that went into writing that song. I used to dance in a company that performed every Friday and Saturday night in a huge nightclub in a shitty part of downtown Boston. I knew all the regular whores on the street, but from time to time I would see really young teenagers, fif-

teen or sixteen years old, hanging out on the phone, trying to get some work happening. At that same time I was baby-sitting for two young girls three days a week. I was taking care of these little girls, getting very attached to them and seeing how traumatic it was for their mother to be away as much as she was.

So, on the most obvious level, I wrote the song because I saw those teenagers on the street and I was feeling maternal about the children I was caring for. But I came to realize that the song was really about the distance between my mother and me. There were certain impasses between us that had never existed before. I wanted to explore the loss but try not to say too much. Writing the song from that perspective seemed to me the most poignant way of getting at the knowledge a mother has that from the second her child is born, she will lose her. That was what was going on in the song, that and the recognition that someday I too will probably experience this loss.

The strangest part of writing from other perspectives is that listeners always assume a song is directly about me when it isn't. Because *Plumb* sounds more like a personal album full of breakup songs, people assume I had a horrible year and ask me if I'm okay. The horrible things that happen in the songs didn't necessarily happen to me. Interpretation's a strange thing. Someone wrote to me about "Dog Dreams," a song about what I imagine my dogs dream about, to say how she was really moved by my feminist song about the subjection of women! I didn't have the heart to write back. I was at such a loss about what to tell her when the song is after all just about my dogs. Nevertheless, I have to take seriously whatever people get from my songs.

Writing in voices other than your own is also risky in commercial terms. It keeps you from entering that huge pop arena. I think you do isolate yourself a bit if you're not playing to the lowest common denominator. I don't aspire to superstardom. If I were Alanis Morissette right now, I'd be really scared. Luckily she has a really strong sense of herself, which will allow her to survive her celebrity, but any number of strong women in her situation have been consumed and spit back out once they have nothing left.

I'm glad my music occupies a smaller category, perhaps a noncategory, that has kept me out of the pop realm. At the same time writing this way is something I don't have that much control over. I don't really know how songs come to me and therefore can't anticipate how they're going to turn out.

I learn again and again from the writers I'm drawn to not to say too much. I'm drawn to complicated, unresolved work. I like leaving the ideas or feelings set out in my work unresolved. I learn from writers I admire to leave things up in the air. I love that quality. It has to be that way. I've been reading Julio Cortázar, the Argentinean writer, who manufactured scenarios that could never actually exist. As a reader you're slowly sucked into

Being on my own has been this amazing stripping bare. I felt completely naked again.

you've written. So what if they think "Dog Dreams" is a feminist song? I like to initiate respect for a listener. "Made of Gold" is a song that doesn't hit you over the head with what's going on. You may figure it out; you may not. You may figure out that there's a woman's voice and a man's voice talking about the same situation, which may or may not have taken place. It's left unresolved at the end whether the undisclosed occurrence is violent or loving, a death or a rape. I know exactly what happened and that it happens every day. It didn't happen to me, but it probably did. That's the kind of indeterminacy I love. That's what fuels me: trying to establish a convincing and effective indeterminacy.

The combination of words and music first hit me when I was nine, sitting on the stairs waiting for my brother outside his girlfriend's house. They had the radio on inside. "Angie" was playing. I didn't know what Mick Jagger was singing about, but there was this pain there, and it got to me. That

this surreal, garish world until you're completely convinced by it. I'd like to experiment more, working outside of realism, writing lyrics that become more complicated exponentially as the song progresses.

The other thing I've learned from writers I admire is not to underestimate your audience. Leave it for them to figure out what

was the first time a song connected for me in that way.

I remember the Mamas and Papas playing full tilt in our house and just loving

Neil Young. I listened to *The Sound of Music* and *Godspell* too. "By My Side" from *Godspell* made me cry every time. I got a guitar

it, singing along. My mom was really into them and the Beatles. My brothers liked Jethro Tull and had Joni Mitchell's *Miles of Aisles*. The Who.

for Christmas when I was twelve and figured out all those *Godspell* songs along with sad Karla Bonoff and James Taylor songs. I was really emotionally involved with songs from then on.

Songwriting is the best job I could aspire to. Emotionally it's enormously satisfying. There's something incredibly emotional for me when a song is good enough to move me deeply. If it does that, I'll keep it; if not, I won't play it. I am a brutal critic of my own work. I'm surprised that there are four albums out there at this point; that I even let those songs through seems remarkable to me. There's part of me that always thinks it could be better and that the song is never really finished or that someone will discover my insufficiency and say, "The joke's over, buddy." It's the phony syndrome. I guess everybody suffers from it to a degree. But does everyone know he's a phony? Are you only a phony if you know you're a phony? Or is it the

> **Are you only a phony if you know you're a phony? Or is it the people who don't know they're phonies who are the worst phonies?**

people who don't know they're phonies who are the worst phonies? Because we think about it, does that mean we're not phonies? Maybe it means we're less phony than those who don't know or don't think about it.

Writing songs is also a way to get at the complicated answers to the question of why we're here or at least why I'm here. I don't know if I'll ever find out something profound by writing songs, but especially in singing them, I find out a lot about myself. I can make sense on an emotional level of what I've written when I perform it.

Writing is dangerous. You risk a lot by trying to get to that deep a place. If you're successful, you'll reach people and they'll respond in a deep way. When a song works, there's a sense that they know you because you know them. It's a real struggle for me to get beyond the part of me that wants to make everyone happy and write songs that people respond to strongly and by no means happily. When I win that struggle, that's the reward.

Although both of my parents were working writers when I was growing up, I never knew until recently what it meant for them to be writers. I never put their writing together with who they were as my parents. It wasn't like they came home and said, "Look at this article I just wrote." What they did at work never emerged at the dinner table, unless I'm blocking it out.

My dad was a journalist and my mom had a column for ten years in the *Christian Science Monitor* called "Looking Homeward," which was mostly about raising kids. My pseudonym in the column was Jodie.

Writing is
dangerous.
You risk a lot
by trying to
get to that
deep a place.

When I was young, I was much more drawn to dance than writing. Something clicked with me through ballet when I was six. I was insatiable. Dance was my main focus for decades. It is something I've clung to fiercely even though I'm no longer dancing. It's so much part of my identity—the way I move, how I stand, how I think of myself— that I'll find myself doing arabesques and pliés while standing in the kitchen.

Dance has a tremendous influence on

me, and it's a huge part of how I came to be a musician and writer. It brings a way of thinking to my music. It brings a discipline that allows me to get through anything. Stamina and the ability to deal with crap: I got those qualities from ballet with its constant evaluations and corrections. When you're a dancer, every day there's something else you're working on, but with that day come a hundred days before when a teacher corrected you. You have to incorporate everything you've learned at every moment. You have to think about a hundred things at once. I brought that ability into my life and definitely to the music as well. I think of it as multitasking. I can do many things at the same time.

I've also transferred from dance the idea of doing the most difficult thing at any given moment. I'm thinking of the melodies I write. They're not simple. They involve quite a range of notes. Writing complex melodies isn't necessarily a smart choice. Difficult songs like "Over Oceans" are still hard to sing. I can't say that on a given night I'll end up in the same key I started in. Still, there's a sense of adventure in imagining the hardest things I can do at a given point in a melody or in asking myself what are the weirdest chords I can use to turn that emotional screw in my heart.

I also think in terms of choreographing for voices. For a long time I had Jennifer's voice to work with, so I could invent a wild pas de deux. We'd sing two parts at once, Jennifer twirling all over the hemisphere, singing counterpoint or harmony, while I sang an entirely different melody. Whenever I think of "Damn Everything but the Circus" or "So Much Mine," I imagine voices moving in an almost dancelike manner.

Because I think of myself as a dancer, I found that I had to get used to the constraints of music. When you're dancing, your body is your instrument. It's the only thing you have. It's your freedom or your constraint. I had to give up dancing cold turkey four years ago because The Story was touring a lot. Sitting for hours, day after day, in cars and on planes was frustrating because I realized I couldn't have the full use of this instrument, my body, any longer. I had to figure out why the music was taking over. Why is music rather than dance suddenly the thing that means the most? How am I going to make it as fulfilling as dancing?

Very quickly I realized that the potential for music is much greater. As a dancer I was always someone else's clay, and while I loved that, it was never something I could derive creative pleasure from. But music has a huge scope and so many different levels you can use to reach someone—whether it's the sound of the group, a partic-ular chord, the melody or a lyric that a listener hangs on to. You've got all these ways to get through that dance doesn't have.

> **I see a beautiful stone cottage in the south of France with a huge kitchen table where we cook all the time. I see tomatoes—tomatoes that taste like tomatoes.**

The other interesting part has been trying to incorporate movement into performances. It's hard to move as much as you'd like to when you're behind a microphone holding a guitar, but on this last tour I put down the guitar for one song and came to this incredible realization that I can actually let the guitar player play and have the freedom to dance. I think there's also a physicality to singing when you access a deep place. There are times when I'm completely absorbed in a song and find a balance that's incredibly physical. I don't know that other people who don't have a dance background would feel it in the same way. It's so visceral and muscular, very deep physically. I'll hear this voice coming out of me that's a very different voice and connected to all the ages. I find more and more how physical singing is and how fulfilling it is in that respect. I come offstage as exhausted as if I'd run a marathon.

I'm married to Alain Mallet. This relationship was the one that snuck up on me. We've been married eight years now. We were introduced by a mutual friend whom I had a crush on. Alain talked my ear off and eventually convinced me to go out with him. On the first date I told him, "Look, you're fun, and we'll have a good time, but there's never going to be more between us than that. Marriage is out of the question." He's from a Catholic background, and I was still very conscious of my background as a Christian Scientist, how important it was to me, that it was part of me he could never understand. That ruled Alain out.

We ricocheted back and forth for three years. At one point I moved to New York to dance full-time. I was seeing another guy and thinking about Alain a lot, but I thought it was just because the other guy was a real lunatic. The lunatic and I broke up, and I called Alain. We had a slow reconciliation. There was always the sense that he wasn't going to go away no matter how many times we split up, that there was always an element there with him to bring me back. But each time we were together, there was something unresolved. The final time we got together, something had resolved. Maybe I had settled down finally and wasn't so worried about needing to be free. Before that I needed to have the sense that I wasn't really tied down and could keep the door open. I finally shut the door. We were both fairly young: I was twenty-four, and he was twenty-five. He knew from the beginning this was going to be the one while I didn't know it at all. I can't say it was love at first sight or I was to-

tally in love from the beginning, but I knew it wouldn't go away. Something between us was very strong and was not going to disappear. We had to resolve it one way or another.

We've been lucky to evolve and change in the same direction. We've also been very lucky in that we understand what's involved in a life in music. Unless you're doing the same thing, it's a very weird life to understand. I don't think I could have married a banker or someone with a very rigid schedule. It would have been impossible with me being away all the time.

It's been a long road, and Alain's been a huge part of all the musical success. He coproduced from the very beginning and produced *Plumb* by himself. His production is great, and no one else would be so devoted to getting it right. It's been quite a labor of love. We try to limit kissing time on the tour bus especially when there are five other guys whose wives are all at home.

Being on the road so much makes for a less than traditional domestic life. When I think what life might be like if I weren't working as a musician, I have an earth mother fantasy. I see a beautiful stone cottage in the south of France with a huge kitchen table where we cook all the time. I see tomatoes—tomatoes that taste like tomatoes. Friends come over for conversation and musical afternoons. There are ten or twenty dogs and some kids running around, family nearby so we're all involved in one another's children's lives. A real sense of community. A kind of rootedness that's not possible given the current all-over-the-placeness of my life. In the picture it's sunny and green and lush.

hat I hear in my music that's particularly southern is the thickness of it. There's a definite consistency there that I associate with home. When I think of life in Mississippi, that rich texture is what I remember: something highly perfumed, pungent even, that's enveloping, warm, unpretentious — and very sensual. We can certainly add that.

I think all southerners experience the thickness of a life comprised of so many different layers, visible and invisible. I'm a true southerner in that sense. Definitely. A large part of the fact life feels this way to us comes from our closeness to nature. I remember going to sleep in my grandmother's room when I was a little girl. There was a plum tree right outside the window, and a few yards behind that some bush. I'd lie there and watch the breeze blow her fine curtain, just the right

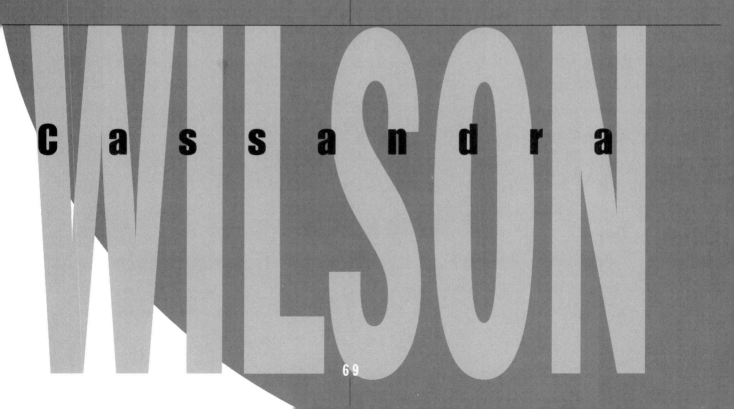

Cassandra WILSON

weight, back and forth over me while I smelled the special night smells and listened to the night sounds, all my senses alive with the environment around me. In the summertime all the children would have to be outside by eight in the morning. We'd run around with no shoes, playing in the woods all day long. At the end of the day we'd eat blackberry cobbler that Mama, as we called our grandma, would make. Being outside all day in the woods and, when we'd come in, blackberry cobbler and a cool glass of water—that was bliss.

> I'd lie there and watch the breeze blow her fine curtains back and forth over me while I smelled the special night smells and listened to the night sounds, all my senses alive.

Another important layer of the South involves the richness that the Africans brought to this part of the world: the knowledge of agriculture and the cycles of the moon, a way of being that includes music and hospitality, all of the ritual around food and socializing. Much of what we think of as particularly southern has been gleaned from our experience, the African experience. We've shared our culture with the culture at large. A lot of southerners might not come out and admit that influence, but they know it's there.

You can hear that richness and complexity in Robert Johnson's music, for example. He's an incredible figure, and he always sparks my imagination. I can visualize what his life was like. He embodies that journey from the plantation to life on your own which is the beginning of the blues. He had to learn what to do when you come to the crossroads, how to maneuver so you can work your way through that maze. I'm drawn to him as a figure who provides an example of how to negotiate so many complex transitions. His music is especially important because of the way it occupies a central place in the movement from blues into jazz. Not many people hear it, but there's an incredible complexity I'm drawn to in his guitar playing. He's really playing the drum which was taken away. It's amazing to listen to him with that in mind. Imagine that movement from the drum to no drum, having to play all of the parts without the drum, including the polyrhythms that are beginning to happen in his music. He's singing on top of all that, which adds still another layer. His music is what I mean when I say "thick."

I'm interested in music that crosses boundaries. To be able to operate in several worlds at once is the result of being open-minded, whether in music or some other part of experience. Breaking down the divisions allows you to access freedom musically, and of

course the music then begins to create the life. There is definitely a lot of divisiveness in every area today as the result of the point we've come to in Western civilization. We're so compartmentalized, abstracted into oblivion. That way of thinking has reached its peak, and we're now witnessing the end of looking at life in those terms. I'm definitely optimistic about the crossroads we're at. You have to destroy before you create. Even when I was a child, my role was the creator-destroyer. That impulse in me goes way back. I was the last of three children, the only daughter, so I had more freedom than anybody else in the house. I still believe that things have to fall apart before something new can

> **I'm interested in music that crosses boundaries. Breaking down the divisions allows you to access freedom musically, and of course the music then begins to create the life.**

emerge. That's true for everything, including music.

One of the things that needs to be broken up is the perception that the senses and spirit are polarized. They're not poles. When we have sex, it's a form of worship. I truly believe that God gave this act to us as a gift to be revered. The body is very spiritual. My interest in the Song of Solomon, which I write about in "Solomon Sang," comes out of that belief. The Song of Solomon likens physical love to the kind of love that we have for God. Both kinds of love come from the same place and give the same kind of fulfillment.

I don't remember precisely how I became interested in Solomon, but the combination of the senses and the spirit I found there really moved me. God knows what guided me to that source. It could have been that one day I saw Solomon once too often or someone mentioned the name to me for the hundredth time. That's how an interest in something usually begins. References to it recur so frequently that you know it's not an accident. I don't believe in accidents, especially when everything and everyone seem to be telling you, "Look over here." Although I remember a few passages from childhood, I'm not really that well versed in the Bible. I was raised in a Presbyterian church, and my grandmother read scripture to us every

> It's amazing that we've been able to survive—and not only survive but flourish and thrive—given all that's been lost. That's a story that has to be told.

day, so it's in me somewhere, but I didn't remember that beautiful, beautiful imagery in Solomon until I reread it. It's so thick you can smell it. All those rich spices and flowers.

The story also interests me. Solomon falls in love with the queen of Sheba, whose name, Makeda, you won't find mentioned in most of the versions of the Bible you read. Her race, which is apparent in the verse where she says, "I am black, but comely," was clearly a problem for a translator. At some point when the Bible was translated, perhaps when King James decided on his version, there was some sort of cover-up and the queen's name and origin were erased. I wish I could read the book in its original language. Translations always worry me. If you read the Ethiopian account

Arabian peninsula but from Ethiopia. Her race is still clear in the King James Version, but her name's been erased.

I write about that process of erasing our names in "Memphis": "History has been arranged / To hide us from / Our secret names." I was thinking of the holocaust, our holocaust, and one of its effects. A lot of us have lost those names because of the loss of the language and the culture. When you lose your name, you find that you're just groping. It's amazing that we've been able to survive—and not only survive but flourish and thrive—given all that's been lost. That's a story that has to be told. We don't even know where to go to find our names. We have an idea—maybe Yorubaland or Ebo, Ashanti or Akai—but we still don't know exactly where we come from. There's also the fact that there's so much other blood in our veins as well. We have to deal with the fact that a lot of us do have European ancestry. That's something that we don't readily talk about.

of Solomon and the queen of Sheba, then you'll see that her name was Makeda and she was not from some mythical place on the

Why am I so drawn to Irish culture and why do I feel so comfortable with the music? I often wonder if that feeling has something to do with Irish ancestry. And then there's Native American blood that's there too. There's a lot happening in many of us. I think you have to celebrate every part. It's what you are. You have to try to find all those secret names.

"Memphis" is also about accessing a tradition of spirituality that we're often cut off from in a way that's not so different from being separated from our names. When the walls of the prison you've made for yourself fall away, you can begin to access that spirituality. I am increasingly drawn to the traditions my grandmother embodied.

When I was in the ninth grade—the first year of desegregation—I remember a student teacher, an educated man, saying "nigra" when we got to the Civil War period of Mississippi history.

She was a devout Christian, but she also practiced an old-time religion too, one that was in touch with plants and the cycles, our spiritual connection to nature. She was always out in the bush beyond the plum tree, picking herbs. This tradition becomes more and more important to me. The older I am, the clearer it is that I'm supposed to be recalling and remembering that tradition, piecing it together. It's a way of re-creating a spiritual structure for myself and, as a result, for my family and my extended family, the community. A lot of it comes to me intuitively, and a lot is reignited by the research that I do.

The more that you recover through intuition or sense memory, the more you want to go out and find documentation that tells you where the rituals you've instinctively developed come from. I don't talk about the way I access that spirituality more specifically than that. It's just for me.

Sense memory also brings back the other side of our story as well. I've been dealing with part of this past by singing in *Blood on the Fields*, Wynton Marsalis's oratorio. It's a brilliant, pivotal work that provides a way for us to unearth this past and look at it plainly. The piece is important for jazz because it incorporates text with music in a very new way that allows you to really focus on the story. There aren't enough stories about the Middle Passage. People still don't understand fully the horrors and legacy of slavery. *Blood on the Fields* is important because it allows all of us, through the music, to recall these events. It's been amazing for me to inhabit a figure from that past, to sing in her voice, and it allows me the opportunity to deal publicly with what she experienced. I do that in my own music too, but this context is very different because the story that's being told is very succinct and heroic.

I think we all experience the aftermath of the history that's described in a song like "Strange Fruit," for example, whether or not we lived during that time. Perhaps the ability to recall those experiences is a result of where we are in the South and the fact that we have been affected by them much more so than people in other parts of the country. That past is much more immediate for us. It's a memory that is easy to call up. The instant we hear someone say "nigger" it all comes back. Everything, for that instant, is recalled. That kind of recollection is more direct than what I actually experienced growing up in the South in the early 1960s although the aftermath of what we went through in the South was still there then as it is now, even if it is in the process of being reworked. I didn't experience anything as harsh as what my

I did experience desegregation firsthand, which was in some ways exciting but also very painful. When I was in the ninth grade—the first year of desegregation—I remember a student teacher, an educated man, saying "nigra" when we got to the Civil War period of Mississippi history. I was infuriated. I recall thinking to myself, *If educated people are still using this word in this manner, then I'm in trouble.* I thought, *This is not going to work.* I just couldn't believe he'd said that. To make matters worse, no one, black or white, called him on it. The regular teacher who was supervising him didn't say a word about it.

The first school I went to after desegregation was a few miles from my home. We had to carpool, but it didn't take too long to get there. Jackson is not really that large. We didn't have to travel miles and miles to get to a school bus. But the school was in another part of the city—a different neighborhood, a different building, different smells,

mother experienced growing up, but I take on all of her memory, just as she took on all of the memories of her parents, and so on. That past is in each one of us.

different everything. For the first two years it was much too tense and there was too much anxiety to allow people to really let their guards down. Ninth and tenth grades were difficult.

Things got better after that. For all of the negative aspects, experiencing things that were different from what I knew was also exciting. One of the benefits of going to that school was the view it allowed me inside another world. That view, among other things, introduced me to different music. In the eleventh grade I got the part of Dorothy in the high school musical of *The Wizard of Oz.* That was the beginning of reaching out to these people and being able to talk to them. Music was the way we came together. We talked about music. There was exchange, at least the beginning of it, and there was give-and-take. We traded albums at school. I remember hearing James Taylor and then really getting into Joni Mitchell. I turned some of my friends on to jazz they

hadn't heard before. I had a group with a couple of guys in high school. They were both white and played guitar. We'd just get together and play music. So the exchange that occurred during those years was eye-opening and important to my way of thinking about music and its boundaries.

I can't recall a specific moment when I first became interested in music because music was always there. We had everything in the house: jazz, blues, Motown, the current hits. I remember listening to Miles Davis's *Sketches of Spain* at seven or eight. I was obsessed with it. It knocked me out. It was so different from the rest of Daddy's jazz collection—so expansive, so wide. I heard music in a way that I'd never heard it before. Later, when I became interested in pop, everyone at home was open to it. I didn't have to sneak *The Monkees* into the house although my mother suggested that I not bring that particular album to the sixth-grade end-of-the-year party. She said, "It wouldn't be too good an idea. I don't think everybody's aware of them."

After that period, when I immersed myself in pop and folk, I started singing with the Black Musical Arts Society in Jackson. That was a very important time for me. That period was a coming back to, a reclamation of, the whole tradition of jazz I'd grown up with. Singing with the society allowed me to put together the history of the music for myself. The society is still there. It's run by a man named John Reese, who is tireless in his efforts to get jazz to the community. He and my father were the ones really responsible for my serious education in jazz. They helped me reclaim jazz for myself.

Since I was a child, music was always there in one form or another. I've performed since I sang in my brother's kindergarten graduation program when I was five. There were seven years of piano recitals when I was taking lessons—a recital each year. I was in the marching band and the concert band. In college I started to perform on my own. So there was a long apprenticeship. Making music is just something I've always done. My father shared his love for music with me, and although he didn't discuss any

particular expectations he might have had, I believe that music is what he ultimately wanted me to pursue. My mother was an educator, so she felt that I should become an educator too. She's not disappointed with what I'm doing now, but for a long time she was concerned because I didn't really begin to sustain myself as a musician until the eighties. Up until then I depended on my parents quite a bit, and she thought I should get a job and work like she had.

Now music has taken over my whole life. My social life is the music. Whenever I go somewhere, whenever I do something, it's usually connected to my work. I rarely have the chance to get outside of it. I used to be able to. Everything was much more manageable three or four years ago. I could step out of it, jump off to Jamaica for a few days, and no one would say anything. Waking up in Jamaica in these incredibly rich sheets, getting in the ocean to cleanse myself, experiencing the wealth of the culture, the music, the food, the sun: I can't just go off and do that anymore. I have to figure out a way to experience that kind of feeling here, so I can regain the kind of balance I had. This is going to sound corny, but however much this life consumes me, however unbalanced things get, I always want to remember that when I look into someone's eyes, I am seeing myself.

Ani DIFRANCO

I'm constantly framed as a stompy, angry girl, the staunch idealist with the big mouth. That's definitely part of my MO—it's an aspect of who I am—but everything else tends to be ignored. When people listen to "Untouchable Face," for instance, they think the phrase *fuck you* in the chorus is the ultimate kiss-off because they only bring one frame of reference to the song. If they were really listening, it would be obvious that *fuck you*

means "I love you desperately; how can you not love me back?" That meaning is clear, but some people have such a simplistic idea of language and who I am that *fuck you* has only one meaning for them.

Everybody's favorite songs on *Dilate* seem to be "Untouchable Face" and "Napoleon"—the two songs with *fuck* in the chorus. Congratulations, Ani! My manager and dear friend, Scot, is always asking if I can think of another word to use. Sure I can! It's not that I have a limited vocabulary. So why does *fuck* show up in the choruses of those two songs? Because I wrote the lines as I would say them. To speak that way was my

instead of playing the FCC's game or listening to some internal censor. Yes, I *could* think of another word, but wouldn't replacing the

real impulse, so why shouldn't I sing the lines in a way that's true to that feeling? So the songs could be played on the radio? I'd rather live in my own world

original thought with something less genuine be a teeny step on the road to writing for some reason other than honesty or personal fulfillment? I'm not interested in making decisions for the sake of becoming palatable.

Last night I was having a conversation with the band about censorship. We don't experience institutional censorship in this country, but there is a kind of self-censorship in a capitalist system where the goal is to move units. Nobody's literally holding a gun to your head and telling you what you can and can't say, but the extreme focus on fame and fortune creates its own kind of censorship. You start to tell yourself, *Maybe I shouldn't say that.* Would you rather have a word in a song bleeped out when it's played on the radio or water down what you write to make it radio-friendly? The staunch idealist in me has a grand resentment for the self-censorship that occurs within the context of capitalism and is an inherent by-product of that system. We have as much mushy radio fodder as we do because it makes money. Even if a writer isn't deliberately making mush, those subconscious tendencies toward generic lyrics that are acceptable and salable is very strong.

One of the worst things for me is when people say I write for shock value, that my songs are unsubtle or heavy-handed. That response probably comes from feeling threatened. We expect to hear certain things and when somebody talks outside the parameters of acceptable conversation or writes songs that aren't about the usual topics, people can become defensive. It's instinctive: "She said 'tampon'; I'm feeling a little tense." Listeners tend to focus

I'm not interested in making decisions for the sake of becoming palatable.

on what makes them uncomfortable, so they don't notice or acknowledge all the other things that are going on in the songs.

I've become aware of a subterranean perception that first, it's "wrong" to talk about certain things, like abortion or whatever the taboo subjects I write about are, and second, if you're going to take on those subjects, you're supposed to do so with a tone of sadness, shame, and apology. The poem "Tiptoe" is a prelude to an abortion that I put on *Not a Pretty Girl*. When I was recording it, there were these really funny outtakes. The poem begins with me walking across the room to the microphone, but in my sneakers, the footsteps weren't loud

> So many of us, myself included, need to keep our sense of personal outrage in check. Each human being's position on the planet is one of intense humility.

enough, so I borrowed my friend Ed's boots, which are twice the size of my feet. I started walking across the room in the pitch black because I always record in the dark. So I'm clomping through the studio, tripping over things and laughing hysterically. I put those outtakes on the album because they were so funny, but several people asked me, as if they were addressing Satan Woman, how I could be talking about an abortion and laughing. If this is my life, then what I do is my prerogative. I should have the personal freedom to react emotionally without having my response restricted or dictated by anyone else. Don't tell me I have to be somber because I'm reading an abortion poem or say to me, "Okay, you can have a relationship with someone of the same sex, but you have to hide it and be full of shame and terror." No way, man. It's a good time. I don't want to be told how to think about the "unacceptable" things I do.

When I write about subjects that aren't the usual topics of songs or use language in an unexpected way, a red flag goes up for some people. They can't get over that defensive response, so they place the song in the shock writing category. To have someone frame my writing that way is the biggest insult because I work hardest on crafting songs. Writing is very important to me. It's the focus of what I do. That's where the real work is. Jamming with the band—now that I have one—allows us to come up with little riffs and rhythms ad nauseam, but to make any one of those ideas into a song is the hard part. It doesn't just happen. I obsess over every line. It's got to be perfect. I know that makes me sound anal, but if it's not *just right*, it's hard to live with.

There's a line from "Buildings and Bridges," which I wrote four albums ago, that keeps coming up with my audience: "eyes the size of snow." I intended the image to mean eyes as cold as snow, but I wanted the alliteration of "eyes" and "size." I just liked singing it that way even though it's not the best possible wording to get the meaning across. I thought, *Oh, well, it's just a little ditty, so let it go.* I've had nothing but trouble since. The conversations I've had about that line are encouraging in one sense because they show that my audience is really listening but . . . The other night after I played the song, some guy yelled, "What does 'eyes the size of snow' mean?" Okay, it's dumb, but it's only one stupid fucking line that I let slide. So there's the lesson: Obsess over everything.

I'm anal about what I write, but I also think you have to have a sense of humor about your work and everything else in life. More and more, life and humor are inseparable for me. When I was a teenager first

writing songs, I was too scared and in too much personal jeopardy to see that things were funny. Just trying to pass in the adult world and take care of myself was hard enough. I wasn't as much of a good-time gal as I am now that I'm not as threatened by everything that comes along. So many things are funny to me now. Even the most heinous things have their funny side. There is a certain personal empowerment that comes with being able to laugh at what's most horrible. Without that capacity, we're doomed. So many of us, myself included, need to keep our sense of personal outrage in check. Humor helps us do that, as does humility. Those qualities are necessary to put things in perspective. Each human being's position on the planet is one of intense humility. How significant is any one of us? Very significant and, at the same time, not at all significant.

> I heard that a lot of women were getting off the boat because I fell in love with a guy. The really terrifying thing for me was the thought that those women were here all along because, what, I was a sex symbol?

It seems so self-indulgent to me when people become enraptured by their own sense of personal injustice. In "Joyful Girl" there's a line that reads, "The world owes us nothing." I've always felt that way. I'm basically a middle-class kid who's turned off and maddened by middle-class expectations. Like other middle-class kids who come from this country, an affluent country with one of the highest standards of living, I never really wanted for much. Because of the lucky circumstances of time and place, many of us have always been afforded our basic needs at the very least. I see these fortunate people around me, at the shows, *my* people, and some of them have this pervasive sense of personal outrage about all sorts of things. That they don't recognize how privileged they are is intolerable to me. We think the world owes us all this and more. Eighty percent of the people in the world don't have what we do. Think about that.

Outside a venue where I was playing in Northampton, a friend of mine, a guy named Steve who's part of this very cool group of fans which comes literally to more than half of my shows, was being verbally abused by these young white middle-class women. Steve is the sweetest man. To know him and then picture a scenario where these women are abusing him, saying things like "We've been taking shit from men all of our lives, and now it's our turn" is unthinkable. There is no right target for that kind of self-indulgent bullshit. I was so angry when I heard about what happened. Nobody told me until after the show because

My guitar was my only company for a long time.

they knew I'd get up onstage and rant about how those people need to fucking get over themselves.

Dilate is kind of funny to me because I am so consumed with my emotions and the melodrama of my own circumstances in the songs on this album. Indulging in the melodrama of my personal life was never really my thing. I didn't have much of an attention span for my own emotions until I developed this incredibly strong feeling for someone I

dedicated to my own thoughts and feelings, but that was always a running joke to me because I never really was. Even though I was this symbol of strong convictions and despite the fact that I was supposedly very angry, I was an easygoing, happy person. But then that feeling of being colossally in love came over me for the first time, and everything seemed essential. In one verse of "Shameless," where I write about imagining the bones beneath our skin, stripping things bare, there's a kind of urgency that's about recognizing mortality, its character, form, mass, and velocity. At that moment of desire and love, nothing is as it seems. We put on our little uniforms and play our roles, we walk around steeped in connotation, but then suddenly everything becomes fresh again because of the way love makes you take nothing for granted.

Lately I've been experiencing this whole new terror because *Dilate* is mostly about that ridiculous, essential experience of

supposedly couldn't have. I didn't think that I could make it through that feeling. Until that point in my life I'd always been pretty happy-go-lucky. I was perceived as being

falling in love. The object of my affection happened to be a boy, and that fact gave rise to a whole wave of disillusionment in the dyke community. I had fallen for a guy, so I was suddenly the straight queen of the universe. I heard that a lot of women were getting off the boat because I fell in love with a guy. They saw that as the ultimate betrayal. The really terrifying thing for me was the thought that those women were here all along because, what, I was a sex symbol? That's the thing they got out of what I do? Whoa. I'm still grappling with that thought. It's the ultimate terror to think that there's no difference between me and Mariah Carey other than the people I'm attracting. Some people's work is about sex, but for others it's about something more,

> **I'm trying to figure out if it is possible to supersede your intelligence and stumble forth in life with a sense of innocence.**

something bigger, that includes sexuality but isn't about selling sex. If the fantasy of a relationship with me that listeners might have is shattered, isn't there something else in the work to hold their interest? Are they actually hearing anything that I'm trying to say? If there's nothing about my work beyond the sexual fantasy for people, then when I step up onstage, I'd feel like a joke.

I hate the cliché that you have to suffer in your life for your art, but unfortunately I find it's true for me to a certain degree. Trying to balance life with my work is something I've been grappling with a lot lately because *I'm in a relationship.* It sounds so funny for me to say, "I'm in a relationship," because it's so much not my thing. But now I have a really close friend and we spend all of our time together. It's nauseating. It's ridiculous. I'm part of that tribe of couples now, I guess. Most of my life I've had no one to talk to. I've always been pretty good at being alone and staying independent. I certainly veered towards loneliness and despondency a lot of the time, but therein lay the creation of all those songs. Because I literally didn't talk to people, certainly not about things that were really important to me, I wrote a lot. My guitar was my only company for a long time.

Now when I have a thought or a reaction, I have lots of conversations with what's his face instead of writing so many songs. It's terrifying: Whoops, I'm not suffering anymore, I'm actually kind of happy, and I have somebody I love, so I guess there's nothing more to say. Of course it's not completely like that. I'm still writing songs, but I'm not writing with the same careening, car-crashing desperation because I

have something in the world other than myself and my guitar. I'm starting to feel this slow burn, a maddening sense of artistic constipation, because days go by when I'm not writing. When I do finish a song, I feel a real sense of fulfillment and let out a big, heaving exhalation. The days when I'm writing are very good days.

In writing and in relationships with people, I'm trying to figure out if it is possible to

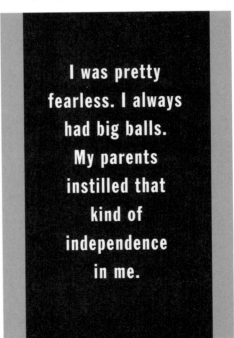

I was pretty fearless. I always had big balls. My parents instilled that kind of independence in me.

supersede your intelligence and stumble forth in life with a sense of innocence. I worry most about whether I'm too calculating because I can gauge the consequences of my actions ten or twenty steps ahead. I try to shut off that knowledge so I don't manipulate the outcome so much. That's hard to do in the writing process, for instance, because I know exactly the kind of reaction every little thing I write is going to get. Even in relationships with people, you know how someone is going to react to certain things, so you calculate your actions accordingly. I want to be able to ignore that knowledge, to turn it off and regain a sense of genuineness and innocence even though I know a little bit too much.

That's one reason I still find the coffeehouse culture of folk music preferable to the posturing, glamorous world of rock and roll. I've been inadvertently sucked into the pop music sphere and exposed to all of the horrible things that come with it, but I've been making a conscious effort to remain con-nected to the folk world's values. We've worked with the same independent little folk promoters all along rather than the big commercial rock and roll promoters so we could sustain relationships with people who believe music has some meaning beyond making money. I like playing folk festivals and coffeehouses where you can talk to people. I don't feel very fulfilled in that screaming and generic rock and roll milieu. I think it's cool that there's a whole community of people who perform *as themselves* without pretension or pomp. I'm much more attracted to that sort of genuine and simple form of musical expression.

There are constant checks and balances when I'm deciding what to do with my music to make sure it remains genuine. Scot and I examine every possibility that comes up by asking ourselves why we should or shouldn't do something. I question everything, like whether I need to worry about being played on commercial radio. My radio exposure has been exclusively on college and community stations because they're the only ones playing whatever they want without commercial or corporate interference. When you get into the commercial radio sphere, the rules of the marketplace are very much in effect. Commercial radio has not played me because I have no leverage in the industry. It's not like Jack at Warner Brothers calls up WXYZ and says, "All right, we got the new Ani DiFranco single, and we want you to play it. If you do, we'll give you the exclusive rights to the U2 worldwide simulcast and giveaway tickets for their next tour." That's the way it works. It's preciously close to bribery. There's an exclusive club, and I'm on the outside, so no commercial airplay for little me.

Scot has been telling me that the only way these radio people are going to acknowledge me at all is if I go to the stations and meet them. If I sit down and play them a song, maybe they'll think I'm all right and pay attention. In a

sense that idea attracts me. Why should people play music on the air? Because they want to. Because they believe in it. Because they met the musician, heard her play, and think she's good. That seems to me a very genuine way to interest people in what I do. But then I think, *I don't really enjoy going to radio stations and doing interviews, so why should I?* To get more airplay. Why do I need more airplay? I don't want to go talk to some person at a commercial radio station who doesn't really love music. Of course they're not all like that, but it really makes me uncomfortable to be in a situation where I get the claustrophobic feeling that it's about money, not music. It's like finding yourself in a demeaning conversation that you didn't intend to take part in.

So I question everything and fight it all. I fight doing every interview. I make life very difficult for the folks at Righteous Babe Records because I leave them without the tools to do their jobs. There's no marketing publicity or buzz clip video to work with. Unless I'm willing to go out personally and talk to everybody in a grass roots fashion, there's not much they can do to promote the records.

I'm used to being independent and call- one who wasn't in trouble. I was well adjusted, so I was easily over-looked. My mother and father afforded

ing the shots, so none of this is odd to me. I was pretty much on my own from the time I was a kid because in my family I was the me a lot of independence and just assumed I would rise to the occasion. It was a really good way for me to be brought up—or not brought up, as the case may be—because I

was always a very independent person, the stable one in a very fucked-up family. That role seems kind of funny now because I'm perceived as this freak from hell. But when my family was in a state of chaos for a long time, I was the well-adjusted daughter who could serve as a sounding board for my mom. Of course there was the mother-daughter element of our relationship, but more than that, we were friends and I was her confidante. She would say, "You're the only person I have to talk to," and then spew out her perspective. My father and brother had very little emotional relationship with me other than the flux and struggle we went through day by day.

I was pretty fearless. I

always had big balls. My parents instilled that kind of independence in me. And I was a happy kid even though I'm sure I shouldn't have been. That independence allowed me to deal with the fact that everything's always in flux. When people ask about the significant days or turning points in my life, I can't answer because I don't see anything in terms of milestones. For me, everything is interrelated.

There's an infinite sense of reality down in the subway. That's why I still play there. It's one of the most real things I know. When I was living on the West Coast a few years ago, I was miserable. I realized it was because I didn't have the subway. Playing there is something that I have to do or else I get ill in the head. It's therapy for me.

Busking has been an education in understanding people, and for everything you see down there, it's made me feel more positive about humanity. It reminds me not to stereotype people, not to judge books by their covers. I used to play a little game, trying to figure out which person was going to put something in my case. I'd look over the butt brigade—the people who keep their butts to you while you play, just looking up for the train—and think, *This dude with the long hair and the freaky jacket will be the one who*

LORD

Mary Lou

gives me the buck, not the guy with the briefcase and the suit. And then the businessman would turn around and put some money down. At first I was surprised that the longhair wasn't necessarily as appreciative as the guy with a briefcase, but it didn't take long to realize my preconceptions about people were too strict.

I also love the fact that I can keep songs alive by playing them for people down there. Songs only exist when someone hears them. I especially like to play songs that have never been recorded, are stuck in some archive, or hidden away on an unreleased album. Lately I've been playing "I Figured You Out," a song by Elliott Smith, my favorite songwriter right now. He was going to throw it away because he thought it sounded too much like an Eagles' song. I told him that it didn't sound anything like an Eagles' song to me and asked if I could record it. He agreed to let me. The song is a reflection on bitterness that carries a humble kind of anger, and I really feel that emotion when I play it. I know other people get some-

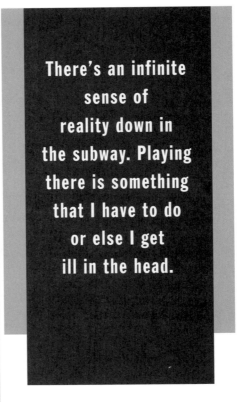

There's an infinite sense of reality down in the subway. Playing there is something that I have to do or else I get ill in the head.

thing strong from it too. It's just such a great song that I didn't want Elliott to throw it away, to let it disappear. Even though a song like that isn't necessarily getting airplay and the listeners probably don't even know the name of the writer, during the three minutes I'm playing it for the people standing around at the subway stop, the song is living again, right then and there, in real time.

It takes a lot of work to research songs and find great music that isn't available on the radio or in record stores. If you're a busy person with a busy life, you're not going to spend time seeking out that kind of stuff. I've tried to make it available. My reward is when someone likes what I play enough to come up and ask, "Who wrote that?" or "What's the name of that song?" When I put out records, I include covers on them, songs I love which are hard to find, for the same reason.

Playing songs, whether I wrote them or not, is a very cathartic and personal thing for me. Even if they're not mine, they're still my story. They're real to me. If you're not faking it and you're playing for no other reason than your belief in the music, then this life can be a beautiful thing. I never felt I had to scramble to get ahead or make contacts; the process was natural because I was doing it out of love and respect for the music itself. That may sound like a romantic idea, but it's a fact. What is romance any-

way? In part it's about love, and I love songs, I love playing, so in that sense I guess it is romantic.

I've been fortunate too because people have respected what I do. Those who have helped me out along the way knew I was into music for the right reasons. It was almost as if it was impossible for them to disregard me because they knew I was doing the right thing. By incorporating what I did into their lives—whether by giving me a gig or letting me record for their label—they were doing the right thing too. I don't want to sound like I'm some saint. What I mean to say is that it's been very natural to come to this point with my music because of the way the music itself, outside of my own ego and interests, is at the center of what I do and who I am. The people I've been lucky enough to work with understand that too. They're just respecting songs and music in their hearts like I am.

Joni Mitchell says that songs are like children. When I wrote "His Indie World," I was trying to illustrate that fact. I was hanging out with these kids who were listening only to current indie music and I'd ask them

they loved Sebadoh and Lou Barlow. Lou Barlow adores Joni Mitchell; without her in-

if they'd heard Nick Drake. They'd say, "No." Then I'd ask if they listened to Joni Mitchell. They'd say, "No, and we don't want to listen to her." Yet

fluence he wouldn't be writing the songs these kids love so much.

And then there are any number of indie musicians writing songs inspired by someone like Lou Barlow who don't even realize they're producing songs that are the grand-children of Joni Mitchell's songs. They haven't even listened to her work. It's important to know the history behind what you're doing as a musician, to know where your songs come from, whose children and grand-children they are. I just adore songs, and I adore songwriters. It's taken me a long time to realize that not everyone feels that way. Not everybody wants to be an archivist, someone who keeps great songs alive. Songs aren't like children to everyone.

The paths music takes are fascinating to me. I began by listening to lots of folk music, then moved into rock and pop. I've been listening lately to a lot of rockabilly. I've almost gone through the whole genre now, listening to different kinds of rockabilly. My interest in it started when I was getting more and more into pop songs, the kind of music the Beatles were exploring in the early sixties. So I asked myself what the Beatles listened to, what they were influenced by. They listened to Gene Vincent and Carl Perkins, for instance. I followed that line of rockabilly back to country music by people like Ernest Tubbs, Jimmy Rogers, and Woody Guthrie. Now I've come full circle. I started with folk and ended up back with Woody Guthrie after a long detour that led as far away as the progressive rock genre. It's all interconnected. It's all part of this big family tree.

The music I play is a combination of the different musical directions I've taken. If I had to place it on that family tree, I'd say it's the offspring of folk and low-fi. It's close to folk in spirit, but it's not as finely crafted, not as densely worded. I'm very respectful of the craft and skill you need to play real folk music. It takes years and years to master those skills. My music isn't that polished, but it does have the simplicity of folk. It also takes a more pop-influenced, low-fi direction. Even though I was playing mostly folk, I was always interested in the punk crowd and the indie movement. Once I heard Lois and Daniel Johnston, I understood how close their music is to folk because of its simplicity and the fact that a lot of it is acoustic. But it's also got that three-chord pop structure and a certain quirkiness. When friends turned me on to the low-fi stuff, I went in that direction. That's the kind of music I was going out to listen to every night after I'd played folk music all day. The resulting mix is more popular now than it was then, but in the end, no matter what it's called—low-fi, punk, folk, indie—the music has to be real and the songs have to be honest.

In the beginning, when I was in high school, I wanted to be a DJ, but the managers at the college station where I had a show wouldn't let me play the songs I liked. They came up with a playlist that was ridiculous. They wanted the DJs to be programmed machines instead of people. I played what I wanted anyway and wrote the names of the songs on their playlist in the station log. They discovered what I'd been doing and kicked me out. Before I left, I told them, "I don't want to spin goddamn vinyl anyway; I want to make what's on it." I didn't believe I could, but I knew I wanted to do something involving music.

> If you're not faking it and you're playing for no other reason than your belief in the music, then this life can be a beautiful thing.

After high school, I went to Berklee College of Music in Boston as a voice major, but when I tried to switch into the production-engineering track, I was told I couldn't get in. I found a school in London for audio engineering and went to England before I found out that they taught everything through simulated equipment. It seemed like all I did for four months was draw flowcharts. I didn't want to know how to fix the stuff; I just wanted to know how to use it. But I'd already paid for the course, so I took my flowcharts into the subway to study because it was warmer than the unheated squat where I was living. I'd sit near this busker so I could listen to him. One day he asked me to watch his stuff while he went to the bathroom. I picked up his guitar after he left—my roommate from Berklee had taught me a couple of chords—and played what I could. Someone threw money in the can, and from then on I was sold. I got a guitar and played one little tune over and over again and eventually learned some more songs. After school in London I came home with the desire to play.

When I was just back from England, I decided that I didn't want to wake up one day when I was thirty-five and realize that I had never tried to be a musician. Up until then I'd wanted to be a producer or an engineer, but I realized that it would be very difficult to step into those roles without first spending years doing crap jobs at a studio. So I proceeded to experiment with myself instead of waiting for the perfect artist to come by and ask me to produce him. I served as my own A and R person, my own producer. I think the experiment worked because I've never tried to bullshit myself or anyone else. Because of that, I've gone a lot further than I ever thought I would.

During that period in the late eighties Suzanne Vega, Michelle Shocked, and Tracy Chapman were really changing the system and the way music was being looked at. They were tremendous role models for me, as they were for so many people. They influenced a lot of young women who are playing and writing music now. Of course people had been playing acoustic music for ages and ages, but it just so happened that the record industry really pushed it at that time. That push allowed many young women to hear these artists and identify with them. Before that, I don't remember, aside from Rickie Lee Jones, many high-profile women singer-songwriters.

> They discovered what I'd been doing and kicked me out. Before I left, I told them, "I don't want to spin goddamn vinyl anyway; I want to make what's on it."

the right people's favorite songs. When I say the "right people," I mean people I would want to talk to, people, like Robert, who really cared about music, people who were journalists or DJs because music was so important to them. So they would come up and talk to me.

Inspired by that climate, I decided to give it a shot. My motives for playing had changed from the desire to make a few bucks because I was broke to playing songs as well as I could and getting better each time. One night I was trying to play a Sandy Denny song—I was truly awful—when this guy from WERS I'd met once before, Robert Hague, came up to me and said, "Oh, there you are—struggling." Even though I was terrible, I was playing

Soon after that, Robert Hague introduced me to Shawn Colvin, and from that day on I was so moved by her music that I wanted to help further it in any way I could. This was well before she had a tape out or a record deal. It was important to me that people heard what she was doing. It became my mission in life to turn the world on to Shawn Colvin, and in the end I think I did introduce her to a lot of people. Support is very important when you're starting out; you can never get enough encouragement. There have to be people behind you because there isn't always a lot of radio play and label attention to keep machines. Now Shawn and I are friends; I feel about her the way she must feel about Joni Mitchell when she

you going at the beginning. The industry is ass-backwards. It relies on formulas. But real music has to come from people, not adding writes in the liner notes of a record, "You master, me slave."

From that point on I completely committed myself to playing, to getting better and putting the songs I loved out there. Of course I missed out on a lot of what people in their twenties normally do because I was standing in a goddamn subway every Saturday night. Sometimes it got to me, playing there, eleven o'clock at night, cold, smelly, all these happy couples walking by, kids dressed up to go out, and there you are with your dirty fingers, dirty face, bums coming up to you. . . . Still, if I could do it over again, I wouldn't have it any other way. Those are the dues that I paid. I learned so much. I have that now. I did the work.

The more I played, the less social time I had. I missed going to the clubs with my friends, all that shit you do in your twenties. What the hell do

> I took my flowcharts into the subway to study because it was warmer than the unheated squat where I was living.

people do in their twenties? Some go to graduate school, I guess; others get married, have kids, get divorced. Instead I was standing there singing. When I stopped playing for a few minutes and finally started to meet people, they were the ones I would want to meet. It was as if I'd been sending a message out while I was playing: "This is me. This is what I do. If you're cool with it, come talk to me." When you play songs, you're giving someone a gift. If they recognize that, hopefully they will want to give it back. That's what made the life I was living worthwhile: the way I could give and people would give back. When I came back from England, most of my old friends were gone, but by playing, I eventually made new friends who were into the same things I was.

When I was growing up, I was a com-

plete outcast like a lot of artistic people in their hometowns. They're just not quite in step with everybody else. Once you get older, it can be really cool to have been different, but when you're in the middle of it, it's awful. What's most important is the way you're treated by your family when you're beginning to find out who you are. If you have support from your family, it's cool to be different; it's okay to be artistic or gay, whatever. You can remain consistent in your oddness. But if your family is against you, as well as your friends, then it can get really confusing and painful; it can fuck you up for a really long time. But that's life. Growing up was difficult for me, but I guess it is for everyone.

I'm the very last of five kids. There's a nineteen-year gap between my oldest sister and me, so I grew up in a family of three different generations. I had a lot of freedom, maybe too much freedom. I was left alone a lot. I felt neglected, and now I can get pretty angry about it.

My mother worked the night shift, and I didn't see her very much. I asked her recently why she didn't work during the day so she could be with me when I came home from school. She said, "Because I worked the night shift."

By the time I came along, she had already had kids for nearly twenty years; she was forty-two and just wanted to hang out. Being at work was her social time. It was factory work, but she loved spending the night shift with her girlfriends, smoking and shooting the shit for eight hours. So I was supposed to be taken care of by my sisters and brothers, but they usually did their own thing. They were teenagers, and they left me alone a lot. There was too much time to think. I developed a love of music because I could sit in the middle of all that sound and feel less lonely. From early on music had the power to make me feel really good.

Songs were the backdrops for what I felt as a kid. I remember my mother cleaning the house on Saturdays and blasting Burt

Bacharach, the Carpenters, and Herb Alpert. She used to sing along, screaming at the top of her lungs, "This guy's in love with you," dancing around with the broom. Those were the best times. Mom was home, and I knew she was happy because she was singing. So whenever music was on, people were happy. When the music wasn't playing, I knew somebody was unhappy. It went hand in hand. From the time I was very young, I associated music with happy times, and I still remember what I've done, feelings I've had through songs.

Later on my father had a CB radio that I'd use. I'd meet friends on the CB, and we'd find some channel that no one was using so that we could talk. I'd ask if they'd heard a particular Led Zeppelin or Jethro Tull song.

> It was as if I'd been sending a message out while I was playing: "This is me. This is what I do. If you're cool with it, come talk to me."

If they said no, I'd get all excited—"You've got to hear this!"—and put the CB mike up to this little tape player I had, so they could listen to it. We'd spend hours trading songs back and forth over the air. I was really into heavy music, and the people I found who liked it too—my new CB friends who smoked pot and had motorcycles—were all living a more or less white trash lifestyle like me. We weren't listening to Bananarama like the preppy kids. We thought the same way. We liked the same music and used it as an escape. They became my new friends in high school because they had the same background as I did. Most of them had older siblings and came from big, messy families. I felt comfortable with them because I didn't have to be ashamed of where I came from; their lives at home were just as messed up as mine.

My parents had expectations for me, but it was difficult for me to relate to them, especially because they didn't have any expectations for themselves. They were living one way yet expecting me to live another. They wanted me to be a prep and go to college even though they never encouraged me by their example. Of course they didn't want me to go out with the boy on the motorcycle or get pregnant, but they weren't providing much of an alternative by the example they were setting.

My mother and I would go

> **I was really into heavy music, and the people I found who liked it too—my new CB friends who smoked pot and had motorcycles—were all living a more or less white trash lifestyle like me.**

shopping on Saturdays, and she would buy me belts with sailboats and pants with whales. My mother would always ask me if I was going to call my friend with a father who was a lawyer. She wanted me to hang out with the yacht club kids. What could I say to the kids at the yacht club? We didn't understand anything about one another's families, and when you're a kid, all you have is your family. I didn't realize then that a lot of families, however rich, were run poorly too, because they only tell you about the good stuff, you only see the good stuff. So you think that things are going great for them when they might really be going wrong. There's so much bullshit you can't get through when you're a kid. Everybody's just full of it.

Whatever was happening in other families that I didn't see, I don't think too many

ing and screaming. Sometimes my brothers, who were eighteen or nineteen, would take me out with them in-

kids were up until three o'clock in the morning, listening to their alcoholic sisters fighting and screaming. Sometimes my brothers, who were eighteen or nineteen, would take me out with them instead of leaving me home alone. They would rush me back before my mother got home from work at one or two in the morning, then get me ready for school the next day because she would still be asleep. There were days when I'd only see my mother for five minutes after I came home from school and before she left for work. There wasn't much time to say, "Guess what, Mommy? I was up until one again last night cruising around with my brothers." So the whole cycle would start again, and the next day I'd be falling asleep in class. The teachers screamed at me and then began to think I had attention deficit disorder when it was just that I didn't sleep enough. I became addicted to sugar because it helped keep me awake, and because of that, I got really fat. That whole time in my life was just ridiculous.

I was an awkward kid, and I had no confidence in myself whatsoever until I began to sing. I joined the Salem Chorus, a group with kids from all the different schools in the city. There was a tryout for a solo on "You Light Up My Life," so all the girls auditioned. After I sang, my teacher stood up and took my hand.

In front of everyone she said, "Now that was the way the song was meant to be sung; Mary Lou will be singing the solo." I was amazed that I'd done something well.

Then, in high school, there was a tryout

for an all-state concert choir. By then I didn't care much about that dorky chorus stuff, but a girl in my group named Christine said, "Come on, Mary Lou. You should really try out." I told her I wouldn't make it and that I didn't care about that music anyway. But she insisted and helped me prepare a song for the audition. I kept singing it the wrong way, and she would scream, "Get it right!" until I did. Christine, another girl, Kelly, and I went to Beverly High, in the next town over, on the bus together for the audition. I was a long shot, and they were pretty sure they'd get in.

About three weeks later I was called to the office at school. I was high as a kite and thought, *Now I'm in serious trouble.* I looked in the office windows and all these geeks with their cellos and violins were sitting there. I thought, *They can't all be in trouble,* so I went in and asked, "What's wrong?" The principal said, "We just want to congratulate you for making the all-state chorus and tell you that your picture's going to be in the paper." I screamed, "Oh, my God!" When I went to class that afternoon, I think some of the kids were pissed at me for getting a spot when they didn't. I worshiped everyone else in the chorus and thought they were all better than me, so making all-state was a real surprise and a

> **A lot of the time I still think I'm nothing, but then I remember that a label gave me a lot of money to make a record. When that happened, I thought, *Well, maybe I'm not as worthless as I think I am.***

119

confirmation. It told me that I couldn't have been the only one to pass the audition if I had been worse than everyone else.

A lot of the time I still think I'm nothing, but then I remember that a label gave me a lot of money to make a record. When that happened, I thought, *Well, maybe I'm not as worthless as I think I am.* I know it's fucked up that it takes money to convince me that I'm any good. It was like that in the subway too. I kept telling myself how bad I was, but when someone pulls a bill out of his pocket, that money does not lie. I know that's an awful way to think, but that's how I felt. I was lied to a lot as a kid, so I didn't really trust what people said, but every time a person put something in my case it reaffirmed for me that I was okay, that I was doing something right. It's the same with being signed to a label.

I was really fortunate in getting a record deal. I met this woman named Tinuviel at a party. It turned out we had a few mutual friends like Kath-

> **I'm learning to listen to my head a lot more now because I already trust my heart. I already know it's fully functional, even if it does sometimes get me into trouble.**

leen Hanna from Bikini Kill, who recorded for her label, Kill Rock Stars. So we hung out one summer when she lived in Boston and became good friends. When she went back to Seattle, she called me and said she really missed my voice and asked me to send her a tape. I made a compilation tape for her on a boom box and sent it off. Once she'd listened to it, she called back and said she really loved the tape and wanted to put a song on a Kill Rock Stars compilation. So they put the song right from the tape onto the record. When the compilation came out, my song got quite a lot of attention because it was this wimpy folk thing recorded on a box sandwiched between all this hard stuff—Bikini Kill, Team Dresch. I went out west to visit Tinuviel and decided to move out there. I stayed for a couple years, put out a seven-inch with Kill Rock Stars, and played here and there.

One night I was opening up for Sebadoh in Olympia when Margaret Mittleman came to the show. She's a music publisher at BMG who was thinking about signing them. My friend Slim Moon told her to make sure she didn't miss my set, so she came early and really liked it. I didn't know what a publisher was, and I didn't really care, but she kept sending me tapes of this guy Beck, who she was about to sign. I'd listen to him and think, *She can't be an ambulance chaser because this guy is totally weird.*

Around the time I signed with Margaret, she got Beck a deal with Geffen, and his first record did really, really well. All these record companies came barking up her tree because she was the one who found Beck. They asked who else she was working with, and she told them, "There's this new girl, Mary Lou Lord, who I just signed." So all of a sudden the record companies came running to me. I was really fortunate to get that attention. I talked to all these different labels, and it took me a year before I decided to sign with the WORK Group. I finished recording *Got No Shadow* with Nick Saloman of the Bevis Frond, who cowrote a lot of the songs. I'm a huge fan of his and it's really amazing to work with him. I think it's a really good record, and I'm proud of it.

So I'm slowly letting go of the idea that I'm worthless. I'm actually starting to believe that I'm okay now. I don't need so much proof from outside anymore. I'm becoming much more comfortable with myself. I un-

derstand now the importance of being truthful to yourself and treating your friends and family well. If I'm not lying to myself, if I focus on the real things, then I'm fine. That's the bottom line for my life these days.

I'm learning to listen to my head a lot more now because I already trust my heart. I already know it's fully functional, even if it does sometimes get me into trouble. I just let the heart work on automatic pilot and try to engage my head when I need to. I'm trying to make better decisions about how I live, to live the way I've always wanted to. If you do that, you end up respecting yourself more and treating people well. I've always been honest about at least one thing, which is music, and now I try to bring that honesty into the rest of my life. I don't even want to think about what things would be like if I didn't have music. I'd be working in a lightbulb factory, I'm convinced of it, or I'd be dead.

Mary Chapin CARPENTER

There I was in my little room at the back of the bus lounging with my dog, Cal. He was sitting there looking so cute I just had to kiss him. I got on the walkie-talkie and said to everyone up front, "Hello. Chapin to anybody. Would you think I'm completely sick if I told you I wanted to kiss my dog on the lips?" And I did it—kissed him right on the lips, on that scrunchy mouth of his. I thought, *I'm completely nuts*. Then the com-

ments started coming back fast and furious over the walkie. Someone shouted, summing up the general response, "I really think you need a vacation."

Seriously, though, it's not a surprise that having Cal with me on the road means so much. I've always relied on the companionship and unconditional love of animals. We had lots of animals in the house when I was growing up. During the period of time before I got Cal, I was particularly lonely. I can't imagine now how I ever got along without him. Because Cal's companionship gives me as much pleasure as anything in my life, it's so important to have him with me.

One of the biggest sacrifices I've made, doing what I do, is a homelife. I haven't yet allowed the time for that sense of putting roots down, settling in, the strong feeling of being part of a community. It can be romantic and breathtaking seeing so many places, having the chance to send your music out there, but you miss the other side of it. For some people it doesn't matter where they are, but home means a great deal to me. A perfect day for me is to wake up in my own bed, with the dogs rarin' to go out, take them on a run, get a couple of song ideas started, have the kind of conversation with a friend that fills my tank, prepare a great dinner, watch a video or plow through a great book, and then crash. Even though I can't always have those days, I try to provide, in very tangible ways, some sense of home for myself. It's a way

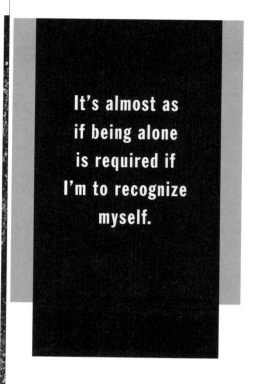

It's almost as if being alone is required if I'm to recognize myself.

to counter this transient, peripatetic existence. So home can be a place you take with you. Like George Carlin says, "You've got to have your 'stuff.'" I always bring some pictures, my pillow, some favorite books—the familiar things that personalize a sterile hotel room or that small space on the bus. I'm also lucky that I've played with a lot of the same musicians over the years. Having the same people with you also gives you a sense of family and makes being away from home less difficult.

For all that I try, though, it's tough to balance everything all the time. I have this secret, occasional fear that I can't be with someone else because I'll lose track of who I am when I'm doing what I normally do. Although I've been in love and have had long-term relationships, I still don't believe I know how to be completely myself when I'm with someone else—as if I'm a different person within a relationship. I haven't learned yet how to make those two selves coexist. I wonder if I've sabotaged or walked away from relationships because I hadn't figured out how to fit into the picture. It's almost as if

being alone is required if I'm to recognize myself. I don't mean that to sound self-pitying. I don't want to believe that I have to be alone to do what I do—that's such a cliché to me—but I wonder if it isn't true nonetheless. I can think of any number of people who live very balanced lives that include healthy, ongoing relationships whose work is egocentric as this work is. It's possible to have it both ways. I know it is. I just need to work at getting there.

Relationships can be amazingly difficult puzzles. They're like complex math problems that need to be solved if two people are going to be able to communicate. God knows why it's so hard. On *Shooting Straight in the Dark*, songs like "Can't Take Love for Granted" and "What You Didn't Say" are pretty bleak. Songs often seem to be windows into what I'm going through at the time. That record definitely reflects where I was then. Although I don't necessarily feel that pessimistic now, there are still peo-

> Connecting with people through songwriting is the ultimate. Communicating, in all its forms, is the thing that I find so hard to do. When I feel that I've connected, I'm grateful.

ple I just don't get through to, and I'm sure they feel the same way about me. Perhaps the longing to connect is what makes it so fulfilling when someone tells me they "get" a certain song. Connecting with people through songwriting is the ultimate. Communicating, in all its forms, is the thing that I find so hard to do, so it's a great reward when it happens. When I feel that I've connected, I'm grateful.

The idea that I could get through to people through songs came later than the initial impulse to write because for years I wasn't playing for anyone but myself. Writing was an outlet. It soothed me and created a vent so things could come out. That was

about looking at life and trying to make sense of why I did a certain thing. It's about a lot of different emotions and responses, though perhaps when I'm writing, I'm not clued into all of them. When I begin to collect the songs for an album, a theme isn't necessarily clear to me. But by the time I've finished, a thread that runs through and connects each song makes itself plain. The emergence of that thread is a magical process to me. Even when you're not always sure about what you've done, writing serves a lot of purposes.

For me, the desire to communicate hasn't anything to do with confession. The confessional female singer-songwriter stereotype is a snore. I've never liked the word *confessional* anyway. If I have something to confess, I'll let you know. I've never written something that I later felt revealed too much. I don't think of a personal song necessarily as confessional. I take the meanings of these words quite literally. *Confession* to me means

an undeclared motivation: to provide a way for what's inside to come out. Songwriting has become the way I make sense out of my life and the lives around me. It has always been there, to help me sort my thoughts, work through my emotions, express humor and pain and the occasional outrage. It's

admitting something you've done for which you seek forgiveness. I think of songwriting as a vehicle for *expression* rather than *confession*. Writing can be personal and emotional without being tied up with guilt and the need for absolution.

Someone asked me recently what I thought about the fact that women in rock have become the new "flavor of the week" in music. Being a woman definitely informs my songwriting. Being a woman is a central fact of my existence. It's inescapable. It's what I am. I have written some songs that are undeniably from the vantage point of a woman, songs that I think could only have been written by a woman. But there are just as many that I believe speak to all of us, and as such they could come from a woman or a man. When songs are utterly autobiographical, they're obviously going to be from *my* point of view—that is, a woman's viewpoint.

But because I never felt I wrote more one than another, I've always been uncomfortable with being tagged as a "woman's writer." The best part of songwriting is the feeling that I'm connecting with anyone and everyone,

men and women. We share a lot of the same experiences and emotions, and I'm often more interested in what we share than what makes us different.

How many times have you heard a writer advise that you should "write about what you know"? I believe that it's in the exploration of what you *don't* know that exercises your mind. I want to stretch as a writer as much as I can. Hell is writing the same song over and over again. Two of the songs I'm proudest of, that made me feel as if I had stretched, were "John Doe No. 24" and "I Am a Town." When I was writing those songs, I felt completely inside them. I was in "the zone." "John Doe No. 24" was inspired by the obituary of an anonymous ward of the state of Illinois who was found wandering the streets in 1945. I carried that obituary around for a long time, not because I thought I would write about it but because

I was haunted by the story. I couldn't stop thinking about John Doe because something about his isolation rang a bell inside me. Then one day I was working at my desk and the first verse of the song came out. I found something affirming in his story because he accepted his circumstances with dignity and grace. Given all the scenarios one would have to guess at imagining his life, I was amazed to find out later from people who had taken care of this man that I had been on target. They told me that he dressed himself every day, that he had a great sense of humor and was very dignified. That song has always felt like a gift from somewhere.

The thought of writing a song in the "voice" of a town was another idea that found me out of the blue. In this case it was the power memory, unbidden, that gave me the initial glimpse of the song. I was driving on the Washington Beltway, this congested, noisy bypass. It was the middle of the summer, and there was that certain light you see when the seasons are changing. I don't know how to explain it, but it seemed more like an autumn light, even though it was summertime. There I was driving down the highway on a hot Washington day and the light in the sky made me think of the ocean and the Outer Banks of North Carolina, where I've gone every September for the last ten years or so. I started thinking about the drive from Washington to the Outer Banks and what you pass on the way and how the highway eventually becomes a two-lane road that goes through all these little hamlets. I started seeing all those places in my head, and I wanted to speak in their voices. It was another example of what can happen when a feeling, a smell, a sight reaches back inside you, reminding, retelling, returning you to places you had surrendered to the passage of time. By choice or necessity, we consign our thoughts and experiences to the farthest corners of ourselves. Moments become shadows there, and feelings are replaced by a chalk outline, until something jars the senses. Suddenly the shadows evaporate and the moment comes back into full focus, as your eyes squint into the light. The chalk outlines are filled in, and the feelings are as muscular and true as they ever are.

I didn't think about being a musician as a young girl. Music was just one of my hob-

> My seventh-grade science teacher used to gather his students together after school and play guitar. That was the first time I ever felt I was a part of something, that I belonged somewhere.

bies. There was always music in the house. My parents are musical, but in a recreational way. Dad's a jazz freak, and Mom loves all things operatic and classical. We had a piano to bang around on. I became interested in the guitar because my mom and sister played. Mom had an old gut-string Goya, and my sister had a bass uke that I liked to fool around with. A bass ukulele has the first four strings of the guitar, so it was an easy jump to the guitar. Along with the atmosphere at home, my seventh-grade science teacher used to gather his students together after school and play guitar. That was a big deal to me. That was the first time I ever felt I was a part of something, that I belonged some-where. It made me want to write songs to ex-press myself to others.

The confessional female singer-songwriter stereotype is a snore. I've never liked the word *confessional* anyway. If I have something to confess, I'll let you know.

I always played music, but it never oc-curred to me that I could earn a living that way. It wasn't even a fantasy. Before the age of fifteen I proba-bly spent more time figure skating than anything else. I was a jock. I was either skat-ing or playing sports at school. But as I grew older, I was also playing the guitar more and more and then scribbling down songs too. Increasingly, playing and trying to write songs took over completely. I don't know if it became more fulfilling because I had become an angst-ridden teenager, but I found more and more that I relied on the escape that mu-sic provided.

Trying to write was a big part of the escape. My parents divorced when I was seventeen, and I was already pretty withdrawn. I have a lot of the same fears now that I had then, but they've grown up. I still contend don't know how to articulate them. I was very shy. I was confused about "what it all means" and what we're doing here. Big ques-

with them in songwriting. They are those big-theme fears, like abandonment and betrayal. As a kid you tions. What made me happiest when I was younger was feeling a respite from confusion. That's not so much a state in itself but a reaction against a state. I felt best when I didn't feel shy, of course. I loved riding my bike, just being outside, having fun with my sisters, and being with animals. I loved being loved by our animals.

My father and mother didn't impose on us or communicate expectations beyond their basic wish that we make the most out of an education and be independent. They let us find our own paths. They conveyed somehow that they felt we could do anything we wanted to do if we worked hard. If we developed an interest in something, they usually provided the opportunity for us to follow it. When I got out of high school, I took a year off because I wanted a break . . . from routine, structure,

you name it. I worked a couple of jobs. During that year off I went to an "open mic" night at a bar. I didn't play my own songs. I sang an Emmylou Harris song. She's always been a big inspiration to me. It was very frightening but not so much that I wasn't willing to try it again.

There wasn't a single point when I decided to try to create a career in music. I didn't have some epiphany one night. It just kind of developed slowly. Perhaps my lack of expectations served me well in the sense that I might have lost my courage if I had a timetable. By not looking at things in that way, I didn't leave

> If the contract with the record company fell through tomorrow, I know I would still write music. That's always going to be there, and it will always be a part of me, whether I sing songs for an audience of one thousand people or for two dogs and their water bowls.

myself open to feeling like a failure when I didn't accomplish certain things by a certain time. I didn't have to compare my "progress" with someone else's. But it wasn't wisdom on my part not to have expectations; it just happened that way. I had the belief that I'd keep doing this as long as I could take pleasure in it. Each time something positive happened, I knew it was the combination of really good luck, of being in the right place at the right time, along with hard work and persistence. And the day's going to come, I'm fully aware, when I won't be able to buy myself a gig. I know that although I might not perform forever, songwriting doesn't have to end as well. The

> A friend once remarked that I have an excruciating sense of fairness. Even when people cut in the checkout line, it makes me crazy. I want to hip-check them out of the way.

audience is the key part of the performing equation, but I also know that I started doing this without one and I'll always write for myself. It's the beauty of it all. I didn't get into music because I wanted a record deal. If the contract with the record company fell through tomorrow, I know I would still write music. That's always going to be there, and it will always be a part of me, whether I sing songs for an audience of one thousand people or for two dogs and their water bowls.

A friend once remarked that I have an excruciating sense of fairness. Even when people cut in the checkout line, it makes me crazy. I want to hip-check them out of the way. I want them to account for their behavior. It makes me nuts when people take negative actions and then don't have to account for those actions. There's nothing that makes me crazier, whether it occurs in the supermarket or on Capitol Hill. Okay, I'm showing my judgmental streak. I can't help it. The anger still comes out all this time after discovering in my vulnerable years that life is not perfect. It was hard to accept that not everyone is treated equally and not everything is fair; that some people have neat, tidy lives while others have messy, chaotic lives; that some people don't have money while others do; that life is full of ugliness and unfairness. Only when I hit my thirties did I gain the belief that along with all the shit out there, you find a lot of wonderful things too. Life looked a bit better once I got that part.

That appreciation also helped me to understand that we can do things, however modest, in the face of life's imperfections. Even though I always had deeply held convictions and strong feelings, I was never very assertive about them. In the past few years I discovered how easy it is to merge a kind of activism with my vocation. Last year I wanted to raise funds for CARE on their fiftieth anniversary and decided to put together a different kind of tour book—not your typical ten pages of glamorous glossies—which included essays of mine and photographs by Bill Campbell, who'd been touring with us off and on for a couple of years. The profits all went to CARE. It gave me a great chance to shoot

> If art is about
> keeping faith,
> I understand why
> I need it so.

my mouth off about things that are important to me. It's a real privilege actually.

I can't say, though, that I've ever thought of my song-writing as a moral project in any sense. I suppose in order to do so, I would have to think of myself as a topical writer. Good topical writing is an art form in itself. I would end up hitting people over the head with a message about a right way or wrong way to think about something. I've always thought of myself as a writer whose songs are kind of plain in their structure and meaning, but I hope not pedantic. If I get the details right, I'm happy. There are a lot of different ways to write a song, and mine feels like the nuts-and-bolts approach, which feels right for me. I don't feel as though I offer a voice that represents a generation, a gender, or a political position. If it's true that, as W. H. Auden wrote, "Poetry makes nothing happen," then repressionist regimes wouldn't exile their artists. Even if you're not a polemical writer, your work can make something happen. I recently read a piece about Seamus Heaney which described his writing as a way of "keeping the faith." I love that description. So, if art is about keeping faith, I understand why I need it so.

I am constantly reminded, by personal experience and by the examples of others, that answering a creative need within affirms one's self-worth. To leave this need alone, as something yearned for that either out of fear or failure or mixed-up priorities gets pushed out and away, is to experience a slow and gradual death of spirit. Not all artists are interested in recognition for what they do. As for those who do seek some sort of recognition, it is an ongoing struggle with rejection, an uncertain livelihood and constant internal questioning. But creativity enriches our lives beyond description, and that enrichment leads always to a better understanding of ourselves.

lot of my writing is not terribly civilized. Sometimes I listen to songs by very smart writers who assume that the world is a civil place with certain formalities that people follow, but I don't see things that way. My own experience tells me that life is not like that. That's why I write the way I do. I grew up with people in my face, pulling my hair, saying, "You're the whitest girl I've ever seen." At one point, after I cut my hair short, I was mistaken for a gay boy and got beat up for that. I couldn't win! Although the degree of uncivilized behavior I experienced might have been in part a product of the neighborhood where I grew up, I find that the world as a whole is not particularly civilized.

I didn't go out looking for fights as a kid, but if it was necessary, I'd fight. Fighting was a daily thing where we lived. It was more than being a white girl in a very mixed

VEGA

Suzanne

neighborhood, I was a target because I was a particular kind of girl. I was always reading and interested in books. I didn't like the world of the street because I wasn't well adapted to it. I was better suited to the worlds I read about, so I developed a fantasy life. But I also knew that if I didn't fight, I'd get picked on even more. Fighting was necessary to maintaining my own self-respect.

My family lived in East Harlem for five years before moving to the Upper West Side. Right after my mother's first marriage ended, she met my stepfather in Los Angeles, they fell in love, and he took her back to New York, to East Harlem, where my stepfather's mother had a house. My mother had never been to New York—she grew up in the Midwest—so "Harlem" didn't mean anything to her. She didn't know what she was getting into. When I asked her recently what she thought when we moved in, she told me she was just happy we were living in a three-story house instead of an

A lot of my writing is not terribly civilized.

apartment. We lived there because there wasn't any other place to go.

I'd fall down our narrow red linoleum–covered stairs all the time because I was off in my fantasy world instead of paying attention to what was in front of me. I remember coming face-to-face with the little nails sticking up out of the linoleum on many occasions. I liked to play in the front yard, which was a plain concrete patch enclosed by an iron fence topped with little spikes, but I really adored playing in the backyard with its weed tree. It was *A Tree Grows in Brooklyn* kind of tree, a tree with no name, that would drop little seeds that I loved to play with.

There were caterpillars on the branches that I'd get to walk up my arm. Beyond the tree was a part of the yard that was dirt. Because we were in a courtyard, whatever people would throw out their windows landed there. My mother didn't allow me go to that part of the yard, but every so often I would do it anyway, travel all the way across our lot to the place where most of the stuff was. I was fascinated by all this junk. I loved finding little fuses back there. You could clear away the dirt from a fuse's window and see a little blue thing inside. I'm still a bit of a packrat. I collect stuff and keep it with me. Some of what I collect now is intellectual—ideas or facts that I keep in my notebooks—but some is still

physical—little things that I hold on to.

I was the oldest child, and both my parents worked, so I had a great deal of responsibility from a very young age. We occasionally had baby-sitters, but they weren't always available. After we moved out of East Harlem when I was a bit older, I would take care of my brothers and sister for hours. That was the way things were. Even though I was dealing with the daily realities of life, like taking care of my siblings, I was always in my own dreamworld as well. I'd baby-sit by putting on puppet shows for my brothers and sister. I was always inventing characters and making up stories.

I had some fears as a kid, but I was also relatively fearless. Maybe that's a result of living half the time in reality and the other half in fantasy. I found it frightening when my parents would argue, which they did constantly. My stepfather had a very explosive temper. That's the one thing I feared above everything else. The rest of the world was fine compared to that. I wasn't afraid of going places or doing new things. I would do just

> **I grew up with people in my face, pulling my hair, saying, "You're the whitest girl I've ever seen."**

about anything or go anywhere. I'd get a notion in my mind and just follow it.

When I was eight, I decided I'd had enough of living at home. I was going to live in the park. I thought I could live on grass and certain weeds that grew there. So I walked uptown to the park by myself, eight years old, through Harlem from 102d and Broadway, where we were living by that time. When I got to the park, a black boy of twelve or so came over and asked me what I was doing. He said he was looking for a girlfriend. I told him I couldn't think of anybody. At one point he kissed me on the lips, just a little, gentle kiss, but I started to cry and began to think that maybe I didn't want to run away after all. That scary feeling of being out in the world by myself and seeing gangs of men hanging around on the street has stayed with me. It was frightening, but I kept going anyway.

Once I got to the park, I realized it wasn't going to be quite the picnic I thought it was. Still, I stayed for several hours intead of going back home right away. By that age I'd already taught myself not to feel fear and pain by stripping down what I felt so I could put a line around those feelings. If I gave fear a shape and a texture, I could "handle" it. I could describe the sensations I felt to myself and, by putting a name on them, make them less overwhelming. The problem with using this technique is that you find yourself doing the same thing with joy and happiness as well. You limit the pleasure from good things because the minute you feel something you say, "This is what it is," and squash it with a name. My intellect has always been more responsible than my emotions for how I respond to the world. Emotion is something I've become gradually more familiar with, but as a kid I wasn't really sure what my feelings were. I felt safe in the world of ideas and imagination, and that's where I continue to feel safe most of the time although as I've grown older, I've begun to feel more.

Both of my parents were political, and their politics came out of the neighborhood. It was a politically charged time. I remember the Kennedy campaign coming through East Harlem. The booklet about Lyndon Johnson's War on Poverty included a picture of my sister looking out the window. We couldn't

> For the first time in my life, I felt that I'd found a tribe I could belong to.

get away from politics. They were everywhere. So I grew up in a very politically active and aware household. My stepfather was always trying to teach us what lay behind advertising, for instance. He had a real hatred for America's corporate mentality. No Walt Disney. No Barbie. My mother was interested in feminism, and she and my stepfather wanted to make us aware of the roles men and women assumed in society. My mother wanted me to understand that as a woman I could do pretty much whatever I wanted to, that I didn't have to use sex or sexuality to define myself. For example, she encouraged me to play ice hockey when I was twelve. Why not? But the organizers of the team wanted me off the ice. They said, "What if she gets a scar? Who'd want to marry a girl with a scar?" Who *cares* if a girl has a scar? This was twenty-five years ago, well before sports were as integrated as they are now. That's just one example of how my parents tried to let me know that being a woman shouldn't turn

you into a stereotype. I took those lessons seriously growing up because they were such a big part of the atmosphere at home.

My stepfather felt that being an artist was the only sane thing to do in this society. My stepfather was and is a writer—novels, short stories. He wrote constantly. When he wasn't writing fiction, he'd make up songs for us. Although I remember standing on a box in the backyard and singing "I love you, yeah, yeah, yeah" (the wrong words) to "She Loves You," the first song I really responded to deeply was one my stepfather wrote for my brother Matthew. It was loosely based on Dylan's "A Hard Rain's A-Gonna Fall"— "Where have you been my blue-eyed son?," that format. It was in a minor key, and I thought it was so beautiful and very serious. He put me in the song too, which made me feel really special. I remember the verse: "'Who will you marry my handsome young man? / Who will you marry my dear?' / 'I'll marry my sister, her name is Suzanne. / She has a butterfly fan.'" I felt celebrated; he'd written about *me*. Every so often he'd go off to teach or take a job of some kind, but he would realize pretty quickly that he couldn't stand to be hemmed in and come back to writing full-time. He'd write all night and sleep during the day. I had a great respect for his work and the life he led as an artist.

He loved it when I started writing poems at six or seven and encouraged me to keep at it. When I was seven, he saw me with a book and asked if I had been reading the stories he'd given me. I said, "No, I don't like those kind of books." He asked me what kind of books I liked, and I brought him the unabridged edition of Mark Twain's *Huckleberry Finn*. He didn't believe I was really reading it, so he asked me to read two pages out loud. After I answered his questions about the meaning of what I'd read, he called my mother over to tell her that I was actually reading and comprehending *Huckleberry Finn*. They thought it was a little odd for me to be reading like that at seven, but they were proud that I could and encouraged me.

Given the artistic environment at home, it wasn't surprising that I went to the High

School for the Performing Arts. I loved it there even though I was something of an outsider. It was very disciplined and gave me a real structure, which I liked because my family life often had none. There was always a bit of pandemonium at home, so I really responded positively to the strict routine at school. I focused on dance. I loved the atmosphere of the dance studios—the wooden floors, the big mirrors, everyone dressed in pink or black tights, the musicians accompanying us—and the feeling of ritual the classes had. You were considered a serious artist at that school. When classes ended, I went to a private studio on scholarship, so on a normal day I danced for seven hours. That helped me learn about the discipline art requires. I took dancing very seriously and was very ambitious. I was considered aloof. In my junior year other students grumbled because they thought I was acting like a prima ballerina. They'd call me Prima because I sat in front, off to the side always, but in front. I was extremely competitive and in my own world.

Even though I graduated with eight academic awards and was in the top five of my class, I was disappointed because my prospects as a dancer weren't as promising as I wanted them to be. I knew my technique would never be as good as that of the best dancers. At eighteen you're mature enough to know whether you're going to reach that

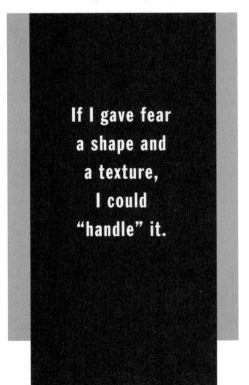

If I gave fear
a shape and
a texture,
I could
"handle" it.

level and I realized I couldn't. In my disappointment I gave up performing as a dancer. My teachers encouraged me to do more academic work and not to have all my hopes in dancing.

Besides dancing at school and the studio, I'd written all these songs and had begun to play them at auditions. I felt I'd have a chance to shine more if I focused on writing instead of dancing. One of the pianists for my dance classes knew I wrote songs and told me that I wouldn't do well in the world of commercial music because I was so shy and the music business was so horrible. He suggested that I buy the *Village Voice* to find out where the little coffeehouses were and then go audition at them. He said it was a very gentle scene that I'd be comfortable with. So I read the *Voice* and went to one coffeehouse in a church basement on Eighty-sixth Street. There was a woman there named Mary Grace in a long white dress playing an autoharp and singing "Wild Mountain Thyme." I said to myself, *Okay, I can do this.* Mary Grace

liked my songs, and she gave me a booking seven months from the date of that audition—the following year— January 2, 1976. So that was my first gig.

Once I started auditioning at music clubs in the Village at eighteen, I realized that I was surrounded by men who were mostly in their thirties. In that world I was very young and precocious whereas in the dance world I was already considered mature, nearly too old to get where I wanted to go. I felt happy playing and hanging around at folk clubs in the Village. I'd heard that the way to break into the scene was to try the Bitter End first, then graduate to Folk City, and, finally, if you're really good, play at the Bottom Line. I took this advice as strict gospel. So I went to the Bitter End and tried to get a gig there for two years. I'd go down once a month or so, sing my songs, get rejected, come home, and prepare for next month. I'd come back with new songs or a different outfit—the most ridiculous costumes—and the same guy, Stefan, would be there. He'd say, "Oh, hi," then listen to me sing and say, "Well, no."

Finally after two years of this it occurred to me that I could try Folk City, just

association with Bob Dylan, but to my surprise, I found a great group of people there I really liked and who liked me. We could talk

forget the path my friends had told me about and jump ahead to the next club. I found the idea of playing at Folk City really daunting because of its

about songwriting together, which I found to be really exciting. I loved the group of people at Folk City. For the first time in my life, I felt that I'd found a tribe I could belong to.

Even though I wasn't a typical folksinger,

nobody really cared. It was the Village, and everybody was into poetry anyway. I was never considered a folkie in that scene; I wasn't asked to play the big folk festivals because I wasn't well known enough and my style was considered very idiosyncratic. That's why it was shocking to me when I got the record deal and found myself being touted as a traditional folkie. I wrote "Cracking," for instance, in 1980, when that kind of song was considered anomalous and more than a little strange in the folk world.

During those years I was also in college. Out of everything I was doing, I was least passionate about studying. I faked my way through a lot of assignments. I bluffed my way through my first philosophy test and, to my surprise, got an A, so I thought I could

There was a moment when I had to choose between starting a family or signing a record deal. I chose the record deal.

fake it all the time. It worked until my adviser pulled me out of my junior colloquium and told me that writing stream of consciousness wouldn't do. She asked me to drop the course and take it again when I felt like reading the books. She kicked my butt. She was right to. I wasn't doing any of the work. Instead I was hanging around the theater and performing music wherever I could get a gig. There were also boys. I was always attracted to someone new. I was completely infatuated by people. I'm still that way a little; I fall in love easily. I have a reputation for being aloof, but I really become very infatuated—with bands, people, characters—and then let an infatuation take over for a while before I return to my neutral corner.

When I graduated from college, I worked at a publishing company. I didn't give up my day job until about ten months before I actually signed a record contract. Even then I gave it up with a lot of hesitation. I felt that it was stupid to quit a good job for some pipe dream. I wasn't convinced I would get a deal, but my manager finally insisted that I give up the job and play more regularly. There was also a moment when I had to choose between starting a family or signing a record deal. I chose the record deal and gave up that particular relationship— along with the possibility of having a family. That decision stayed with me for a long time, but now I have a family, a husband and daughter, so I didn't have to give up that part of life in the end. Even though I gave up the chance back then, I have a different version of it now. Other than that, I couldn't say what I've sacrificed in order to do what I do. Perhaps I could

tell you twenty-five years from now. It's something that I wanted to do so much that I put everything aside for that one thing.

I still feel conflicted because I don't always get to spend as much time with my daughter as I'd like, given my work. It's not always easy to balance time with my family and working on the writing and singing. Music comes as second nature. I've been a performer for twenty-five years. Being a mother and being a wife is more difficult for me. I've been a mother for two years and a wife for one year, and I find that there are some things involved with those roles that I'm just not trained for. It takes as much discipline to be a mother and a wife as it does to do anything else. It takes all your imagination, all your involvement, so much more energy than you'd ever dream. But then you have a nearly perfect day that makes it all worthwhile. Maybe it's a Sunday, like one we had a few months ago, when the three of us are actually home together with no pressing issues, commitments, or illnesses. Everything's peaceful. All three of us are happy. We get to spend a lot of time with Ruby, who eats right on schedule, then takes a nap. Those are great days.

Being pregnant really changed my sense of myself as a woman. I was really big. I know some women who stay small even when they're pregnant. If they're very thin beforehand, they stay thin throughout the pregnancy and then go back to how they were. I assumed I'd be like that. I wasn't. I was much bigger than I expected to be. When you're pregnant—especially the way I was pregnant, which was *huge*—you can't hide it. I had a sense of myself as a very big person in the world. When I walked down the street, people would move out of the way.

> I have a reputation for being aloof, but I really become very infatuated—with bands, people, characters—and then let an infatuation take over for a while before I return to my neutral corner.

In the past I might have been anxious about how big I was, but in this case I felt great. I started to wonder how big I could possibly get. It occurs to you that you'll lose control completely and keep expanding until you're inconceivably enormous—out to *there*. I felt like one of those sexy Italian women you see in pictures. That was a lot of fun for me. I felt comfortable and womanly.

You can't pretend to be androgynous in that state. In the beginning I thought it would be cute if I could dress like a potbellied man. I'd see one and feel a kinship for the silhouette. I could wear my suspender pants, the really big baggy ones, with an undershirt and look like a paunchy man of fifty, but by the eighth month you're not interested in looking like a potbellied man. All you want to do is get dressed and go eat something. Your breasts are too big, your rear end's too big to pretend you're a guy. It's not useful.

It's not necessary. I was biggest in June, and I found I was more comfortable in dresses and sandals. That wasn't my style before.

So you eat, you sleep, and then this wonderful child comes out, but you don't feel like you have any control over that process, over her, over her character and who she is. It seems to me she was born fully formed. When you're writing a song, you can manipulate things a bit more or throw out what you don't like. Ruby, on the other hand, is her own creation. Maybe it's just that she has an unusually strong personality. I've seen children who were more subject to the editing process than she is. With her, I have a very strong sense of negotiating with a person whose will is as strong as mine. To see so much of myself in her was kind of shocking when she was only three days old. You figure, *She's a baby; of course she's* going to be cooperative; of course she's going to breast-feed, but then you find you're facing this really strong-willed person saying, "No, I won't." She'd go thirteen hours without eating rather than give in. Songs don't normally resist that strongly. She has her own coded way of dealing with the world. She'll arrange her dwarfs in perfect symmetry; if I mess the pattern up, I'm in trouble. I can never tell when she's in one of those moods when things have to stay just as they are. Her code is not the same as mine, so I have the sense of working at a puzzle. Ruby's a big mystery to me.

The fact that *Nine Objects of Desire* is more sensual than some of my other records is directly related to my pregnancy. The new sensuality made me feel really weird at first. I wasn't prepared for it. When I was pregnant, I felt filled with life, and I felt really happy. I ate well, and I slept well. I felt much more useful than I'd ever felt before. That was the climate this album was conceived in, and my feelings at the time are reflected in the work. For example, "Birth-day," which is about giving birth, is a song that had to be written by a woman.

That said, I've never thought the fact that I'm a woman was important to my work. I've written songs that men could sing. I've written songs that women don't necessarily identify with. I've had men come up to me and say they completely identify with "Small Blue Thing" while some women tell me they don't feel any connection

> When you're pregnant you can't hide it. I felt like one of those sexy Italian women you see in pictures. You can't pretend to be androgynous in that state.

to that song at all. A song like "Cracking" could have been written by a man or a woman. But then there's "Birth-day." I think that I can go either way. I don't think gender is aesthetically defining for me.

That's not to say that being a woman isn't an important part of my identity. I still consider myself a feminist. I don't go to demonstrations as often as I might, but I still feel strongly about the movement that first affected me a lot when I was twelve or thirteen. Books like *Sisterhood Is Powerful* have stayed with me. I'm not sure why feminism is such a reviled thing in so many quarters today. Perhaps it's because of the stereotypes associated with it. To me, a feminist belongs in the same category as a humanist or an advocate for human rights. I don't see why someone who's a feminist should be thought of differently. The humanist umbrella covers all of those things whether you're working for children's rights, women's rights, or social justice. Gloria Steinem is still as vital a presence as she ever has been. She's been consistent as a good leader, a good speaker and writer. She's reasoned and balanced. There's nothing hysterical or shrill about her work. She's not any of those things people would have her be. When it comes to feminism, what people are responding to negatively is the caricature of someone who's militant or doesn't shave—that kind of thing. It's only the caricature that's outdated as far as I'm concerned.

I wouldn't characterize my work, however, as directly political. I'm not trying to make a point as a feminist, for instance, when I write a song. I write most often about things that are very personal to me. When I'm writing, I'm dealing with what's in front of my face. Of course, sometimes when you write personally, you are also writing about society, obliquely reflecting topical issues, but not in

> I write about romance at least as much as I write about, say, psychic amputees.

a way that people would expect you to or in the way that someone trying to make a point would. I don't care about making a point.

So it was a big surprise to write a song like "Luka" that became so popular in part because it was written from the perspective of a boy being abused by his parents. I suppose you could see certain songs I've written as products of more than a purely aesthetic impulse. You could say that "Cracking" is about mental health, "Fifty-Fifty Chance" is about attempted suicide, or "Men in a War" is about posttraumatic stress syndrome. I don't know why "Luka" should take off, and not those songs. Maybe at that moment it touched a nerve in society that the other songs didn't, at least not in such a widespread way. I got a lot of letters from people in child abuse agencies complaining to me about "Luka," saying that I'd written it "incorrectly" and that the correct thing to do is empower the child rather than make him feel bad. I didn't follow that way of thinking about the issue. Because they made me so angry, I kept those letters for a while before throwing them away. My correspondents wanted me for a cause and felt I hadn't expressed myself according to their rules.

There are other songwriters who have written about child abuse in the "correct" way by taking the point of view of the neighbor, for instance, and describing the situation in a civilized way. As I said before, I don't think being civil as a writer is always adequate to the reality. There are moments onstage when I cringe at the prospect of having to sing my own words. They're not always pretty, but they reflect something I've seen or understood, however unseemly it is. I do write about horrible things, but not exclusively, and when I do, there's another level there as well. Yesterday, for example, I was being interviewed by a very young girl on television who asked me, "Why do you write about suicide and ampu-

> **I favor T. S. Eliot's aesthetic of impersonality. He doesn't have to blurt out his intimate feelings to make the *Four Quartets*, for example, deeply moving.**

more about a psychic state than a man with no leg. But trying to explain that in the heat of the moment when the microphone is in your face and the camera's rolling can be sort of daunting.

I don't think my writing's limited to "those kinds of things," as my interviewer dubbed them. I do write about a wide range of topics. Not everything's about the painful side of life. I write about romance at least as much as I write about, say, psychic amputees. But I never want to get to the point where I write a safe song or one that misrepresents my sense of a subject in order to appear civilized. There has to be some kind of urgency there. What I like best in other writers' work are the lines or passages where the urgency behind the words makes the language really sing itself.

When I was preparing to write a song for the *Dead Man Walking* sound track, I read the book by Sister Helen Prejean on which the film is based. There were a few pages where you could really feel her fear

tation, things like that?" I tried to explain to her that I was not writing so much about literal amputation in "Men in a War" as I was using amputation as a metaphor. I'm writing

and anxiety in the words. She describes what she sees, how she feels—all her physical sensations—when she went to the jail to meet the killer for the first time. In those descriptions the words begin rhyming, that sparkles on the page. I knew those descriptions were where I needed to go in order to write the song. Because the rhymes were already there, it was just a question of

seemingly of their own accord. There's really beautiful alliteration pulling them out and putting them together. The experience of making a song from that heightened, urgent passage was much more powerful than if I'd chosen some other moment. If I don't feel that something really needs to be written, I'd rather not write it.

When I was pregnant, I was having a great time, so there was no reason to report back to the notebook that I felt happy. It was enough to feel good, to eat breakfast or—and I found great pleasure in this—eat two breakfasts. What was I going to write, "I had sausage today"? That's not something for the notebook. It was probably the most... *contented* is not the right word because it makes you sound like a big cow in the middle of a field eating grass . . . let me say instead it was the most joyful I'd ever felt. I just didn't feel like writing anything. The urgency wasn't there, so I let it go.

That doesn't mean that what I feel compelled to write is always directly about what I'm doing at any given time. Writing is always personal in some way but not always in a direct way. Writing dramatic monologues, which is exactly what I'm doing in many of my songs, allows me to put on a different face. Every single song that I've written from a character's point of view mirrors something that was going on in my life but not always in an obvious way. In "Casper Hauser's Song," for example, I'm telling the truth about Casper Hauser, and I'm also telling the truth about myself. What I make the character say about himself has to be true to that character and at the same time reveal something about my own life. I'll work it both ways by using a line like "I want to be a rider like my father," which Casper Hauser actually said while he was playing with a toy horse. In my life I want to be a writer like my stepfather. In that line it's a play on words—"rider" and "writer"—that creates the connection for me. I love the doubleness of words. Certain kinds of jargon, the language of physics, for example, take on a double meaning when you use them in a song or poem. There are certain words that sing to you out of these other disciplines. They leak, in a sense; a phrase that means something very specific in one world becomes poetry when it enters another world. It's like creating a secret code.

There are some songs that work exactly like that and others where the double meaning is more about experience than wordplay. When I wrote "Calypso," I didn't take on the voice simply to pretend to be a figure from Homer. There was someone I was involved with who was constantly leaving at the crucial moment. So by writing from Calypso's perspective about losing Odysseus, I was also expressing my own point of view. Almost all my songs have that double quality. I've been inventing voices like that since I was a kid putting on puppet shows. You

All of a sudden I started to understand the feelings in operas where people are singing to one another across the stage.

could have different characters talking to one another, but of course each character was also in your own voice. Writing this way allows me to step out of myself. It takes me away from my own ego and leaves room for listeners to put themselves into a song. Writing in other voices is almost Japanese in the sense that there's a certain formality there which allows me to sidestep the embarrassment of directly expressing to complete strangers the most intimate details of my life. It allows me a neutral place to put the stuff about myself so that someone can talk to me about Luka or Casper Hauser without my completely revealing myself.

This distance creates a form of politeness or discretion that acknowledges the fact that we're not all intimate. We can be friendly, we can be pleasant to one another while we talk, but we're not intimate. In society today I find myself puzzled sometimes by having to look at the body of someone in an ad or a movie, for example, who's not my lover or child. Why should I have to look at her breasts? Do I know her? No. For some reason, the climate in our society right now is one of premature intimacy with everyone wanting to get to know one another quickly, right away, with all the details. Ultimately that kind of knowledge doesn't mean much. It makes life like having a stranger sit down next to you on a bus and tell you all about the most intimate details of her love life, leaving the bus right away and being replaced by the next person, who does the same thing. That's not a relationship. It's not even very human, really.

It's striking how commercially viable that impulse for instant intimacy is right now, especially in songs and writing. Just spill your guts and you're on. I love my niece and think she's a wonderful girl, one who's

very passionate and eloquent about her feelings, so I'm interested as a close relative in her emotional life, but if I were a stranger and she were a performer, I wouldn't pay twenty-five dollars to see her throw a fit. I don't want to pay to see a stranger purge herself. Writing in voices other than your own allows you to organize yourself and arrange an experience in words that have a form. I favor T. S. Eliot's aesthetic of impersonality. He doesn't have to blurt out his intimate feelings to make the *Four Quartets*, for example, deeply moving. I prefer to arrange a song in a way that has order and beauty.

There are other things I need to work on as a writer. How do you write about those moments when you are fulfilled or feeling completed? Maybe you need to write more anthemic songs, like U2, to do that. I haven't found a way to write about falling in love with my husband, Mitchell. How do you match that feeling of almost operatic passion? We weren't able to fling ourselves to-

gether in the way that we might have were we younger or in different circumstances. He was married. I didn't want to be involved with someone who was married. Plus we were working together in a professional situation, so we stayed apart. There was that odd feeling of being apart but feeling this thing growing that neither of us was talking about. If I could have walked away from the relationship, I would have. It should have been the easiest thing to do because he was everything I didn't want in a person: a producer and a keyboard player who was married with a child. No way! At the same time there was this amazing sense of inevitability, a feeling that this was something that had to happen. It took six or seven months before we were finally able to work everything through. All of a sudden I started to understand the feelings in operas where people are singing to one another across the stage. That made sense in a way it never had before. Some of the emotion was because of the restraint we had to exercise. There was also a great feeling of risk. How do I write about that? I don't know. How do I write about those six months when I was feeling things I never felt before? I don't know yet. That's the job. The older I get, the longer it takes to filter experiences so they can become songs. "Tired of Sleeping" took eight years; "Stockings" took ten; other songs take fifteen. By the time I'm seventy-five I should have it all worked out pretty well.

Holly PALMER

hat I remember of growing up is often as real to me as what's happening in my life now. My past is made up of disjointed pictures. I've created a whole reality based on the way I recall certain events. When I talk to my sister or my parents about my childhood, I realize that I've embellished the experiences I had. Those embellishments, the past that I've stored and augmented in memory, emerge in the songs. What comes across is my sense that as a child I was fearless and loving, as were all the children around me. We were completely open to all the absurd, violent, and wonderful things that happened to us.

I have two people inside me. One comes from my father, who's Italian. The other comes from my mother, who's Finnish. My parents are about as opposite as people get, and my personality combines aspects of them both. On one side, I feel things very strongly, and I'm not afraid of that. The other side is shy, quiet. In my writing, those two things come together. What I write about tends to be potent, but I try to couch it in imagery that's a bit opaque.

When we lived in Santa Monica, my parents, my sister, and I were very close. We also had extended family nearby. My mother and father had a very passionate relationship when I was growing up. I used to see them tongue-kissing around the house. They had it in bloom when I was a child. I'm the youngest. My sister is two years older than I am. She's more of a thinker and I'm more of a feeler. To avoid making the wrong decision by simply going with my heart, which is what's natural for me, I find myself thinking in circles and not really solving anything. Then I have to go back and listen to my heart, which I should have done in the first place. It usually steers me in the right direction.

Growing up in Santa Monica

> **As you have new experiences—new pain and new joy—what came before begins to fade into the background. It's there if you want to look at it, but what's right in front of you is really what's important.**

was weird. Along with the usual earthquake and fire drills, every year we'd be told at school that if a guy in a white coat wearing a stethoscope comes to the back fence and says that your mom told him to pick you up from school, don't go home with him. Our school system felt strongly enough that being kidnapped like that was enough of a threat to justify bringing it into our consciousness. As

bia of Redmond. Still, it wasn't entirely blissful. There was a lot of chaos at home, but at least we were all together as a family. After a year all hell broke loose. My parents split up and everything changed. It was tragic that they couldn't work it out between them and stay together. Even though they split up so long ago—twenty years—it's still hard to think about what we all lost. It's been cathartic to write about that loss, and I'm finally ready now to move on to other things. As you have new experiences—new pain and new joy—what came before begins to fade into the background. It's there if you want to look at it, but what's right in front of you is really what's important.

My mother was always the breadwinner, and my dad worked at different jobs while he was writing. After they split up, my dad started writing a novel called *Fuck Yes*. He worked on it for the next seven years. We weren't usually allowed to have friends over because he needed quiet. He would bang on

a result, I was always afraid of being kidnapped.

In 1978 we moved from California to the Seattle area. We lived in the rural subur-

the walls if we were too loud. He was always writing. We became insular. We didn't know that many people. I missed my friends in Santa Monica, who were the people that I'd known all my life. I didn't understand the new kids I met when we moved. I went inside of myself. I entered the world of books. My mom bought us books by Roald Dahl, Madeleine L'Engle, Laura Ingalls Wilder, always in hardback, and I devoured them.

My father would try out bits from his book when we went for rides around Lake Sammamish. It's a hilarious story. This crazy guy, the Reverend Wing F. Fing, starts a religion called Yes,

He just looked at me with these eyes that went right into my soul and said, "If you want to be a singer, then sing. If you want to be a doctor, then do that." I decided to sing.

The Holy Church of the Slippery Word. He talks about how *fuck* is the opposite of *yes* because *yes* means accepting everything and *fuck* means fucking with people. When I was older, he would ask me to read drafts. He would ask me questions about them. I'd say things like "Pa, I don't understand this transition. This part makes total sense to me, but how come he's already at the beach when he was being chased by the police back here?" He'd say, "Shit, Holly!" then go back into his room and come out four hours later with a revision. Working with him in this way gave me insight into the process of writing.

When he wasn't working on the book, my dad would sometimes play and sing Beatles' songs like "Norwegian Wood" for us. I loved that stuff. I always knew I was a singer. The way that my father lived by his artistic standards is the way that I learned to live by mine. Because he was following his muse, I felt I could too. There were other people in my life who were motivated by a need for security. I'd seen how unhappy they were. Witnessing that unhappiness convinced me that I was not going to be a slave to the nine and the five on a clock.

My dad never asked me to do anything specific as far as academic achievement or career goals went. I brought home straight As one time, and he just sort of giggled. He thought it was cute. It was more important to him that I be thoughtful, responsible, and conscientious. The first summer I wanted to play softball, I

asked him if I could join the league. He said, "Well, yeah, I'll give you the money, but I want you to do something for me. I'd like you to learn to meditate because I think that will be really useful to you." He was concerned that I find a balance between the side of me that was entertained and the side that was thoughtful. By then I was involved in so many different things—

sports, music—that he worried I didn't have enough quiet moments. After that we spent part of every day that summer practicing yoga or meditating. This year I've begun practicing yoga again, and once again it has slowed me down and opened me up.

In high school I felt like I was a freak. Aside from music, I didn't have much in common with anybody else. I'd go to football games and get wasted, try to do those typical high school things, but I didn't enjoy them very much. I had one close girlfriend, a singer and piano player, and we played a lot of music together. One time we put a band together for a school dance and played things like the Aerosmith/Run-

> As a writer I want to pull someone, regardless of who it is, into an experience. I want to rub them up against different textures, give them something they can taste, something that allows them to use their senses.

D.M.C. version of "Walk This Way." Oh, man—I did the Steven Tyler part, and I really hope nobody has a tape of that. I had a few other good friends in band and a band director about whom I can't say enough. His name is Gary Evans, and he created a music program in which people were encouraged to try anything. He gave us courage through his love and fearlessness. In Gary's world, the uncool thing was to laugh at somebody, and the real cool thing was to try. He transcribed some incredible Nancy Wilson/Billy May arrangements for me to sing and gave me a double live Sarah Vaughan record, which I wore out. I was most fulfilled as a person through music at school. It's such a bizarre age. Every year that goes by, I'm more and more glad it's gone.

Even though I was most passionate about music, my mom would tell me that I could be a doctor and do music on the side. I told this plan to Mr. Jones, my junior-year English teacher. I said I was going to go to college to study medicine or prelaw and sing on the side. He just looked at me with these eyes that went right into my soul and said, "If you want to be a singer, then sing. If you want to be a doctor, then do that." He phrased it much more beautifully than that, and what he said really rang true. I decided to sing.

After high school I went for one year to Pacific Lutheran University, where there was a great vocal arranger named Phil Mattson. I was singing jazz. It was hard but fun to sing second soprano with him. Because I had played second tenor in the jazz band, my ears had begun to get used to those dissonant sounds. During that year I was corresponding with a friend who was studying at the New England Conservatory in Boston. He kept telling me what an incredible place it was, that I had to come out there to sing with this band or that band. Since my mom worked for the airlines, I got a free ticket and went to Boston to visit him and check it out.

During that weekend I fell in love with the energy, all those musicians running around, and decided I wanted to be there.

When I got to Berklee the following year, I lived with two friends of mine who played trumpet, so I ended up hanging out with all these horn players. I really got into their world. It changed my thinking about music. I started to think of my voice as more of a horn, more of an instrument, as opposed to just part of my body. The improvisational nature of jazz became part of my nature. I need the space to create from an intuitive place. I make sounds and melodies and rhythms out of the moment and what's happen-

I wanted to take this icon of lust—the dirty old man—and say, "That's how I feel about you sometimes." You know, that state of being so turned on that you're actually drooling?

ing next to me, what other musicians are doing. Anything can happen. I love that about music. Along with the jazz I was immersed in at Berklee, I fell in love with soul music and seventies R & B. I started listening to singers like Al Green and Aretha Franklin, improvisers who put their whole souls into their songs and never just sang down the melody.

Even though I feed on the interaction, the warmth and inspiration that you feel in a band, after singing with different groups, I realized that I wasn't really sustaining myself creatively. The music we were making wasn't always coming from a genuine place. Too often we were just trying to bridge the gaps between our influences: my passion for jazz and soul, the guitar player's Neville Brothers influence, the drummer's thing for the Pixies, the bass player's love for The Band. I hadn't found a situation that allowed me to feel I was really contributing something honest and sincere, something out of my heart.

to pay attention to the quality of the words I was writing, to capture what I saw. I wanted my lyrics to have some of the features I found in the work

So I started to write my own songs. I became serious about the process and tried

of poets I admire, like Maya Angelou and Sylvia Plath. With Maya Angelou, every word counts. There's such potency, sharpness, and motion in her work. She can really communicate. I find Sylvia Plath's imagery lush and full of life even when she's writing about the darkest things. I admire her sense of irony. There's so much more to her than the image of the suicide poet in black that

excruciating joy and pain. From her, I drew the license to write out of heartache. We don't necessarily share the same type of pain, but I respond to the way she wrote about the subtle, very real peculiarities of growing up. Like many others who are moved by her work, I also feel a connection to Plath as a woman.

My voice is necessarily that of a woman, and the fact of my gender is more central than incidental to what I do. At the end of the day, however, I'm a human being with struggles just like

many people have reduced her to. She's making fun of herself and everything around her while she's experiencing

anyone else, man or woman. It's important to acknowledge the differences between men and women—that's what feminism at its best tries to do—but that knowledge should allow you to understand the person across the table from you, whatever that person's gender. Really strong writing by a woman should not only appeal to other women but invite men into women's experience as well. The focus on women in music today is perplexing to me. In the bit of promotion I've done for my record I've been asked several times what I think of this "new trend." Half of me wants to say, "Where have you been? Women have been kicking ass for a very, very long time." The other half of me wants to ignore the question completely because I don't want to recognize this divisive idea. I don't want to ride that train of thought. However, this is a very complicated issue because I also value the attention and opportunities women have received recently. But I do know they have come as the result of a lot of hard work. In an ideal world artists would be judged by the art that they make, not on the basis of their being black, white, women, or men. Finally, my job as a writer is to bring what

I know to life for anyone who wants it.

As a writer I want to pull someone, regardless of who it is, into an experience. I want to rub them up against different textures, give them something they can taste, something that allows them to use their senses. I don't have a conventional sense of beauty. I love wrinkles on people's faces, what their eyes can tell you about who they really are. I'm not concerned with beauty when I write; I'm concerned with showing something that I see, something that may not be at all pretty. I want the experience registered in a song to be obvious, to be right there, so a listener can fall into it. When a song comes from my guts and my heart, I can let it out.

I'm interested in images that exist for me already rather than ones I have to force. I don't assign meaning to what I write or try to control a song thematically. When the process is working, it's much more fluid than that. "Five Little Birds" is a good example. The opening image just came out: "I reached be-tween my legs / And found a silver screw." It was one of those rare moments when you're writing and something you hit on feels ab-solutely right. That song is basically a stream

wanting to share myself with someone. The song contains a list of what I went through to get to that point of being an adult, of being ca-pable of intimacy. But I didn't think about

of consciousness set to music. If I were to tell you what it means, I might say it's a song about being grown up and

meaning when I was writing it. The chorus is like a mantra—"Everybody's gonna be al-right"—that's soothing after the chaotic im-ages of the verses. A lot of my songs walk that thin line between consolation and collapse. I'm drawn to that kind of duality.

I like the way that words can allude to sex without knocking you over the head. Liz Phair makes so many people happy because she's sexy and strong in a fresh, entirely direct way. She wasn't afraid to say, in effect, "fuck and run." In "Lickerish Man," I wanted to take this icon of lust—the dirty old man—and say, "That's how I feel about you sometimes." You know, that state of being so turned on that you're actually drooling? People have asked how could a woman see herself as a horny *man*. The Lickerish Man is a metaphor—the fact that he is a man is incidental. That feeling is universal, I believe. Sex is a huge playground, and that song represents just one lit-

> I can imagine myself in a cabaret, Paris, 1940. I'd have wavy hair, very long eyelashes and fishnets, singing ballads in a dark, smoky room accompanied by a piano player.

tle corner of it.

To a degree, I believe the maxim "Write what you know," but I seem to resist straightforward autobiography too. I want to open my songs out, make them go past that impulse. To do that, I'll write in another voice or in the third person about a character I've invented. It's tempting to think about writing as the observer as an easier task, but you not only have to see what you're describing but conceive of the situation in a manner compelling enough to communicate something essential about it. I spent three long weeks at my desk writing "Sal the Gardener." The first week I tried to write a love song and scrapped it. It was trite, a throwaway. During the second week this

character, Sal, and his story started to emerge. I still don't know why he came to me, but I got to that place where an intuitive voice came out. The story told itself to me: "Singing songs Sinatra sang / Sal the gardener is drunk again / She is gone but he remembers / Polka dots and breathing hard / He dances with an angel in the yard." Even though I hadn't experienced what Sal had and despite the fact that he isn't someone I knew in a literal sense, I understood what I needed to say about him. I tried to see through his eyes and to live in his skin. During the third week I went back and edited the story that had come out, shaping it and polishing the lines. In the end, by following a possibility that came out of nowhere, what had been simply a name that wanted to be in a song conveyed a full experience, a life, to me.

What determines your subject is often unexpected. In "Come Lie with Me," I used some lines from Lawrence Ferlinghetti which are themselves adapted from Christopher Marlowe's "The Passionate Shepherd to His Love." Ferlinghetti takes it in a different direction than Marlowe did. He describes an idyllic scene but also gives it a dark feel, a kind of murkiness. I transcribed the poem into my journal because of its beauty and ease. It's one of those pieces of writing that I want nearby at all times. On the open page next to it were some lines of my own. When I went into the studio one day to work on some new songs, naturally I had the cookbook with me. Kenny White, my coproducer and writing partner, started to play these beautiful chords for a verse, and when he got to the chorus, he played this melody that just cried out to be sung right

away, and the only thing I saw on the page were those lines from Ferlinghetti. They just floated onto the melody so beautifully. When I went back later to write words of my own for the chorus, nothing I could come up with was as perfect for that melody as his lovely words.

I'm compelled to sing and write. I don't really have a choice. It is what I do; it is who I am. Even though I miss academic pursuits and worry about my intellectual breadth, there's nothing besides music that I can devote myself to. If I'm not able to give my all to something, I don't do it at all. Clinical as it sounds, that's the truth. Whatever place, whatever time, I believe I'd be a singer. I can imagine myself in a cabaret, Paris, 1940. I'd have wavy hair, very long eyelashes and fishnets, singing ballads in a dark, smoky room accompanied by a piano player. We'd probably be doing a really slow version of "Embraceable You."

Everything is holy. There's a fly crawling on the window right here. That this creature exists in all its complexity, with its thousand eyes, is an amazing thing if you really stop to think about it. It's something that man, however brilliant, cannot create or synthesize. We can't do it. We can never fully understand creation, the element of it that's inexplicable and inimitable. Seeing that single fly as something extraordinary is only a tiny example of what I mean, but trying to live in a way that allows you to perceive the spiritual dimension of everyday life is, for me, something essential.

Our culture is steeped in a history of seeing ourselves as separate from God—that old guy with the long beard in the Michelangelo painting—and seeking to be reunited with Him, to be worthy of Him. I understand that tradition because I was raised in it, but it seems to me now that thinking of ourselves at such a distance

Joan OSBORNE

183

from what's divine impoverishes us. To try and recognize the miraculous in the mundane is a much richer way to live. I'm not saying that I've achieved the ultimate Zen state where I feel that I can do that all the time, but it's definitely something I strive for. When I was in India, I learned more about Eastern philosophy, which says that everything you do—even common activities like cleaning a home or cooking a meal—can be a form of prayer if you're fully conscious of what you're doing and put the right energy into it.

The kind of religion practiced in much of America is of course very different. Coming from Kentucky, I

> Sometimes I feel that I'm a puppet of a wish that I made so long ago and was committed to for such a long time that it started pulling my strings instead of the other way around.

know that there is still a very strong presence, not only in the Bible Belt but all over the country, of traditional Christianity and religious fundamentalism. That's still very much a part of our cultural fabric even if we don't see it reflected so often in the mass media. So I was not all that surprised when "One of Us" became controversial. I was somewhat taken aback by the vehemence of certain responses to the song because I felt it was asking a question that could be answered any way the listener chose rather than trying to make a particular point. Despite the fact that the song didn't have an agenda, many people thought I was trying to push a secular way of thinking, and they reacted very strongly against it. I even got death threats in the mail, none that I took

mitted to for such a long time that it started pulling my strings instead of the other way around. It's a weird dynamic. It makes you feel awkward when you see a representation of yourself in the media and know that's not really you. The image that's put out there might go against something you really believe. You feel violated when that happens. You want to say, "Everyone *thinks* that's me, but no, it's *not* me." You don't have much control over what you're identified with. The fact that you're portrayed in a way that isn't true to who you are makes no difference. If I were better at manipulating the media, I might be a little more satisfied with the version of myself that's out there. I'm relatively satisfied with the three-dimensional version of who I am, but the two-dimensional version needs a little work.

very seriously, but that was definitely a little unsettling.

Sometimes I feel that I'm a puppet of a wish that I made so long ago and was com-

Going through the process of becoming successful in the particularly public way that music artists do takes a lot of getting used to. It's almost like reliving adolescence. Suddenly everyone is looking at you and judging you. They don't make any bones about the fact that they think you're ugly or don't like the clothes you wear. It's kind of like walking through the halls of junior high school all over again. You're judged on a very superficial level. I'll be walking down the street and total strangers will scream my name, sing a line from "One of Us" at the top of their lungs, or point at me like I'm some animal in a zoo. This kind of attention makes you incredibly self-conscious and guarded; you just want to protect yourself. The junior high years were not my favorite part of life, so it's not particularly pleasant to revisit them in this way.

I wrote something for *Interview* on Janis Joplin not too long ago. I wanted to write an appreciation that discussed the contradictions and complexity that she, like all of us, embodied instead of writing about her as a fan who may only respond to her image. I used to resist all the comparisons between us. The connections

people made seemed a result of lazy thinking: Just because I'm a white chick, sometimes sing with a raspy voice, and have similar hair, I'm the new Janis Joplin. I used to resent those easy categorizations, but I found I had a lot of opinions about her, especially concerning the fact that what she represented to people eclipsed who she really was. She was much more conscious of the image she projected than most of us give her credit for. It's easy to latch on to the incredible sense of freedom she embodied, but I think there was a lot more going on there than simply getting loaded, going up on stage and wailing away. That wild freedom was definitely part of who she was, but it wasn't the whole story.

It's more interesting and more human to understand that we live within contradictions and in so doing accept ourselves and our own

> **If you're able to accept that the world is not a place with a black-and-white code of morality, you discover a landscape full of gradations that enables you to accept yourself and your own contradictions.**

contradictory natures. For me, the world is not a place of black-and-white extremes. I used to be very confused by conflicting feelings. I thought that I was a bad person when I felt more than one way about something, especially if I knew the "right" way to feel but felt equally drawn to the "wrong" way. Those kinds of contradictions made me feel a lot of guilt. If you're able to accept that the world is not all one thing or a place with a black-and-white code of morality, you discover a landscape full of gradations that enables you to accept yourself and your own contradictions.

When I write, I like to find contradictions in the songs. I use a method of fleshing out an idea which is based on the form of a spiderweb. I take the central idea, write it down in the center of the page, and let myself go off on a mental fugue. I'll put down all the things I associate with that central idea, and it's often best if they're contradictory things. I end up filling the page with images, ideas, or scraps of information that relate to that central subject. Then I draw lines—this one connects to that one; this one rhymes with that one—and I choose the images, lines, or ideas that are most evocative. That's how I try to build a song out of association and contradiction.

> One of the things I like about writing from a character's point of view is that it allows me to have an empathic connection to someone outside of myself. I think that's a very human thing that we all need to do.

The musical equivalent to working with contradiction in the lyrics is synthesizing different traditions in the songs. On the first record I wanted to put together different kinds of American roots music, and now I'm looking to integrate Qwaali music and hip-hop as well. I'm not abandoning my interest in American roots music because it's a tradition that I know pretty well and is particularly suited to my voice, but I want to extend the synthesis to other traditions. I'm also trying to make the music a little more fun this time. One of the things about the last record that bugs me when I listen to it is that it can sound a little ponderous. Playing the songs live can point up that weakness. You want people to release themselves and fully participate in the music with you. It's a good thing when you can get them to move their bodies and stop listening quite so hard.

It's important to learn new things when

give the same satisfaction it did when I first started out. That's something I always guard against. It would

I write so that the process of creating stays alive for me. I don't ever want writing and performing to become just a job that doesn't

be a real shame to end up punching a clock and going through the motions. So I try to do things which allow me to keep pushing myself, not because of some noble ideal but because it keeps me excited about and engaged in what I do.

I sometimes worry that what I do for a living makes me selfish because I am so often the focus of my own thoughts. I have to explore my own ideas and reality as an essential part of what I do, but I worry about focusing on myself to that degree. I suppose I can justify that self-absorption because it enables me to do something that other people ultimately enjoy. The process itself may be selfish, but the end product is more about other people than it is about me.

I also write less about myself than most people might think. The assumption is that if you're writing in the first person, the "I" in the song is you. That's not necessarily the case. It's very freeing to write through someone else's sensibility. One of the things I like about writing from a character's point of view is that it allows me to have an empathic connection to someone outside of myself. I think that's a very human thing that we all need to do. Even if you can't answer for that person's thoughts and feelings, you can try to understand them. To look through someone else's eyes and understand how they feel is ultimately a very political act as well. Writing songs that relate the experiences of people who don't tell their own stories is one way of writing a political song. The politics may not be expressed as directly as those you find in a song by the Clash, for example, but they are there nonetheless. To the extent that I can understand someone else's life when I write, I feel good. I'm not suggesting that I can understand someone else completely (I can't even understand myself fully), but when I succeed to some degree, the world feels like a more knowable and welcoming place.

I don't understand exactly why I'm drawn to particular subjects. Why does my mind make up details to fill in certain stories? Why isn't it interested in inventing the details that would fill in other stories? I don't know, and I don't have to know. There are just certain things that spark my imagination. "Pensacola," for example, is based on a story a friend told me years ago about her father leaving home when she was very young and how she always felt she was waiting for him to come back to get her. As a child she'd expect him to pick her up from school or drive to her house at night and take her away with him, but he never came. I imagined what it would be like if she found her father many years later after envisioning him as this great force in her life. What if she saw that he was just a fallible human being in a situation that really spoke of his smallness in the face of what she had imagined was his largeness? I don't know why I was drawn to a story like that, but I was. Take it for what it's worth.

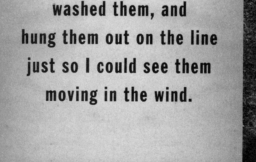

I rented a house in the country last summer, and the first weekend I was there I took all the clean sheets off the beds, washed them, and hung them out on the line just so I could see them moving in the wind.

Then you think about the responsibility you have as an artist. Think about the situation that Martin Scorsese found himself in after he made *Taxi Driver.* A very unstable person latched on to the character of Travis Bickle, set out to imitate his actions, and attempted to kill the president because of his obsession with this film. Obviously you can't hold Martin Scorsese responsible for this person's actions, but if Scorsese had never made this film, maybe this person never would have picked up a gun. We don't know. Like movies or books, songs can give people who listen to them energy and ideas. It's difficult to know what form that energy and those ideas will take or whether they would have come up at all if they hadn't been engaged by the song. Art can have results that not even the artist can predict.

Thinking about art in terms of film is natural for me because I'm very visual. I rented a house in the country last summer, and the first weekend I was there I took all the clean sheets off the beds, washed them, and hung them out on the line just so I could see them moving in the wind. I've always had pictures of things in my head, and I try to write in a visual way so that the person listening to the song sees something unfold in front of him. Being able to direct the video for "St. Teresa" was a lot of fun because I got to use my visual sense in a direct way. Before I started singing and performing seriously, I wanted to make films and went to film school at New York University. Making films is a very com-

plicated process and one that involves lots of other people, equipment, and money. When I was trying to put myself through college, I just didn't have the kind of resources that would have allowed me to make films in the way I wanted to. It was very frustrating. Singing was an alternative that was very freeing because I hadn't invested as much in it, and I could do it without worrying about all the complexity and expense of making a film. With singing, you open your mouth and there it is. Of course you have to work at it to improve, but the act of producing the sound is very simple and organic. After worrying so much about the mechanics of filmmaking, I was so relieved not to think so much, to open my mouth and let the sound come out. That freedom and simplicity is very attractive to me.

Singing was always something I loved

> There were a couple of instances when men would act towards me in ways that were overtly sexual. I know now that I was just starting to read the handwriting on the wall. It said, "You're a grown woman, and this is what it means."

and knew how to do. When I was in school, I did a lot of singing in the chorus. My music teacher started to single me out, asking me to sing solos and perform at the state competitions. I was excited to be asked but kept wondering why the other kids weren't doing those things as well. I figured everyone could sing, that it was just something people could do. It was weird for me to find out that singing was a special ability.

In something like the same way, being an artist seemed a natural thing for me even though as a kid I didn't know what being an artist really was or that it had a name. I knew all along there was something different about me. I don't think it was any big surprise that

I ended up doing what I'm doing now. I've always had artistic ambitions. Being creative was an important part of who I was. It's not that I'm uninterested in doing different things. Other people might fantasize about being a rock star while I fantasize about leaving the music business and becoming a marine biologist, a profession that seems like it would have a lot less pressure. God knows music careers are so short that I can expect mine to last for about another five minutes. I could be free to live out my underwater fantasy anytime now.

When I was growing up, my secret ambitions were more artistic than the ambitions my parents had for me. We didn't talk too much about that kind of thing. The day-to-day mechanics of raising six kids was pretty overwhelming for my parents, and that was about all they had energy to do. Because of that, a lot of my emotional life was private, and I guess it still is. My mom and dad were aware of the fact that I was intelligent, and they may have

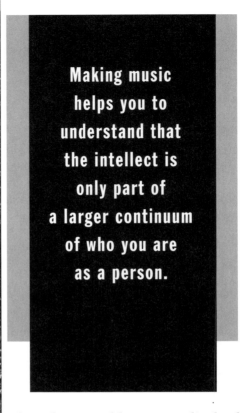

Making music helps you to understand that the intellect is only part of a larger continuum of who you are as a person.

thought I would go to medical school or become a teacher. I started teaching my little brothers and sisters how to read before they went to school. I liked to play school and be the teacher, so it probably seemed logical to them that I would end up doing that. It was a little disturbing to my parents when I started hanging out in New York City bars until three o'clock in the morning and singing the blues. I think they felt I was lost back then.

At home I was the second mommy. As the oldest girl I was called upon and volunteered to do a lot of the mothering of the family—making lunches and breaking up fights. In addition to helping with a lot of daily tasks and activities, serving emotionally as a second mother seemed to be my place. Raising that many kids is a lot for anyone to take on, so my role was a necessary one and one that I usually liked.

I loved being a part of a big family. I remember how all of us kids would build forts together. We would take blankets and some furniture and go off into the woods to construct our own little house. I loved being in nature and still do although I don't get to experience that nearly as much as I would like to. It's very reassuring and spiritual to be connected with something larger than yourself and the inside of your own head. I loved to sit on our back porch near this huge old maple tree. We had cats that we liked to play

with. We lived next to a trail, and we'd watch the horses go by. We had one of those big old console stereo systems. It was next to a cabinet where my dad kept all his bar accoutrements. I would sit next to the speaker and open the door of the cabinet so it would make a little box I could sit inside with this big speaker playing music. I would stay there for hours and listen to records and sing along. I knew the entire score of *The Sound of Music* backwards and forwards.

I also remember that I'd wake up in the middle of the night with this strange consciousness that the room was suddenly all out of proportion. My hands felt really large and heavy even though I could hold them up to my face and see that they didn't look any different from the way they usually did. That used to scare me badly, and I would go sit in the bathroom, turn on the light, and wait until the feeling went away. I've never understood what made me see things in such a weird way, and I never told anyone when it

happened. It was the middle of the night, and you don't want to go wake people up and try to explain something to them that you don't even understand yourself. I was afraid they'd think I was nuts. I also knew that telling my family about it wouldn't make it go away, so I kept it to myself.

When I was older, about fifteen, I became aware that men could be predatory, and that scared me in a more profound way. There were a couple of instances when men would act towards me in ways that were overtly sexual. I felt appalled and threatened by that, especially when it was my father's friends acting that way. That really shocked me. I know now that I was just starting to read the handwriting on the wall. It said, "You're a grown woman, and this is what it means."

I don't think that I was an ordinary kid. Part of being different came from feeling responsible for my younger brothers and sisters. If anyone picked on them or threatened them in any way, I would become irate and do battle on their behalf. That sense of responsibility gave me a social consciousness. I definitely developed a sense of justice that was easily offended. I got very angry about things I saw as being unjust, even if the injustice was something I read about or saw on TV. I was just a kid, so there was only so much I could do about what I felt, but the strength of those feelings certainly served to define me. I don't think it was only my role in my family, however, that determined the fact that I was not an ordinary kid. I was aware that I was very smart. I knew that I could outthink my parents in certain ways. I also realized that I caught on to things much

more quickly than most other kids my age. That sense of myself also made me feel different.

I definitely trust my brain and have always relied on it, but as I get older, I'm trying more and more to trust my instincts. Brains are wonderful things, but they're not everything. Making music helps you to understand that the intellect is only part of a larger continuum of who you are as a person. That's one of the best aspects of playing music for me. Music enables me to stop overintellectualizing everything. It forces me to deal with the emotional and sensual aspects of who I am.

Lucy KAPLANSKY

I came to New York to be a folksinger in my late teens. It was going well. I got a great review in *The New York Times.* I was building a nice name for myself. There was, of course, a lot more work to do—it wasn't like Columbia Records was beating down my door—but things were going in the right direction.

All of sudden I freaked out and decided that I was very unhappy, that I wasn't doing what I really wanted to do, that I wasn't us-ing my real talents. A couple of things caused that reaction. First, I was only performing other people's songs, and the fact that I was born with the ability to sing didn't mean any-thing to me. I didn't feel that I'd really be ac-complishing anything if I had success as a singer. Maybe it would have made a differ-ence if I'd been able to write my own songs, but I wasn't capable of doing that back then. Second, I was really scared, and I didn't know it. This was partly because of who my peers were. When I was starting out, there were some unbelievably talented people beginning their careers. It was an extraordinary scene. Suzanne Vega and I hit the Village at the same time. Shawn Colvin came a year later. Bill Morrissey, Cliff Eberhardt, David Massengill, really gifted people were all there. The Roches, coming from the same scene, had just become hugely successful.

I was really scared that I wasn't as good as they were. If you know that you're scared, you can fight it, but if you don't know you're scared, it can be really crippling. I opted unconsciously to avoid ever finding out if I was good enough by not following through. I

> He said he'd really like to do a record with us—a moment which is every musician's dream come true—and I said, "Oh, no, no, thanks. I don't want to make a record. I want to become a therapist."

told myself I didn't want to do this. That was a lie. I really *did* want to do it. For years I had the fantasy, a very convenient fantasy, that if I'd kept with music, I would have been successful and famous. The trouble is, the fantasy doesn't make you happy. I was still miserable.

But I convinced myself that going back to school (I had dropped out of Barnard) made sense. I decided to become a therapist because I was in therapy myself and interested in how therapy worked. I also wanted to heal myself, which is why a lot of people become therapists. I said to myself and to everyone around me that I was quitting music to go back to college. Except I didn't really quit. I kept singing. I didn't pursue a solo career after that, but I did a lot of backup singing and sang in a couple of duos, one with Shawn Colvin that was going well. I was acting very differently from what I was saying. I said, "I'm going to be a therapist; I'm not interested in music," but I was still singing.

That conflict eventually came to a head when a record company guy approached Shawn and me one night at Gerde's Folk City. He said he'd really like to do a record with us—a moment which is every musician's dream come true—and I said, "Oh, no, no, thanks. I don't want to make a record. I want to become a therapist." Shawn looked at me in shock. She had no idea that I wasn't pursuing this career seriously because I was acting as though I were. She said, "If you're not going to pursue this, I guess I need to." She wasn't being mean; she just realized she couldn't stay tied to me if I wasn't as committed as she was. That was the end of our duo.

I still did some background singing. I let gigs come to me; I didn't pursue them actively. I was very passive, which is the way I've lived most of my life until recently.

That's been one of my major conflicts. Then I decided to go to graduate school. That's when I really stopped singing. I stopped playing gigs and hanging around with musicians. I disappeared.

But Shawn and I remained friends. She had always wanted to produce a record and one day said, "Why don't we make a record? We'll get some money, do it live in the studio; it will be really fun." And I thought, *Fun, fine, sure,* but didn't take it very seriously. I thought it would be fun to work with Shawn, so we made the record. Again, I took a passive approach. We worked on it together, but she was really the creative mastermind behind it. It turned out to be a really good album, and we started shopping it to record companies. I was back in therapy with a new therapist at that point, and I said to him, "I wouldn't want what Shawn has" (she was already becoming very successful, and I was referring to things like recognition, money, accolades), and he asked me, "Why not?" No one, including my previous therapist, had

ever asked me that before. I started to say something like "She's away from home so much," but I stopped and said, "I don't know why."

Unless somebody asks you something that simple, you may go through your entire life not questioning your basic assumptions. That was the beginning of my understanding that I'd been lying to myself. I also saw that I wasn't being truthful to myself when I saw

Shawn on the Grammys. She had been nominated for Best Pop Vocal, an enormous honor. I was filled with despair and envy even though I had supposedly made the decision to leave music to be a psychologist. I was miserable, really depressed. My response helped me understand that something was wrong.

So I discovered finally that it was nonsense to pretend I didn't want to be a musician. Once I understood that I wasn't telling myself the truth, things began to change in a

dramatic way. Suddenly I couldn't lie to myself anymore. I saw the truth, and there was no turning back. The record was finished. Red House Records picked it up. I started pursuing a solo career.

I still have all kinds of internal struggles about the choice I've made. It's a very scary thing to have to see if you're any good. It scares the hell out of me. Every day I wonder whether I'm good enough to do this and if I'm going to find out that I'm not. At this point I don't have a lot of choices because if I didn't pursue this now, I'd never be able to live with myself.

One of the reasons I was conflicted about being a musician had to do with the narcissistic gratification of being onstage and being applauded. It felt a lot safer to be in a helper role as a therapist, much like it felt safer to be a backup singer out of the limelight. Like many others, I became a therapist because being the mediator was my role in the family. I was always taking care of everyone, looking out for everyone else's feelings. Becoming a therapist was a natural, though not necessarily a healthy, thing. You don't necessarily want to perpetuate a role that wasn't entirely good for you in the first place, a role that serves to hide other parts of you. It can be very frustrating, but it was much more comfortable. Performers who are unabashedly narcissistic are not going to have this conflict. It would be fine with them to be the center of attention in every area of their lives, including onstage. But for someone who isn't comfortable being the center of attention, being recognized onstage can be a conflict. Still, after all those years away from music and not getting any recognition as a performer, it feels very good now when it happens. It's something I can finally say that I want.

"The Tide" is angry, and it's certainly about feeling depleted, but it's not about resignation. It says, in effect, "I have nothing for you, but I have a lot for me." I wrote "The Tide" with my husband,

Rick Litvin, after I started to see that for my entire life I had always been passive and compliant, unable to let myself be angry. With that recognition, suddenly I started to change. I was

discovering a lot of new things in myself. The song is about saying, "I'm not doing it anymore. I have to look out for myself." With that assertion the whole world opens up. We were using the idea that in nothing is everything. You have to burn away what you *thought*

> You have to burn away what you *thought* was true until you're left with the truth. It's incredibly gut-wrenching and frightening, but that process also gives you life.

working on it in my own life. I focus less now on the interior, on the hard purging, and more on rebuilding. That part of the process is more apparent in the songs on my second

was true until you're left with the truth. It's incredibly gut-wrenching and frightening, but that process also gives you life. If you are living lies, which is what I did for most of my life, you're not alive.

In part, "Somebody's Home" offers a metaphor for therapy, an incredibly important element of my life that has helped me come to some kind of recognition of what and who I am. That process destroys, and it gives life: destruction and creation. I'm still

album, *Flesh and Bone.* In "Scorpion," there's a line that reads, "I want to give you everything," and "Still Life" says, "I cannot live in bronze or stone / I must live in flesh and bone"—that's more of a reflection of where things are now spiritually, psychologically. I'm saying, in effect, *"I'm here now."*

Singing makes up a large part of my identity. I was the singer in the family even when I was very young. At six I would sing with my dad, who played the piano. We didn't listen to records as a rule.

205

I would sing along to the music he played. He was the rehearsal pianist for the University of Chicago Gilbert and Sullivan troupe, so we'd do a lot of songs from those operettas. He also loves popular songs from the thirties and forties, so we'd do a lot of those together too.

I have one vivid memory that let me know I had some talent as a singer. My family went to the Canadian National Exhibition in 1967, and while we were there, we saw a show with a theme song. On the way home no one could remember the song except for me: "A place to stand, a place to grow, Ontari-ari-ario." My father was very impressed that I could

In "Scorpion," there's a line that reads, "I want to give you everything"— that's more of a reflection of where things are now spiritually, psychologically. I'm saying, in effect, "I'm here now."

sing the whole thing from memory.

Then, a few years later—and this is a testimony to how much I really loved singing harmony—I would record myself singing and then sing harmony while I played the tape back, just for fun in my room.

The image of singing on the tightrope in "The Tide" is a very powerful image for me. There were so many ways that I was shut down for most of my life, but the one thing I let myself do was sing. It was something I was able to feel sort of free about and allow myself to be recognized for. For me, singing is a powerful symbol.

To think that for ten years I couldn't admit how important singing was to me. How sad and scary. I would only let myself sing country-western songs at parties where no one would listen. That was my experience of myself singing. To be able to experience singing as something artistic which people really *hear* is very important to me now. The voice is an instrument and something with which I can be more creative in an unconflicted way than I can be doing anything else. If I go into a studio to sing a harmony, there are things that come out of me from a completely subconscious place that can be really beautiful and creative. I can reach that level more often now when I'm singing the lead. There's a way in which the voice is both an instrument and a vehicle for artistic expression.

I started listening to the radio when I was eleven. "The Night They Drove Old Dixie Down" was a hit that year. I also remember sitting around the campfire at summer camp, singing Cat Stevens and Jim Croce songs. During seventh grade I started to learn how to play the guitar so I could sing Jim Croce songs.

I really started to listen to music seriously when my brother turned me on to Joni

Mitchell's *Blue* at fourteen, right at that time when I was really ready to hear it. That definitely changed my life. There was something completely captivating about how personal the songs were. I loved her singing. I wanted to be her, to sound like her. In fact, I recently listened to a tape I made when I was with a group in Chicago a few years later. I was trying so hard to sound like Joni Mitchell that I was embarrassed to listen to myself. I even sang "block" so it sounded like "bl*u*ck"—just the way Joni does. So my musical taste shifted, and I started listening to Jackson Browne, Joan Baez, and every Joni Mitchell album I could get my hands on. I was so cheap that I would check out records from my high school library. I listened to all of Joni Mitchell that way before I bought anything. It was so hard for me to let myself buy records. Still is. Really weird.

When I was in high school, a friend who'd heard me sing introduced me to a musician named Elliot who had just graduated from the University of Chicago. We met, sang together a few times, and formed a band. We played the Chicago clubs for a few months before reading a feature article in *The New York Times* about a folk revival in Greenwich Village—it was 1977—and decided to move to New York. Actually, Elliot decided, and because he completely dominated me, I said okay. I was seventeen; he was twenty-three. My family was not happy. Until then I was the most compliant, well-behaved girl. I'd never done anything bad. In fact, it was only in my last week of high school that I cut a class. I was *so good*. I got straight As throughout school. Then, suddenly, I meet Elliot, this guy six years older than me, start having sex, and decide to move to New York instead of going to college. I went to this very high-powered, very competitive high school that was part of the University of Chicago. All anyone cared about was getting into Ivy League schools. *Everyone* went to college but me. All

of this freaked my parents out. They were not thrilled.

Still, Elliot and I went to New York to join the folk revival we'd read about in the

Times. At first we lived with his parents for a while in Manhattan. The city was a very scary place to me, especially as I'd never been there before. I was frightened and lonely. Elliot wasn't good to me, and the relationship was very unhealthy. After a year in New York I decided that I would go to school because my parents would support me if I did. I went to Barnard, but I was not into being in college. I was playing at Folk City and other clubs more than I was studying, so I dropped out. Shortly after that Elliot and I broke up and I started playing solo.

I began to make friends who were part of the Village folk scene. It started to feel like home. I was working menial jobs at three dollars an hour, so it wasn't all fun. Then I got a job in 1980 waitressing at Folk City and was promoted to bartender. That was a wild period in my life when I was drinking every night and doing all kinds of other things. I was definitely out to be bad and have some fun. And I did—sort of.

Although I was living in Greenwich Village, I didn't know much about the sixties folk boom that had taken place there. I learned about that stuff later—like the first place Dylan played in New York was Folk City. I only knew about the folk music of the seventies—James Taylor and Joni Mitchell—which had nothing whatsoever to do with New York. I was excited by what was going on in the late

> There were so many ways that I was shut down for most of my life, but the one thing I let myself do was sing.

seventies, early eighties, when I was there, by musicians like the Roches, Steve Forbert, David Massengill, and, a little later, Suzanne Vega. The success of the Roches galvanized this scene, and it was very exciting to be a part of it all.

When Elliot and I had a duo, we were included on the Cornelia Street Songwriters Exchange album, a collection of work by a songwriters' group that had been meeting for a few years at the Cornelia Street Café. The manager of the café decided to make an album featuring some of the people who played there: Cliff Eberhardt, who was driving a cab back then, David Massengill, who was washing dishes, Elliot and I, Michael Fracasso. The album was reviewed in *The New York Times* by John Rockwell, who wrote that we were the highlight of the album. I didn't read the *Times* back then, and I remember Suzanne Vega calling me to say, "You're in the *Times* today." That was a very nice moment. Later, when I was playing solo, John Rockwell

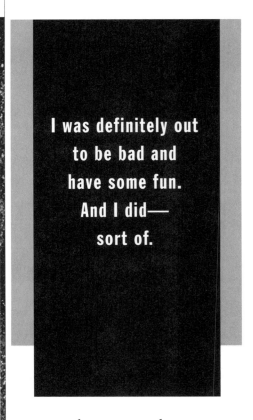

I was definitely out to be bad and have some fun. And I did— sort of.

came to hear me and wrote a very positive review. That was a major thing.

I listen to music because it fills some emotional need in me. I listen to be moved. Any kind of artist who can move you is serving an active purpose for a lot of people. It's a different purpose than the one being fulfilled by a psychotherapist or an engineer, but it's every bit as valid and useful.

I remember the effect of hearing the Roches' "Quitting Time" when I was feeling miserable for all kinds of reasons: a job I hated; a relationship that had gone bad. I walked down the street singing that song, and there was something healing about

it. Even though I couldn't pick up and leave a horrible situation at that moment, singing that song about picking up and leaving was amazingly cathartic. That song held out some hope for me, and because of that, it was important, it made something happen. That's what I'm trying to do when I write a song.

When I first started writing, it was from a pure desire to express something musically. Now writing is complicated by the fact that I have to write. That gets confusing for me. The necessity of writing makes it more of a struggle. Necessity aside, I want to express something emotionally in my songs. There is a feeling I get when I'm singing my own words rather than someone else's that makes for a deeper, more emotional experience. I write to get to that level of feeling.

The most important thing to me is writing songs that are emotionally truthful, that say something honest in an interesting rather than a trite way, so that people can respond emotionally to what they hear. When I listen to John Gorka, the songs I particularly love are the ones in which he hits some unbelievably powerful emotional note. I get chills when he does that. To be able to touch people that powerfully: That's what I'm going for. If I can do that, I'd be very happy.

One thing that's wonderful about writing and performing this kind of music is that you can do intelligent and interesting work that has an audience. Enough people come to your shows and buy your records so you can make a living. That's not true in other arts. I thank God I'm not trying to be an actor or painter. A singer-songwriter doesn't ever have to deal with a major record label or make a music video to be successful. It's a privilege to do this and make a living at it. The folk world is one place where you can get away from mainstream popular culture and still succeed as an artist.

The problem with a lot of pop music is that it doesn't resonate emotionally. There's nothing particularly truthful or interesting there beyond the standard, pretty clichés. I'm not interested in that. I don't know what people are responding to, what moves them about that kind of music. It doesn't move me.

I try to resist the tendency to simplify that I see at the core of contemporary culture and not only in music. For example, the kind of therapy I believe in and the kind I practiced until I left psychology to pursue music full-time is very long-term and difficult. It involves peeling off layers, understanding some very compli-

cated things that go on inside you. People don't usually want to do that. Patients sometimes asked me to give them homework to speed things up. They want the process to be easier. I understand that desire and wish there were easier ways. I'm envious of people who've been saved by religion. If walking into a church could make everything become just as I want it to be, I'd go inside in a second. But that kind of answer just doesn't work for me. A lot of people are very unhappy. They'd like to feel better. Others have capitalized on that unhappiness by coming up with quick, superficial solutions that don't really help. My therapist said to me when I was ambivalent about continuing therapy, "You have a root canal because you *have* to, not because you *want* to."

Writing about a "good girl" carrying "buckets made of stone" in "The Tide" wasn't a conscious attempt to depict women in general. It was very much an image of myself. But I don't think it's a big coincidence that as a girl I did—and to some extent still do—carry an emotional burden in my family. Girls do that a lot in families, as do women in marriages.

Women are encouraged to be emotionally vulnerable, to express their insecurity. More women, for example, say they're depressed than men do. Women simply experience themselves in a different way emotionally. When I think of all the music that women make about their vulnerability, it doesn't surprise me because women are more comfortable expressing

> I'm envious of people who've been saved by religion. If walking into a church could make everything become just as I want it to be, I'd go inside in a second. But that kind of answer just doesn't work for me.

themselves artistically in a confessional way. Nor is it surprising that women would receive such strong responses when they open themselves up like that. It's a way of expression that we're allowed, for better and worse.

I think, though, that the feeling of isolation I was writing about in "The Tide" is somewhat universal. A hell of a lot of people feel overwhelmed and stuck with whatever it is they carry with them from childhood. I'd like to think that whenever you come up with something that is emotionally true, it is universal by definition. Somewhere someone else has experienced that emotion. We're not so different from one another.

I'm shy to talk about why people seem to like what I do. I don't want to sound presumptuous. I only know for certain what my intentions were when I started to write and play. At that point in my life I felt crushed by a desire not just to pass time anymore or waste myself on merely surviving. I couldn't stand seeing so many of us wasting ourselves that way, reduced to living hand to mouth, all of our pride gone. We're noble creatures capable of curing diseases, creating art, appreciating beauty, and most of us don't even get the chance to see that. And I thought, *God, if it's this hard for me, a young white girl, imagine how hard it must be for people who have to face racism, for example, or a handicap, or prejudice because of their sexual preference.* Wasn't I—aren't we all—worth more than worrying about how the rent is going to be paid or if we are going to be fed? I started to feel life wasn't

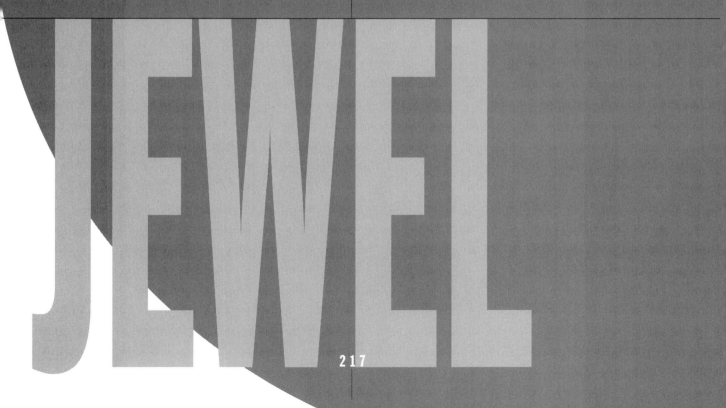

JEWEL

worth it if there wasn't anything beyond that. I'd reached the point where I couldn't accept such limitation and pain all the time.

I needed to find a permanent way out of it, to persevere. This tenacity gave me the strength to say, "I'm going to live my dream." To get there, I would have to take responsibility for what I was thinking. I was spending most of my thoughts on fear, on limitation, on "Oh, poor me, I'll never get out of this." It was thinking like that which was creating the limitations. So I made trying to think of other things into a game. *Can I actually think about excitement rather than pain,* for instance? *Can I allow myself to think that something great is going to happen rather than something bad?* As I was able to do that more and more, I started turning things around. I think anyone can. I realize we're not taught to think about ourselves on our own. That's debilitating. Instead we think we have to go to other people who'll think for us. We go to therapists or psychics to be understood, God to

be forgiven, lovers to be liked. But when those responses don't come from within, we handicap ourselves and become dependent on others to keep us in line. As a result, we're not intimate with ourselves, we're not intimate with our thought process, with our emotions or spirit. Very often we don't even know the difference between fear and anger.

I write about the need to think for yourself in my songs quite a lot. It's something that intrigues me, the fact that your hands manifest thought. What is pollution? It's thoughtlessness. You don't pollute your own neighborhood unless you're thoughtless. War? Thoughtlessness. Instead of treating things like pollution, war, untrustworthy politicians, and the fact that thirteen-year-olds are killing themselves as separate issues we need to think of all these things as manifestations of thoughtlessness, a lack of intimacy with the spirit and the divine. When the spirit is weak, it makes us vulnerable to neurotic, negative, and otherwise contrary behavior. There are few leaders who teach us to know our hearts and

> Wasn't I—aren't we all—worth more than worrying about how the rent is going to be paid or if we are going to be fed? I started to feel life wasn't worth it if there wasn't anything beyond that.

our spirits without dogmatic, fear-based, or segregated thinking. But in our hearts and in silence all answers may be accessed. In silence the whispers of God are heard, and the answers to prayers are given.

Ultimately we are responsible for how we act. On the front of *Pieces of You,* I included a line that reads, "What we call human nature is in actuality human habit." Often we let ourselves off the hook for what we do by saying, "Ah, I'm only human." Only human? We're divinity in the form of flesh. *Only* human? We're spirit as well as a physical body that allows us to manifest thought. That's a gift, not a weakness. I spent most of my life up to this point feeling that it wasn't a gift, that it was a burden, that to be spiritual, you had to transcend your body, live on a mountain, and eat only brown rice with nothing on it. I believed all those ideas people have about spirituality—you can't be rich, you can't wear makeup, you can't have sex—but it's really not that way. We are divine in our form. We are capable of anything. There is no limit. People like Einstein shouldn't be uncommon. All our minds have that potential. It's a matter of cultivating it, of taking responsibility for it.

Plato's *Symposium* was very important to me when I was fifteen or sixteen. I also credit Kant and

> **We go to therapists or psychics to be understood, God to be forgiven, lovers to be liked. But when those responses don't come from within, we handicap ourselves.**

Pascal for my mental awakening. But reason isn't God. In the *Symposium* some believed that through art you could achieve immortality. The idea that a life could be a work of art is a really interesting idea to me. Then what happens? If you're not just making art but making yourself and your life into art, do you become immortal? Years after I read Plato, I wrote the song "Painters," which is about the relationship between art and immortality, but I couldn't complete my thought then.

Standing up there at the American Music Awards, I realized that the only thing that sold my record was sincerity. It was encouraging to think that the world is headed to a place where, despite all the cynicism, a quality like sincerity has some

value. We need to recognize the problems but stay mercilessly focused on discovering where change is possible. There's no true cynic alive; they've all killed themselves, as the saying goes. Even the most cynical people must believe in something, even if it's only themselves, or else they wouldn't be around. Not even the most cynical of us can live without some hope. And so hope and faith are an antidote.

When I was living in my van, I had chronic kidney infections. They were really bad, but there were doctors who just wouldn't see me. I was amazed that I could be that sick and they wouldn't even look at me. Poverty makes you realize your dependency on people, which is frightening and also a reminder of just how much we've lost touch with the fact that survival requires relationships with others. These doctors, for instance, felt absolutely no responsibility for anyone who didn't have the money or an insurance policy. That's just one

example of the kind of thing that happens every day.

Each of us affects hundreds of people we never see and who never tell us about the effect we've had on them. Small acts of kindness do really add up, and on the other side, one suicide is made up of a thousand little cruelties. We can change each other's lives by really focusing on our human interactions day to day. I want to live responsibly in my

We are capable of anything. There is no limit.

life. It doesn't have to do with whether you're onstage every night or not.

"Who Will Save Your Soul" begins with the line "People living their lives for you on TV." Although it wasn't the case when I wrote the song, I'm in a position now that might allow someone to live through me rather than living for themselves. It's a strange feeling, and at the same time, it isn't strange at all because even though my surroundings change, I'm still inside of myself. Some big mystical change doesn't occur because I'm on the cover of a magazine. Fame exists in other people's minds. I can't experience my own fame at all, but I experience it in other people's eyes when I look at them and I see that they're scared or intimidated or overjoyed or whatever. The whole fascination

I realized that the only thing that sold my record was sincerity.

with fame as evidenced by TV gossip shows is disconcerting. That fascination makes me uncomfortable.

The focus in entertainment and the media on perfect bodies also creates a dangerous and degrading gap. I'm all for women doing whatever they want with their bodies—and men as well—but celebrities have the means to do things nobody else can, from the extreme of removing ribs to the luxury of having a personal trainer. That the media promotes looking perfect when looking perfect really means being rich enough to buy the right body is a really disturbing fact. Bulimia and anorexia are such rampant problems; 60 percent of the people in my high school were bulimic or anorexic. There are fourteen-year-olds being so mean to themselves, as I was at that age, and it's still so hard to get over. If I can't look like those women, am I a bad person? Does the fact that I ate some Ben & Jerry's last night make me bad? Trying to be human and being in the spotlight, I'm realizing that perfection is at the root of all evil. Trying to achieve the media's standard of perfection causes a lot of problems for people.

It's also interesting to see your life squeezed into a few paragraphs in a press kit bio. I'm usually answering questions that people ask me based on those paragraphs, but there are important things that are much closer to my heart that don't fit into a press release. The influence of my mother and teachers, for instance. At twenty-two you want to be flattered and think you've done everything on your own. It's flattering when people ask, "How can you be so young and have so much insight?" It's also easy for them to say, with hind-

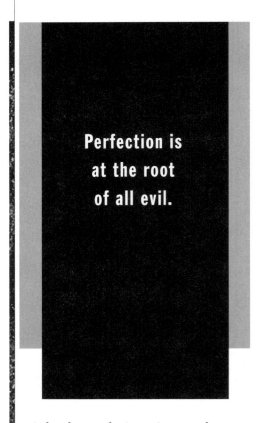

Perfection is at the root of all evil.

sight, how obvious it was that you were destined to succeed. But the emotional and spiritual groundwork for any success is the product of people's interest and devotion to you long before it happens. I had tremendous teachers early on, and I was influenced by several obvious and salient features that molded me into what I am now.

I was very fortunate and blessed to have

those things and people in my life. My mom, first of all. I have described her as grace. She's an extremely refined and brilliant woman. It's so hard for me to begin to describe the effect that she's had on my life or my connection to her. I might be in some spotlight, but I can't take too much credit because she has crafted me into such a good person. She's everything a parent and a good person should be. I feel so blessed to have someone in my life who was constantly encouraging me to be brave and courageous about figuring out what my heart and spirit needed, someone who helped me fit the world around those needs.

> **Fame exists in other people's minds. I can't experience my own fame at all, but I experience it in other people's eyes when I look at them and I see that they're scared or intimidated or overjoyed or whatever.**

She helped me take every risk and also to know how to back it up. She taught me how to chase my dreams in a practical manner. Not everyone has that kind of support in their lives.

Although I am definitely a curious person who has worked hard to bring about what has been given to me, I am not a product of my own making. I'm the result of my teachers and parents but also of my environment. I was raised in the outdoors. When you sleep underneath the stars, you wake up with more answers than you have questions. Although I'm an avid reader, there are more natural ways of acquiring knowledge than what we learn

from books. We learn things from being out-doors, from the wind, from standing next to someone else. Being part of the natural world reminds me that innocence isn't ever lost completely; we just need to maintain our goodness to regain it. You can always return to your original state, which is pure, at any time you want, no matter what position you are in. That's such a relief for me to remember.

Sometimes I feel so far from my light when I'm on the road or otherwise plunged into all the clichés of rocker life. And even though this isn't what I imagined my life would become, I know that I can always get to the place where I recognize myself. I'm never far from there, never separate from God really—or wherever you find your divinity, your specialness. And it is this understanding that gives me a certain centering and strength that have prevented me from wandering off and becoming distracted in my present realm. My greatest bliss was open spaces where I remembered my freedom and

felt the wind on my skin, felt the wind on my spirit and my body all at the same time.

It's taken time, but I'm starting to get it. I don't always achieve the balance, but I'm not chickening out. I'm not going to live in a monastery. I'm going to learn, and I'm going to set an example. We all can. We're learning how to be bankers and be

> My greatest bliss
> was open spaces
> where I remembered
> my freedom and
> felt the wind on
> my skin.

spiritual. We're learning how to be rock stars and be spiritual. We're learning how to be housewives, how to fulfill our needs as human beings, and be spiritual. I think I'm getting better at balancing the world and spirit. I don't succeed every day, but I'm dedicated to getting there eventually. I think faith has a lot to do with the success of the outcome.

CASH

Rosanne

During the time that I was making *King's Record Shop,* I dreamed I went inside an old gentleman's beautiful house and sat on his couch while he talked to Linda Ronstadt with his back to me. I felt very awkward and self-conscious because he wouldn't turn to speak with me. Finally I tried to interject myself into the conversation by asking a question. The man responded with an icy, scathing stare, didn't answer, and turned back to Linda. I was so humiliated that I got up and left.

I told my therapist about this dream, and she asked me to talk to this old man so I could find out who he was and why he wouldn't speak to me. I closed my eyes, pictured him, and asked those questions. He answered, "I am art, and we don't respect dilettantes." His answer devastated me—it was crushing—but it made me realize that up until that point I had been dabbling when it came to my work. I was not going as deep or committing myself as fully as I could have. I set out some very specific tasks for myself because of that answer and started to work at earning the old gentleman's respect.

be a writer from the time I was nine years old, I didn't realize where that desire would lead or that writing would assume the form it has taken in my life. Years later, after I'd

I can see now that being a dilettante was a form of self-protection. Even though I'd known I wanted to

already had number one records, I still didn't understand fully that I'd chosen this life. One day when I was on the couch, it suddenly occurred to me for the first time:

I'm a singer! I remember that moment so clearly. It felt good to come to that realization, but it also bothered me that it had taken so long to start accepting who I was. Even then I still didn't feel a connection with my voice. To accept completely the fact that I was a singer and feel attached to my voice took a long time.

Part of why it took me so long to recognize who I was involved the fact that my father, Johnny Cash, is such an accomplished and well-known musician. To say that his success and fame caused me anxiety is an understatement. Early on I determined that I wasn't going to do what he did. I didn't want to do anything that could lead to fame because the chief imprint I received as a kid was that being famous destroys everything. For a while I really thought I'd become an archaeologist, but I knew I'd write no matter what else I did. When I learned how to write songs, though, I understood that was what I wanted to do. I didn't care about singing or making records, but I knew I had to write songs.

When I was twenty-three, I went to Germany with some songs, and these record company people there wanted to hear me play them. One thing led to another, and the label offered me a deal which despite what I'd told myself

> You reach that point when you've endured enough sorrow that you can't do anything about, experienced enough pain that you've just had to live with. That and a certain richness of the senses are what defines womanhood for me.

all along about not performing, I accepted. By making a record in Europe, I rationalized, I could stay away from my dad's territory. I told myself it would be okay to complete one little project over here in Germany. Then, on the eve of making the record, I realized I was courting the very things I'd always promised myself I'd stay away from. I'd reached one of those forks in the road of my life and I couldn't decide which way to go. Instead of deciding, I went to bed and couldn't get up or stop crying for days. My friends finally took me to a doctor and asked him what was wrong with me. The doctor said—perceptive diagnosis—that I was depressed.

> **Sometimes writing makes you feel like Persephone going into the underworld; you don't know if you're going to come out with your pomegranate or not.**

I came to realize eventually that I'd already decided to make the record, to choose that path I thought I'd never go down, so I went ahead but not without tremendous anxiety. I was very rebellious for a long time after that. I resented it when people asked me about or compared me to my dad. I couldn't believe they'd suggest a comparison when I was so different from him. I had a ton of resentment and acted out of rebellion. But things change. I've come to terms with who I am and what I do. After working through a lot of stuff, my father and I are close now. Both of my parents are very supportive and play an important part in my life.

When I was in Paris working on the stories in *Bodies of Water,* I spent a lot of time

sarily determined by the fact that you've gone through key experiences like getting married or having a baby, although those things may play a part. What's truly definitive is crossing a certain threshold of suffering in your life. You reach that point when you've endured enough sorrow that you can't do anything about, experienced enough pain that you've just had to live with. That and a certain richness of the senses are what defines womanhood for me. I tried to get that realization across in "Part Girl" when Elsa says, "I am a woman which is to say part girl and part suffering."

The connection between being a woman and a writer is so subjective as to be indefinable for me. It's like seeing the world through brown eyes or being five feet five inches tall. It's cellular. It's part of the DNA. How do you talk about your DNA with any objectivity? Somewhere in the cells being a woman and writing collide. I suppose in that sense a lot of my work is gender-specific and therefore political even though my attitude isn't.

thinking about what it means to become a woman, to grow up. It's certainly not about arriving at a certain age. It's not even neces-

Art should transcend politics, including gender politics, even if what you do is implicitly political. I love the process of trying to gain objectivity about what I'm writing. It's fascinating to try and figure out which part comes der aside. Even though I don't have a sure grip on it, I know there are some aspects of what I write that are intrinsically from a woman's perspective—the way we see men

from a feminine point of view and which part is basically human, gender aside.

Men fascinate and bewilder me. I hate or the way we see ourselves—and others that aren't.

to draw gender lines between men and women, but the fact is there are differences, so you might as well talk about the elephant that's in the room. Even if I can never fully unravel the strands that make up the elements of a song or story along gender lines, I love exploring the possibilities. The idea that rationality is male and the emotive is female makes sense to me only in Jungian terms of masculine and feminine energy rather than as those qualities apply to specific people. Elsa, the same character who speaks about a woman as part girl and part suffering, bypasses the graves of thinkers like Voltaire to visit the chapel of Ste. Genevieve, the patron saint of Paris, and has a very emotional experience. I suppose I was trying to explore the energy of feminine emotion versus masculine rationality, using those associations in the service of the story. I try to balance those energies in my life even though I tend to come down more heavily on the side of feeling. I married a man who's very rational, so he helps me keep my balance, as does the very earthbound stuff of being a mother and having a family.

Finding that balance is important to me, but I don't want to deny my emotions to do it. There's a line in "Bells and Roses"— "the gifts of the spirit shall not be squandered on one man"—that addresses a tendency in women to give themselves away. One thing that I do to counter that tendency is go off by myself once in a while. I like all journeys that have the earmarks of some mythic quest to find yourself, but I'm always reminded of that line from *'Round Midnight* when one of the characters says he's going to Paris and his friend says, "You know who'll be there to greet you when you get off the plane? You." You think, *Aw, hell, it's not going to work,* but you go anyway, and it does work, to a degree.

It's also necessary to keep a certain balance so you can court danger when you write and still come back to yourself when you're done. Sometimes writing makes you feel like Persephone going into the underworld; you don't know if you're going to come out with your pomegranate or not. Writing "Shelly's Voices" was particularly dangerous for me. At the beginning of the story Shelly says, "I do not court insanity, but I flirt outrageously," and sometimes I've been willing to push myself to the edge just to find out what's there, to discover the language that comes out of that place. I'm fascinated by the line between rationality and madness and the process of going deep and learning how to get back. However outrageously I flirt with insanity, I've been adamant about

The anarchists managed to elect me Senior Princess for homecoming. There was a lot of grousing from the football players about my title.

learning how to return from the edge. Too many artists go there and can't get back. The arts have far more than their share of suicides, alcoholics, and drug addicts. But even if you learn to defend yourself against self-destruction, you certainly leave yourself open to the disturbing aftereffects of what you find when you court the darker muses.

As a child I couldn't allow myself to indulge in fear. I just shut it down. Family life was chaotic. My mother was extremely distraught through much of my childhood. I grew up in a household of women, the oldest of four sisters. I took care of everybody and spent a lot of energy looking after my sisters. My dad was chemically addicted and on the road most of the time.

In "We Are Born," I wrote, "The summer I was eleven I felt too big for my body, too small for my heart, confused by the secrets and fears that permeated the very atoms of the air inside my home." That's how you feel when you're in a home where there's an addict. All those secrets and fears. During the period when I was between six and twelve years old, we lived on a mountain in a house perched over the desert. There was a lot of scrub. There were rattlesnakes everywhere. It was very isolated and rather bleak.

an important escape. My mother played Ray Charles a lot. When I chose a record, I would put "Hit the Road, Jack" on the stereo and play it

I don't remember feeling particularly happy very often. I liked riding my bike because I could let go of everything for a little while. Music was also over and over while I ran a loop through the living room, the den, and the kitchen until the song ended. Then I'd do it all over again and again. I was in the second grade when I heard the Beatles on the radio for the first time. My grade-school friend's much older teenage sister was driving us to school. We were sitting in the backseat when "I Want to Hold Your Hand" came on the radio. My friend was talking in my ear, and all of a sudden I just couldn't hear her anymore. All I could hear was this song. I just kept wondering, *How do I find that on the radio? How can I hear that again once it's over?* I know it sounds like a cliché, but hearing the Beatles changed everything.

Except for a period during high school when I didn't care about anything, I was always an overachiever. I still have the classic symptoms: the feeling that I've never done anything and that I have to start over every day. That feeling has been a constant grain in my shell since I was a young girl. I'm sure I developed that attitude, in part, as a response to the stifling lack of expectations that southern parents of my mom and dad's generation had for their female children. I was never led to expect I would work, for instance. There was no thought of having a career. You were expected to get through school and find a nice husband; that was it. I discovered very early on that I wasn't going to follow that route. I remember delivering a rabid speech to my father when I was eleven in the back of his limo to the effect that I refused to grow up to be just someone's wife. It was the first time I told him who I was.

When I was ten and eleven, I was the biggest nerd. I'd get my mom to drop me at the library on a Saturday morning so I could read all day. I started out with teen romances and then read the Cherry Ames series—it was a girl thing—from *Cherry Ames, Student Nurse* all the way up to *Cherry Ames, Country Doctor's Nurse.* My daughter Carrie now has the same series. I graduated to reading literature pretty quickly. When I became a teenager, I started reading D.H. Lawrence, Tolstoy, and Solzhenitsyn. It took

me forever, but I got through *The Gulag Archipelago.*

By the time I went to high school at St. Bonaventure in California, I wasn't as nerdy though I still loved books. I thought I was very cool. I was a member of the Anarchy Society. I guess we couldn't really have been anarchists if we formed a society, but still, for a Catholic school where there wasn't much going on, we were on the fringe. Except for our group, everybody else went to games and pep rallies. The anarchists managed to elect me Senior Princess for homecoming. I didn't have enough votes to become Senior Queen, a position which went to the chief Rah-Rah—that's what we called the pep rally types. Even so, there was a lot of grousing from the football players about my title. They would say things like "She shouldn't be in the court because she doesn't have any school spirit." As you can see, it was pretty rough being an anarchist.

After high school, when I was eighteen, I went on the road with my dad. I got a taste of that life, touring around the country on a bus. At some point during the trip, he gave me a list of one hundred country songs I had to know, and I learned most of them. It was a good apprenticeship in some ways, but I wasn't ready to become a musician at that point in my life. After the tour I went on to college, where I majored in English. I read everything I could and everything I had to, including a lot of things I didn't like. I never warmed to *Beowulf,* sorry, or eighteenth-century writers like Pope, who seemed to me an unbearable misogynist. But I cultivated my interest in literature and learned a lot about what good writing required. Studying English formally was important to my development as a writer.

> **During the *Interiors* tour I really choked. About the third song into the set on the third show of the tour, I froze and thought to myself, *Oh, my God, I don't know if I can do this.***

Even though I feel self-conscious about writing in the first person so frequently, I don't feel that I'm reading my diary when I look at my work. I know the difference between confession and fiction. I know where poetic license is drawn. Although I write very personal songs and stories, doing so doesn't feel compulsive in any way. Writing isn't about naked autobiography for me. I often take a small part of myself and expand it. For example, Amanda in the story "A Week at the Gore" is a little like me, but the quality we share is much more central to her character as a whole than it is to mine. I do share to a degree her sense of

247

loss, but it's not, finally, the same as my sense of loss. That whole story culminates in one line for me. When Amanda goes back to visit her girlhood home in England and the cemetery where her parents are buried, she thinks about her father and wonders, "What would he have been like with love and an education?" My father called me after reading that story. He was very moved by it and said, "I wonder too what I would have been like with love and an education." I said, "Dad, it wasn't about you!" I couldn't have written about that feeling of loss and understanding if I had been writing pure autobiography. One of the possibilities of art and music that I value most is that it allows you to move beyond yourself and your own experience. It's not always easy to do. Writing in the third person is difficult for me, but when I did use that voice in "Part Girl," it allowed me more freedom to explore Elsa's character and the ability to feel more compassion for her.

Even when I'm writing in a more directly personal way, my work is balanced by a really profound sense of privacy about my actual life. I wouldn't tell you about what's going on with me and my husband right now, for instance. My boundaries are strict to the point of isolation sometimes, but

> Joseph Campbell says, whatever gives you constant fulfillment is the same thing that allows you to be of the most service. With that in mind, I try to follow my bliss.

that people are going to read their own lives into what I write and that interpretations will vary from person to person. No matter how personally I write, my experience is going to be filtered through the reader or listener's particular experience. There have been moments, though, when I was so close to the songs that I found it hard to perform them. During the *Interiors* tour I really choked. About the third song into the set on the third show of the tour, I froze and thought to myself, *Oh, my God, I don't know if I can do this.* I wasn't sure I could pull it off.

The period between *King's Record Shop* and *Interiors* was a really important time in my life. *King's* was in some ways a landmark record in country music. A woman had never had four number one singles from an album before. It was on the charts for a year and half. It was a big deal. But all that happened during a very difficult time in my first marriage. I had my youngest daughter, Carrie, during that period and then things

there's safety in the fact that I'm not unique to the human race. Anything that's personal has got to be universal. It has to be. I know

between my husband and me really got hard. We later separated and divorced. It was also a period of change artistically. When I was pregnant with Carrie, I stopped

this new medium. The creative process was exactly the same although the medium was so different. In both arts there is a phase of

writing and took up painting. That changed my life. It allowed me to see and understand writing through

dismantling yourself, doing research; then there's a gestation phase and, if you're fortunate, more inspiration, followed by editing and completion. It was such an eye-opener to see that process through painting and then apply what I'd learned to writing. When I went back to writing, I felt really fresh. I had new inspiration and a lot more commitment. I was also feeling more independent than I did before.

After I made demos of the songs that would appear on *Interiors,* I started looking for a producer, but one producer I approached said, "Why aren't you producing this yourself?" I didn't have a good answer for him. I left that meeting enthused and confident that I could work on these songs myself. I had an idea of how I wanted them to sound and knew they should sound different from anything I'd recorded before. I didn't want to use a full drum kit, for instance, except on a few tracks. I started thinking about the process as though I were painting. I went into each song exactly as I would a canvas. I used the process of painting as my template, and the result was *Interiors.*

Writing and producing *Interiors* closed the gap between my work and my life more than it had been before. It's not my experience that making art takes away from the rest of life. My kids taught me that life and art are inextricable. I realized early on that I couldn't be a parent at one moment, then shut that part off in order to write. It would cause me so much anxiety to cut one off from the other. I need to draw from both worlds to sustain myself. For me, creativity is self-generating. The energy that goes into my work comes back into my life. I just completed a story which was harder to finish than I thought it would be, but once I was done, instead of feeling depleted, I had this tremendous release of energy. I was at wits' end about what to do with that energy. The hard part is figuring out how to channel it productively. I finally said to myself, *The hell with it,* and invited a friend over to cook and eat everything we could think of.

When I finish working, my reentry time into the rest of life is fairly short. After coming out of the studio after an eight- or

ten-hour day, my husband takes longer to come back. I have to lead him a little: "Come on, John, come on." During the break between Christmas and New Year's we had pretty close to an ideal day. We went to the Frick Museum—it was fantastic—then walked back through Central Park, down Fifth Avenue, went shopping, ate dinner, heard some great jazz at Xeno, came home; I can't tell you the rest. That was a great day. We covered all the bases: art, nature, commerce, music, food, and sex.

Work is about pleasure too. And responsibility. The artist is responsible for telling the truth. I try to impress upon the kids how important the truth is and how damaging anything less than the truth can be. I believe that whatever you put out in the world comes back to you. A law of karmic returns. So what you put out there has to be truthful. Telling the truth is also being of service to the rest of humanity. As Joseph Campbell says, whatever gives you constant fulfillment is the same thing that allows you to be of the most service. With that in mind, I try to follow my bliss.

Even when I first got involved with Arrested Development, I knew I wanted to be on my own eventually. That's why I didn't become a full-fledged member. The group would ask me to sing on something they were working on, and I would say, "Okay, I can do that," but my plan was always to be a solo artist. I wanted to make my own decisions, to do what I wanted to do artistically.

Because I decided to leave Arrested Development during the period when they seemed to be doing really well, people thought I was crazy. But things looked better than they were. Artistically I felt that my development was . . . arrested. I'd say that all the time: "Our development is arrested in this group." On top of that, we worked hard, but we weren't making any money. I finally realized I could do better digging a ditch every day. Maybe we got a little bit of noto-

Dionne **FARRIS**

riety, but most people couldn't remember which person was which in the group. They'd ask, "Are you the dancer?" and I'd say, "No, I'm the singer." It became a very frustrating situation.

Walking away was the best thing I could have ever done. That was my revolution. I felt emancipated. Leaving that identity behind, I felt like the artist formerly known as Prince. I *did!* I felt so light. All my burdens were lifted. I was completely energized by the idea of beginning again.

It was only after I wrote my own songs and made my own record that I started to realize the power songs can have. The first time I saw people singing the words I'd written, I was amazed. When listeners tell me that they really feel what I'm trying to say, that lets me know that I've made a connection and that songs are powerful enough to make things happen for people. If I hadn't gone my own way, I don't think I would have realized that music can be such a powerful tool for the positive. A lot of people are just playing music to make money, and they don't really care what their songs say. That attitude is detrimental to so many people, so many communities. I know that everybody can't be positive and that we need to see the negative

> **Walking away was the best thing I could have ever done. That was my revolution. I felt emancipated. I was completely energized by the idea of beginning again.**

to appreciate what's good. I don't want to censor anyone for saying what he believes. Still, I think people need to question themselves more about some of the things that they do. That holds true for musicians. They need to realize how powerful music is and take some responsibility for what they're doing and saying.

Take songs about sex, for example. As a subject sex is overrated. Yeah, we all have sex—big deal. After everybody gets their rocks off, then what? In so many songs, that's all there is. When I hear yet another song about sex, I want to ask the person who wrote it: "Do you think about anything else? Do you have anything else going on in your life? *Anything?* You wake up and have sex every minute of the day? You can't! Nobody can." I really wonder if there's anything else going on in these people's minds. I guess the only other thing they think about is making money. Sex and money—nothing else really matters. Everybody's written love songs; they'll always be here. Now, though, a lot of people equate sex with love. These songs obsessed with sex are their love songs. But love is much more than sex. Love is

three-dimensional, but so many writers make it one-dimensional. Love is spiritual and goes way beyond a man and a woman having sex. That's what I was trying to get across in "Passion." It's sad to me that you can write a song without caring who's listening, that children are listening who know every word, however explicit, even if they don't know what it means. People need to govern themselves better. They need to think less about money and more about the effects of what they're doing.

I want my music to come out of what I feel and what I believe. The songs are a product of what I'm learning about myself and this world I live in. One

> When black artists want to try something very different or just be ourselves, people look at us in disbelief because they can't place us. They think, *Oh, my God, what are you?*

thing I'm learning is how important it is to be true to ourselves even though a lot of times we're not, myself included. I want to believe more in what's true, to live with the truth in my life. We lie to ourselves so often. For example, when people would ask me about "Don't Ever Touch Me (Again)," which is a song about a young girl who was raped, I would tell them that I'd never had an experience like hers. I was lying to the people who asked me that because I wasn't being truthful to myself. I was abused as a child, even though my story isn't the same as the experience described in the song. I finally came to the truth about what happened to me after I had my own child. I learned a lot of things about myself when I became a mother. I realized that I had to look honestly at certain things so that I wouldn't bring them to my daughter. I need to be able to speak up for and to her, and I know I can't do that without coming to terms with the truth. That realization al-

lowed me to stop denying what happened. To release all of that, to get it out, only makes you stronger, more able to cope and survive.

In my life right now I don't have time for the kind of fantasy you get in so much popular music. I'm trying to focus on what's real. I'm supposed to do a video for a new song, so I've been reading treatments. Everybody's saying, "It should feel real." Instead of trying to make it *feel* real, I want it to *be* real. I'm not saying that we should put aside everything imaginative—fantasy is part of life—but when I see what's going on in the world, and especially in the music world, I think, *Gimme a break.* When I watch videos, I wonder what's going on here; they're so far from life that I don't even want to *be* in a video. But since we are going to shoot one, let's make it a slice of life rather than a fantasy.

Being real is even more difficult for black musicians because there's less tolerance for the ones who defy the few established musical categories available to them. I was watching an Alanis Morissette video that's just a film of her face. I thought it would be interesting to do something that straightforward and unusual, but I know that if I proposed an idea along those lines, it would be shot down because there's a standard idea of what I'm supposed to be and do as a black woman. The amount of creativity that black artists are allowed is very minimal. I listen to young white rock groups who write about anything they want and wish I felt that kind

of freedom. I love Tori Amos because she's not afraid to say anything in her songs while I feel that I'm not encouraged to say everything I'd like to. Sometimes when I try to write a very personal or quirky song, I'll show it to someone, and the response will be: "Why are you writing about that? You can't say that." Why not? If I'm thinking about it, why can't I write a song about it? To a degree, that kind of response hinders me from trying to write what I want to.

When black artists want to try something very different or just be ourselves, genuine and real, apart from a preconceived image of who we are, people look at us in disbelief because they can't place us. They think, *Oh, my God, what are you?* There are double standards, especially for a black woman. Being black and a woman is something that I'll always have to live with while I'm on this earth. That makes it twice as hard.

People need to remember that we're all people first. That's what I was trying to get across in "Human": "Before I am black / Before I am a woman / Before I am short / Before I am young / Before I am African / I am human." It's really simple. This is what it's all about, people: You break it down — sex, ethnic background, cultural differences, all the things that separate us — and we're all part of the human race. We're all here. This is it. We don't have to necessarily love each other, but let's be harmonious at least. In the end, however unfair things might be, we have to learn from one another and recognize we're all part of the same race. It's encouraging to me that I've had such a completely positive response to a song like "Human."

> A lot of times we sit in quiet—no music or television, as little of the humming of the world as possible.

I've heard it said that my songs cross a lot of musical boundaries, and I guess that's true, although I didn't set out to do that. I just like all kinds of music, period. If that makes my work more universal, great, especially right now when we are becoming much more separate from one another in so many ways. It's nearly the year 2000, and because we have computers, we don't even need to go outside anymore and deal with one another on a human level. It's scary. There are so many divisions between us. I hope that things take a turn for the better. If music can work to break down some of those barriers, then that's significant.

I've never been a conformist,

> My mother said, "Dionne, let me tell you something, honey. As long as you're living under my roof, you will have to abide by my rules." I packed up all my stuff, put it in my little blue Datsun, and left.

so it's no surprise that I go in so many different directions musically. I was very independent even when I was a young child. It was just my mother and I when I was growing up. My grandparents were nearby, but we lived by ourselves. At home I was the protector. I did a lot for my mom. I knew that she was capable in some ways and not capable in others. I didn't pay the bills or anything like that, but I watched out for her. I still do. I'm her guardian angel. I think my daughter, Tate, is my guardian angel. With Tate, I feel I'm the mother and the child at the same time. Along with being the protector, I was also the jovial one, the spirited individual who brought energy and some of the world into the family. I was creative and a nonconformist. My grandfather couldn't understand why I cut my hair off or grew my dreadlocks. When I'd wear boots, he'd say, "Girl, what you doin' wearin' them brogans?" He couldn't understand any of that! I would wear just about anything to school. I remember one time I left my hair wet after I got out of the shower. It was really curly, and I liked that look, so I thought, *Yeah, I'm gonna go to school like this.* Everyone said, "Oh, man, your hair looks good. What did you put in it?" I told them it was all natural. I didn't even know about gel! As the day went by, it dried and started to puff up like an Afro. Everybody started cracking up, but I didn't care. I wasn't exactly the class clown, but I was a jokester. People would enjoy it when I came around 'cause it was going to be fun. I was and am silly. They thought, *Aw, Dionne's here... cooool!*

Home was easy. We lived in an apartment in a friendly neighborhood where everyone knew everyone else and would wave to each other. Every Saturday all the

kids would be outside playing, free from the fear that somebody would snatch us. We'd be out for hours riding our bikes all around the town. I had to be

home when the streetlights came on. It was a wonderful childhood. Although that wasn't too long ago, I don't think a lot of places are like that anymore. I like living in Atlanta because it reminds me of that neighborhood.

The thing I feared most when I was a kid was getting my mother upset. She wasn't a tyrant by any means, but I didn't like it when she was angry with me. I wasn't really afraid of a lot of things. I played with worms—all that kind of stuff. I wasn't afraid of death because I went to a lot of funerals when I was young. It was important in helping me learn about mortality. I don't think death itself really scared me, but I often used to think that when my grandmother passed, that would scare me a lot, that I wouldn't make it without her. *If she dies*, I thought, *I'm just going to die with her.*

My mother expected me to get an education, do something sensible. She knew I loved to sing. She had wanted to sing as well, and my dad played instruments and sang, not professionally, but in choirs. My musical side came from him. You need talent, but you also need that get-up-and-go, and that came from my mother. She wanted me to be able to support myself, to be independent. She sees now that I am. When she visited me recently, she told me, "I really admire you. I do. A lot of the things that you've done, I could never do." I couldn't say anything. I just thought, *Whoa— my mother admires me.*

It wasn't always that perfect between us. I was going with this guy when I was nineteen. I came in one morning at three o'clock after hanging out all night. My mother said, "Dionne, let me tell you something, honey. As long as you're living under my roof, you will have to abide by my rules. That means you can't be coming in here at three o'clock in the morning." I said, "I'm nineteen years old. I can do what I want." But she said, "If you can't respect my rules, you're going to have to leave." That hurt me. I packed up all my stuff, put it in my little blue Datsun, and left. I didn't know where to go. I was dating this guy, but I wasn't going to stay at his house. He offered, but I said, "No, no, no, no—my mom did raise me right." So I decided to stay in my car at the park. It was an adventure. You had to find a place to go wash up and brush your teeth. During the day my boyfriend and I would go to his house and sit on the porch. My car broke down, so I asked my mom to come pick me up, but she said she wouldn't. Living in the car lasted about two weeks before I went home.

I didn't have a job then or much direction. I wasn't totally committed to music yet. I knew I had to do something to survive at that point. I also knew I was going to keep my integrity whatever I pursued. I wasn't going to sell myself short. Even when I wasn't

> I know that this is a special life I have. Everybody doesn't get the opportunities I've had. I hope I'm doing right by whoever has given them to me.

sure of my direction as a musician, I always loved music. I borrowed a Billie Holiday record from the school library that I never brought back. It's still at my mother's house. I'd seen *Lady Sings the Blues* because I loved Diana Ross. I knew she was portraying Billie Holiday, so I wanted to hear what she actually sounded like. I listened to that Billie Holiday record over and over. Before that, I didn't think anyone could sound better than Diana Ross!

I came to Atlanta because I needed to *do something*. I needed somewhere to go. Music was a part of the decision to move here. I needed a new environment and a new space;

I needed to have new energy around me. I had been in a band with a friend who was working with people in Atlanta. I called him and said, "Hey, I'm here." The scene I became involved in was energetic. I was having fun. I thought, *Yes—I'm in the music business. Oh, my God, yes! This is it.* I was writing and singing. I was beginning to do what I'd always wanted to do. I needed a point of entry, and this was it. But it's been just recently that I've become much more focused about what I'm doing. I'm really centered now. Even though people keep telling me I need to have a manager to do all these things for me, I don't want one. In a few years I'll be thirty. I don't need people telling me that I can't make decisions about my own life. I *can* do that. It's my life, my career, and I have ideas about how it should go. I don't want those ideas to be put by the wayside because of what people in the industry think is best for me.

I feel good about where I am in my career and in my life. I like living in the South. I'm comfortable here. I used to go to Virginia every summer when I was young. My grandmother's mother had an old tin house built from the ground up by her husband, my great-grandfather. I've always liked the country. I like the slow pace of things and the friendliness of the people. I'd like to have a farm, a big open space, eventually, especially for Tate. Of course, you have some of the negative things here that you have all over the country. This is America after all.

When I get up, I straighten my house—I like things in order—and make a nice breakfast for myself and my daughter. A lot of times we sit in quiet without any distrac-

tions—no music or television, as little of the humming of the world as possible. I sit and just listen to her. We giggle. We might go outside. I'll put her in the stroller, and we'll go somewhere. I just want to feel good about the day, feel good about myself and be at peace. If I feel inspired, I'll write something down. If I've had a dream, I'll try to figure out what it means. I might call a friend or talk to my mother. Just live, pretty much, just live. On Thanksgiving this year I had to really speak out and say how blessed I am all around. I know that this is a special life I have. I recognize that. Everybody doesn't get the opportunities I've had. I hope I'm doing right by whoever has given them to me.

Sheryl CROW

I grew up the middle kid in a really close-knit family. There were four of us—two older sisters and a younger brother—and I was the one who did everything as planned. I was constantly trying to make everybody happy by getting straight As and practicing the piano. My role was to take care of everybody, to make everybody feel all right and to have everybody feel okay with me at all times. I'm not married, I just turned thirty-five, and do you know that to this day, even though I've put a lot of therapists' kids through college, the downfall of all my relationships has been trying to make everything okay?

I idolized my parents and needed their approval, but I never got enough because I was working so hard to make them happy that I didn't appear to need it. The desire for approval is an essential preexisting condition for people who want to be in front of a crowd. What else could drive someone to stand on a stage and look to an audience for recognition? Whoever the performer is, that need for confirmation all comes down to the same thing: not getting enough at home. I was the kid who turned into a performer for just those reasons.

My siblings and I were always expected to do the best we could. My dad used to joke that if you showed him a good loser, he'd show you a loser. Although that's a funny saying, it really tells you something about how I was raised. I thought constantly about doing the right thing. I'd get so wrapped up in that voice in my head that I didn't really develop my own vision or know how to make my own choices. Even learning how to drive was a major anxiety for me because I worried I'd do it wrong in front of my father. I'm really close to my dad now and realize that most people have complicated relationships with their parents, but some of his expectations were hard to live up to. For a long time I was someone who went through life not letting myself expe-

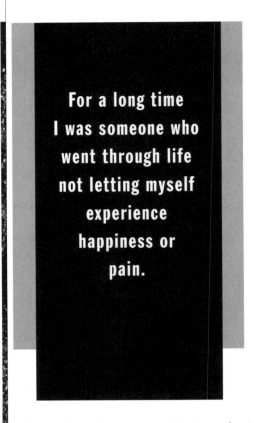

For a long time I was someone who went through life not letting myself experience happiness or pain.

rience happiness or pain. By closing myself off to emotion, I didn't really have to experience anything. In the last few years I've adopted the adage "Hide the pain and you hide the joy." I want to experience all those emotions now.

My dad, both my parents, had another side too. They were very artsy and musical. When I was a kid, they listened to a lot of big bands, swing bands, and crooners. Don't ask me why, but I really related to that music. I can remember lying down by the Magnavox and listening over and over to Judy Garland singing "But Not for Me." I was six years old, and for some weird reason everything about that song represented me. That's my earliest recollection of how music could really strike you at the core.

My dad's best friend was a man named Leo, a musician and also the doctor who delivered me and all my siblings. He played stand-up bass in a band with my dad, who played the trumpet. Leo and his wife lived down the street, and our two families were very close. This guy was walking art, very cosmopolitan. He had toured with the

Tommy Dorsey Orchestra and knew the Hemingways when they had lived twelve miles from our small, rural town. My parents along with Leo and his wife represented something very

interesting and very highbrow to me. After a night out they would come home late to play music and drink. There was this one song, a ballad, that they played. I never knew the

271

name of it, but I would sit on the stairs and listen to that song all night long. It was an instrumental, a really heavy, melancholy tune. It would just break my heart. Later on, as I started picking up songs on the piano, I always gravitated toward the sad ones. One of the first songs I learned was Joni Mitchell's "Both Sides, Now." But that instrumental ballad my parents would play late at night was one of the earliest things that struck a grand familiarity in me. The experience of hearing that song from the stairs when I was a girl is one that never leaves me.

Years after Leo died, I dragged out the record—it was a Buddy Rich song—and listened to it. Some music represents people or times, and that song really brought those days and those friends back to me. There was real, identifiable sadness there, not just in my parents but in Leo and his wife as well. They had run with a cosmopolitan crowd of artists and intellectuals before they were forced to move to a small town to make a living. The same was true for

my dad, who wanted to be a musician but wound up having kids and practicing law in Kennett, Missouri. They all saw themselves as artistic people in a situation that didn't provide the time or the freedom to be very expressive. But because of their love of music, I knew about the power of songs early on.

In addition to their interest in music, my parents loved books and read to us all the time. They raised us to be excited about writing and reading. Instead of letting us watch a lot of TV, they would read to us. I remember my dad playing out all the characters as he read Mark Twain's *Pudd'nhead Wilson.* That was the kind of thing I grew up with, unaware that other children didn't have the same experience. Because I learned to value writers very highly, once I started to write my own songs I approached the process from the standpoint of a writer rather than from the perspective of a songwriter. At a certain point, after you've learned how to put the parts together, you run the risk of thinking about crafting a song instead of focusing on

what you're writing about. When I listen to pop songs that are blithely happy or driven by formula, I know that they are often written by people who really know how to put a song together. But while the writers may be succeeding in terms of craft, they often forget there's more to songwriting than that. Songs have to be more than well crafted. Because I didn't really like or trust my own voice, I would write about characters by default, something that came naturally because all the figures Mark Twain and John Steinbeck created were such familiars in our house.

I still love books that contain great characters. When I was

I pictured myself as a loner off living like a Jack Kerouac character or, worse, someone out of a Charles Bukowski book, one of those down-and-outers who works at a gas station and has no one, no family.

working on the latest record, I read a book by John Fante called *Ask the Dust*. The impact a character in that book, Arturo Bandini, had on me was so strong that I kept seeing people through his eyes and I started to write from his perspective. That was a really interesting way to write a song. I go through life with a sense of awareness about characters. When I meet people or read about characters, I catalog them somewhere in my mind, and they creep up on occasion, like Bandini did. As a writer, there can be real emancipation in separating yourself from the fact that you're going to be singing a song or that someone else is going to hear it and associate it with you. By creating that distance, you don't worry about whether you're going to offend someone or piss off a special-interest group. Obviously the safety that distance provides when you're writing is subject to the anxiety you feel when a song comes out and you're forced to think about people responding to it. While you're writing, however, you can invent yourself in any way you like and gain a lot of freedom.

I've lived a lot of my life without experiencing the kinds of revelations and feelings firsthand that the characters I've read or written about experience. Instead I've created characters who do feel things or act in ways I never did, living vicariously through them, which can be a bit limiting. I was raised around farm people who possessed a straightforward ethical code. I never had a life that touched the underbelly, so early on I imagined myself as a character very different from who and where I was. I pictured myself as a loner off living like a Jack Kerouac character or, worse, someone out of a Charles Bukowski book, one of those down-and-outers who works at a gas station and has no one, no family. Imagining myself through these characters was a way to approximate something without actually feeling it. There have been occasions when I lost someone or felt real pain, and all of a sudden a character I know or invented became me. That's all part of the process, I guess. But most of the time I couldn't feel anything for myself.

Once I was in high school, I realized that music plays a really heavy part in your popularity. I was never terribly popular. Being into the right clothes or the right musicians is very important. I was always a good girl but a bit of an outsider. When you're trying to please your parents, you don't get into too much trouble. The first time I went out with my friends to smoke pot I didn't even get to enjoy it because I felt so guilty. I was also on the periphery because I thought what was going on in music was so dismal—Kansas and Foreigner, all that corporate rock. Every-

275

body knew who the lead singer of Boston was. I just couldn't relate to any of that. I was trying to get my friends into Van Morrison and Derek and the Dominos. Peter Frampton was my first concert. I told my friends I liked him when he was in Humble Pie, and they just looked at me and asked, "Who's Humble Pie?"

There have been very few times in my life when I gravitated to anything other than music. Although ideally and romantically I'd like to picture myself as a fine painter, I'm a terrible artist. I've only felt the pull of music. When I taught school, I really loved it, but I had a great fear that I'd wind up being a teacher all of my life instead of succeeding as a musician. Even after I moved to L.A.

> **I had never been anything but a serious musician, so it didn't occur to me when *Tuesday Night Music Club* came out that people would start speculating about whether my credibility as a musician was real or not or whether I had any credibility at all.**

and was working as a singer, I would dream about teaching, which, although it's the most honorable profession there is, was a sign of my fear that I wouldn't make it in music. I've never really seen myself as anything other than a musician.

Even when I was singing with other people, I always played lots of instruments and made demos on my own all the time. I had never been anything but a serious musician, so it didn't occur to me when *Tuesday Night Music Club* came out that people would start speculating about whether my credibility as a musician was real or not or whether I had any credibility at all. Some even went so far as to suggest that I wasn't present at the sessions for my own album. I never would have guessed that by choosing to make my first record with a group of friends, I would experience the kind of backlash I did. I wound up making the record that way because I really enjoyed the group of people I was playing with at the time. We all needed that camaraderie because we were so burnt out, so cynical, and all of a sudden there was this rare phenomenon of a great musical hang in L.A., where there are no musical hangs. All of us had jammed a couple of times and recorded "Leaving Las Vegas." I was getting ready to make a record, and Bill Bottrell and I thought that working with this group of people would be a really altruistic way to do it.

All the musicians wanted to be there, and everybody knew that this was my record and these songs, although I was open to suggestions, were about my words, melodies, and influences. In fact, we spent a lot of time talking about that. I was really close to these people. Part

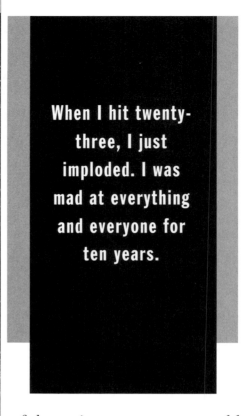

When I hit twenty-three, I just imploded. I was mad at everything and everyone for ten years.

of the excitement was generated by the fact that everybody played a lot of instruments and everybody knew how to record themselves. We'd all been making demos and playing on each other's recordings for years. So making a record together wasn't a big stretch for any of us. It just felt nice to be making music with people you liked outside of a corporate atmosphere.

response wasn't something I had anticipated. It didn't help that a couple of the people involved were really overwhelmed with their own misfortunes and lashed out at me. That's life. At the end of the day you have to accept the fact that people have their own struggles. There are some unhappy people out there whose failures are represented by other people's successes. Some of them you may have worked with and others don't even know you. I read a review by David Frick that was a vindictive stabbing. I couldn't figure out why the attack was so personal; I don't think I've ever met the guy. So whether it comes from someone you were close to or a writer you've never met, you have to weigh what's being said against who's saying it before you accept anything. Once you do that, you just have to let go of it.

Then the greed took over along with a sense of competition when people realized that the record was going to come out. That

I'm learning all of this as I go. When I hit twenty-three, I just imploded. I was furious. I was mad at everything and everyone for ten years. I was standing in the middle of my life wondering who I was. Am I the daughter of my parents? Am I this guy's girlfriend? Who am I? I couldn't figure out the answer. I was completely lost and very an-

trayed by a couple of people I had been very close to and also by the press, which had been particularly brutal to me. The record I made after all the anger I felt in my twenties

gry. The year and a half after *Tuesday Night Music Club* came out was also a time of questioning for me. I was be-

and the things that happened following *Tuesday Night Music Club* is about shedding that skin.

The realization that not everything has

to mean something, that certain things happen which you just have to experience before moving on is behind many of the recent songs. All the characters in them are looking for the same things. Their search reflects something in me even though the songs aren't directly autobiographical. I have a hard time with the self-obsessed lyrics of so much contemporary music. Unless you're a damn fine writer—like Thomas Pynchon or someone that good—you can't deny your own struggles or your own personality when you're writing. That doesn't mean, however, that every song has to be a bare confession. Thematically the first record does reflect who I

> You're either susceptible to becoming jaded and bitter or you maintain a certain degree of wide-eyed naiveté that allows you to underestimate the severity of the things that happen to you.

was when I made it but through stories about characters like a dancer leaving Las Vegas or a young woman running from her hippie parents. Similarly, the characters from the second record reflect the part of me that tries to confront reality and still live in the moment. Writing about characters rather than in the first person isn't a popular way to write songs now. There isn't a strong folk movement to encourage that very traditional form. I'm surprised that people latch on to my records because they're so traditional in that way.

The amount of optimism in my songs equals the amount of optimism I try to carry around in my life. You're either susceptible to becoming jaded and bitter or you maintain a certain degree of wide-eyed naiveté that allows you to underestimate the severity of the things that happen to you. My second record is about identifying that kind of levity in my life. It's about existing in the knowledge that most situations aren't life or death, but also understanding that what's happening at any given moment *is* your life. John Lennon said, "Life's what happens while you're making plans," and he was right. You can get so wrapped up in decision making and worrying about what's best for the future, that you miss out on your own life. I don't want that to happen to me.

The fact that I've become an adult during the last few years also has an effect on writing the songs. As you get older, as your own problems become less consuming, things that happen around you start to become important. I'm more and more amazed by the growing pains America is going through. I'm confused

about whether we're moving forward or backward. It's harder to ignore how inelastic the government is regarding the role of women, for instance, or the fact that we talk a good game but act so badly as a society. Writing lyrics that are heavy-handed can drive people away. I worry that some songs like "Love Is a Good Thing" might be too direct. There's not a lot of imagery or room for interpretation in lyrics like "Watch our children while they kill each other" or "Justice is a fading light." Maybe it's best to steer clear of being that direct, but sometimes when you feel strongly about something, you just can't help it.

"Hard to Make a Stand" was difficult to write without that kind of directness because I felt so strongly about its subject. That song began to take shape when I noticed the reactions people had to a cross-dresser who hung around a coffee shop in Pasadena. He called himself Miss Creation and handed out flowers. He seemed delirious although I think he really knew what was going on. Perhaps he

had been an extremely scholarly guy whose mind was blown by the world. But to watch how people reacted to him was as interesting as it was sad. They were unable to get outside of themselves and see this man as a person instead of as a freak. Right around the same time, a doctor at a Florida abortion clinic was shot. Just the fact that we're still discussing *Roe* versus *Wade* is alarming enough, let alone that religious militants are taking matters into their own hands. The combination of those two things really brought home the fact that we're managing to lose our humanity.

Even when I sit down now to write more personally, I sometimes end up with a social or political song. I was really broken up after splitting with my boyfriend of three years. I thought that writing about what I felt would be cathartic. That didn't go anywhere, so I put down the guitar, sat in front of the computer, and "Redemption Day" came out. The experience was unlike any other I've had writing a song. It was finished in one short sitting.

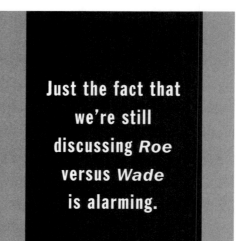

Just the fact that we're still discussing *Roe* versus *Wade* is alarming.

For me, using such a structured form and writing such verbose lyrics, elements very typical of early Bob Dylan and protest songs from the folk tradition, is unusual but that's what came out. I had been in Bosnia on a USO tour, and that experience came to the surface during the course of the eight minutes it took to write "Redemption Day." After going to Bosnia, seeing what was happening in Rwanda on TV, and then watching the elections in Bosnia on CNN, I was disturbed by the fact that we watch from a safe distance without any emotion the same transgressions going down again and again. It shouldn't be like watching *Sophie's Choice* and thinking, *At least it's a movie.* You can't do that when you know what you're seeing is going on at that moment. "Redemption Day" was my response to that recognition, and even though it's very different from anything else on the record, I felt it deserved to be heard.

Other songs are closer to my own experience than I realize when I'm writing them. Beck said that it's bullshit when songwriters tell people writing is a euphoric, cathartic experience during which they're just vessels for some other voice. I was thinking about what he said because three of my recent songs really did come about that way. I didn't know at the time what they were about or what experiences they tapped into, but later on those songs became part of my reality, and I understood their connection to what I was feeling. "The Book" contained a single emotion, which is hard for me to write a whole song about. I didn't

think I'd written anything very good although some people really fought for that song. Later on I realized "The Book," which on the surface is about a lover's betrayal, contains the emotion you feel in your body when you experience any kind of betrayal, whether a lover's or that of a friend who turns what you've revealed about yourself back on you. Now the feeling I get from that song is so close to what I went through that I won't sing it live. I can't revisit that feeling.

"Home" was another one that snuck up on me. I've never been married, so I never experienced the feeling that I describe in the song of having blown away the early years of your life. My parents have been married happily for over forty years, and they've been through all the things that married couples go through: You wake up one morning and can't believe you're actually married to this person, and then two hours later you can't believe how lucky you are to have married this person. When my mom heard the song, she told me it captured for her that profound feeling of thinking about what you might have done had you made different decisions. That's the way I understood the song until I realized that it was also the story of the relationship I'd been in for three years. Those small moments of revelation you sometimes gain through songs, paintings, or some other form of art are a kind of blessing.

If writing these songs was something of a departure, producing the second record myself and making it the way I did was very natural. It was much more in line with the way I've always recorded. When Bill Bottrell left the project a day into it, he told me off. He said, "You don't even need me." His insecurities over not being needed really overwhelmed him, and he left. You can't fault somebody for not leaving his life at the door when he walks into a creative atmosphere. You can't think that you're just going to be businesslike and make a record that way because that's not

how you create. In this particular instance, I walked in knowing I wanted to make a record that was stripped down and very rural. I wanted the sound to be deeply ingrained in the delta. I knew that I could get that feel by using these fucked-up loops. The day after Bill left, my manager said, "What's the worst thing that can happen if you produce yourself? If you don't like it, you can get a producer and do it again. You've recorded yourself for the fifteen years I've known you. Just make the record." So that's what I did, and the sessions felt as comfortable as an old sweater.

I worked with Trina Shoemaker, a great engineer, who I can't say enough good things about. We were like a couple of middle-age cooks in a southern kitchen, sharing a really crazy recipe and pulling it all together. I really honor the aspects of being a woman that enter into what I do. The older you get, the more you appreciate the instincts all women are born with, the sur-

> **I feel like I've passed through a certain door in my life and that I'm standing in a different room now.**

vivalist traits that go along with being a childbearer. Although I've never had children, I feel that survivalist, let's-get-it-done-when-the-chips-are-down kind of attitude, that gut reaction to things. I love that. There are some things I don't like about being a woman. I don't always enjoy the sexual tension that gets in the way when creating with a man. It was a real joy to work with Trina not only because there was that common language and understanding but no sexual tension and no problems with ego. I've never met someone so willing to abandon what she knew, to be able to say, "I know you like the sound of Keith's guitar on 'Gimme Shelter,' and this is the way that Jimmy Miller recorded it, but if you really

want it to sound wild, then let me try it this way." She abandoned everything that engineers grow up learning. I owe a lot to her for the way the record sounds.

It was embarrassing sometimes to catalog myself the way I do in these songs. There are a lot of scratchy places on this record. You try to offer a picture of yourself at that particular point in time, to get something real across that defines your feelings. There were a lot of things on the first record that were real, but there were also a lot that was masked in alcohol and denial; that was all part of how I felt when I was making it. The second record is more direct. It's sometimes uncomfortable and abrasive. That's what I wanted. I don't want someone to be able to sit in a comfortable chair and feel embraced when listening to it.

But those songs are also about the levity I mentioned before. I'm pretty happy with what I have. There are still those days when I'm tempted to crawl into my apartment and forget the whole thing, but I don't feel that way all the time like I used to. I sometimes fantasize about having a farm where I can  live with fifteen dogs if Scout could handle it. I could turn into Brigitte Bardot. No one would ever see me again. It would just be me and dog hair everywhere. That's about as far as my imagination goes these days. I used to think all the time about suicide—stupid thoughts—just because it was part of my nature. I don't have those moments when I feel that way anymore. Life is pretty full. It's mostly about music and not much about explaining. Most days are more inspired than not. I feel like I've passed through a certain

door in my life and that I'm standing in a different room now.

I was always encouraged to be ambitious about whatever I chose to do, and that's how I approach music. When I write a song, I can't do it halfway. I want it to have an edge, something more than the usual pop song. I appreciate a well-crafted hit with a great melody like Petula Clark's "Downtown" or "Monday, Monday" by the Mamas and the Papas. Not every song has to be really deep, but I want to write something that goes beneath the surface. To work for me, a song has to look right when I read it on the page and feel good when I sing it.

My dad, Miller Williams, is a poet who was my mentor and critic, so I've always seen my work from a writer's perspective, not just a songwriter's perspective. When I first started writing, he'd look at my songs, give me his response, and tell me what I could do to make them better. He taught me to recognize what was and wasn't useful to a song and how revising a single word can

WILLIAMS

Lucinda

change everything. I remember that he read the lyrics for "He Never Got Enough Love" and suggested that "faded blue dress" wasn't right. When I changed "faded" to "sad," the song sounded much stronger to me. I learned from him that every word and line must have meaning and not to waste any words, to get right to the meat of the matter. I looked up to him and writer friends of his who would stay at our house: James Dickey, John Ciardi, John Clellan Holmes, and Charles Bukowski among them. I didn't realize at the time how lucky I was to be surrounded by these incredible minds, to be able to listen to them talk about poetry, to play for them, and hear their comments about my songs. I never felt self-conscious or intimidated by the fact that my father and his friends were poets. I wrote for fun the way most kids would be out playing ball.

Because of that creative environment at home, I've always felt I could try to write about anything. When I write, I don't think about whether or not the

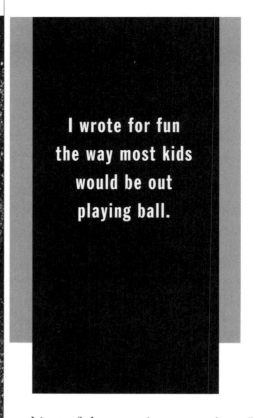

I wrote for fun the way most kids would be out playing ball.

subject of the song is appropriate. It's not as if I sit down and say to myself, *Now I'm going to take on the subject of death.* Issues like the ones raised by "Pineola" and "Sweet Old World" are just part of life.

"Pineola" is about the poet Frank Stanford, who committed suicide when he was still in his twenties. His death had a profound effect on me. It was so sudden and unexpected. I'd known someone else who'd killed himself, but we weren't as close. Frank's death hit much closer to home. I had just gotten to know him. We'd hang out, drink coffee together, and talk. He was a great writer who had been one of my father's students in Fayetteville. I was staying at my folks' house when Frank killed himself. I'd just sat down on the couch when my father told me what had happened. That experience was very hard to write about. In fact, I write about experiences like that because they're so hard, because I need to deal with them. Songwriting is my main way of doing that. There are songs you feel you just have to get out. After I finish, I can move on. When I really start digging into my life and a song comes out, I feel an almost

> I want what I write to be true to life rather than to repeat clichés, and I want my songs to push people's buttons, to make them think.

physical release. I know I've hit on something real when I get that feeling in the solar plexus. When I feel that, it's clear to me I've done something right and the song can convey my experience to a listener.

A song like "Little Angel, Little Brother" took a long time not only because I was writing about my brother, who I really love, but also because I didn't want the song to tell anyone what to think about him. I make a conscious effort not to be polemical in my songs. In that one I was trying to walk that tightrope between being personal and getting something more universal across. I have a new song called "Drunken Angel" that, like "Little Angel, Little Brother," took a long

293

time to write because I had to walk that same thin line. The song is about a self-destructive musician who was shot to death during a senseless argument. I try to look at him sympathetically but not in an overly romantic way. It's the equivalent in songwriting of tough love, I guess. In my mind, he isn't a romantic figure, but in a song he could seem that way if I don't choose just the right words. With "Drunken Angel," I wanted to find a way to be true to my subject without romanticizing self-destruction.

There are already enough songs that do that. I want what I write to be true to life rather than to repeat clichés, and I want my songs to push people's buttons, to make them think.

I'll start any number of songs that I work on for a while before realizing there's nothing to do but abandon them. Some people say I'm a perfectionist. That comes into play when I'm trying to write, but mostly I just think it's because I have high standards. I'm not the type to enjoy a success or relax and enjoy life all that much, and there is a price to pay for being so serious all the time. The inner turmoil never really goes away. At least as a writer, though, I get something out of it. That's the irony: I write because I have these fears, but I'm not afraid to write about them.

> I'd sabotage a relationship if it didn't live up to my overly romantic view of what being part of a couple meant: two people madly in love who live together, make love and art constantly, and inspire one another to do the best work they've ever done.

When I write, that's the only time I'm not afraid. That's one important reason why I do it. There's also a fine line between those who look down into the pit and those who jump in. I'm not on the self-destruct setting—I am ing and jumping. It's healthy for me to write about the darkness because it's there, it exists, and just about everybody has to deal with it.

able to control that tendency in myself—but writing about self-destructive people helps me understand the difference between look-

I work on a J-curve. I won't write for months and months, and then, all of a sudden, there's a rush of writing. Before that happens, I worry that I won't be able to write a song again. I've struggled a lot with a problem many of my friends, particularly women, talk about: the feeling that you can't create when you're content and in a relationship. That idea is of course total nonsense. To think that way is a cop-out, but it's a cop-out a lot of us use. If it's impossible to write and have a domestic life, then how do you explain all the novelists and poets over the centuries who were married, had children, and still produced great works of literature?

The real problem isn't necessarily that your partner is wrong for you, but that you don't know how to be with someone and still do your work. Before I understood that, I'd sabotage a relationship if it didn't live up to my overly romantic view of what being part of a couple meant: two people madly in love who live together, make love and art constantly, and inspire one another to do the best work they've ever done. When reality didn't live up to those unreasonable expectations, I'd go back to my little room alone and start writing wildly

> **The sixties in New Orleans was a special time. It's not surprising that I became a rebel, doing everything a restless kid could do during those years.**

about how things didn't work out. After that phase it's back to another relationship. It just becomes a vicious cycle.

I started playing guitar in 1965. That was the year a student of my dad's brought Bob Dylan's *Highway 61 Revisited* over to the house. I heard that record and said to myself, *This is what I want to do right here.* We moved a year later to New Orleans when my dad got a position teaching at Loyola. The sixties in New Orleans was a special time. Like the Neil Young song says, "All my changes were there." I would hang out with friends and listen to Buffalo Spring-field, Cream, and The Doors. That's when I first heard Leonard Cohen and Joni Mitchell. All my father's students were welcome any time of the day or night. They'd come over for dinner and hang around afterwards, drinking Jack Daniel's, talking about art and politics until three or four in the morning.

It's not surprising that I became a rebel, doing everything a restless kid could do during those years. Even though I grew up in a very supportive household, I still found something to rebel against. It runs in the family. My grandfather was a con-

> There's a fine line between those who look down into the pit and those who jump in. Writing helps me understand the difference between looking and jumping.

scientious objector during World War I who was involved in the Southern Tenant Farmers Union scuffle. My dad worked for civil rights in the fifties and early sixties. George Haley—Alex Haley's brother—is my godfather. He and my dad were roommates in the South in the fifties. He's got some stories to tell about that.

My high school was overcrowded and understaffed—a typical inner-city public high school. I got kicked out a couple of times for trying to change things. The first time I was expelled because I was handing out a list of grievances and demands we'd drawn up to present to the principal. When a black student and a white student would get into a fight, he would suspend the black kid while allowing the white kid to stay in school, that sort of thing. I was sent to the office for distributing these leaflets, and while I was there, the Pledge of Allegiance came over the intercom. Everybody was required to stand up and recite it. I refused and was sent home. My dad found an ACLU lawyer, and I was eventually readmitted.

My father asked me not to do anything that would get me kicked out again, but when I went back to school, there was a big demonstration going on. A group of black and white kids had boycotted classes and was marching around the school. SDS and the NAACP joined the march. At first I just went up to my classroom to stay out of trouble, but when I looked out the window, I saw some of my friends calling for me to come down and join them. The students who were in the room with me were spitting on them. What was I supposed to do, stay up there with them? Hell, no. I went right down to join my

friends. The feeling of adrenaline is hard to describe. We had the conviction that there was a real point to all of this, and we felt an incredible sense of unity. You couldn't be on the other side. It didn't matter what the consequences were. I know it sounds corny now, but that sense of purpose really did exist. The times were different then. Anyway, when the police came and started throwing everybody in paddy wagons, anyone who was involved in the demonstration got suspended.

My family was going to Mexico at the end of the year anyway, and my father understood that things were too tumultuous at school, so he told me to get my books and study at home. I actually read my books for the first time. I also sat in on some classes at Loyola before we left. When we got to Mexico City, I couldn't start classes because I didn't have the right papers. I spent the year I turned seventeen in Mexico City not going to school. I'd spend hours in my room just reading, playing my guitar, learning songs, and listening to records.

I also played my first shows when we lived in Mexico. I performed folk songs with a friend, Clark Jones, at different schools as part of a cultural exchange the State Department set up. At that time I wasn't writing a lot, so we did songs by Bob Dylan and the Byrds, Joan Baez, and Peter, Paul, and Mary, lots of protest and traditional material.

After Mexico, we moved to Fayetteville, Arkansas, where I studied at the University of Arkansas for about a year. If I hadn't become a musician, I would have studied cultural anthropology. I was interested in other cultures because we traveled so much when I was growing up.

I'm very aware of the differences between home and other parts of the country. This is another world and I'm proud to be part of it. I resent the negative stereotypes about the South and southerners that are perpetuated by the media, the idea, for example, that everyone with a southern accent is a dumb hick. The South I know has a rich cultural and artistic tradition. The fact that I'm from the South—I was born in Lake Charles, and my mother's family is from Louisiana— shows in my writing. That I have roots here, that I can identify with a place so strongly is important to me.

For all my fascination with particular places and cultures, my interest in anthropology didn't last long. When I was in school, I

> It got to the point where I realized I had to make music work for me because there was nothing else I could do. I'd devoted everything to it.

already felt the pull towards music as a vocation. My dad had some reservations about my decision to pursue music instead of finishing college. He wanted me to be able to support myself if music didn't work out, so I wouldn't have to go through what he went through trying to live as a poet. It was good advice, but I never did find anything to fall back on. Even though my choice to become a musician didn't make things easy, I had a lot of drive and good instincts. It's hard to say whether I created expectations for myself or whether they came from the family. I know that my father's example was important to me. My dad was so focused on his writing that he'd work amidst the most chaotic situations. It didn't matter what else was going on, he just wrote and wrote and wrote. Writing was at the center for him. I always admired him for that and wanted to be able to focus like he does. It got to the point where I realized I had to make music work for me because there was nothing else I could do. I'd devoted everything to it.

All those years of playing and singing started to pay off eventually, but it took a long time to happen.

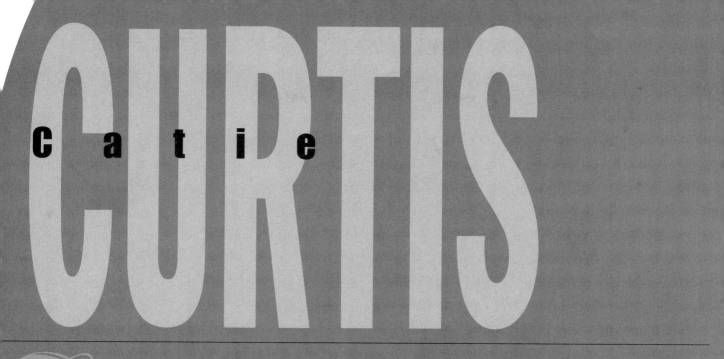

Catie CURTIS

The impulses you hear in my songs to escape, on the one hand, and to confront reality, on the other, don't seem that polarized to me. First, I don't think I'm writing primarily about escape. I'm describing going *to* something as much as leaving something. And I don't see that impulse as the opposite of reality or truth.

I think of these different aspects of the songs as a tension between the kinds of expectations I grew up with and the reality of what my life has been like. There is the me I've always known who grew up in Maine nurtured by a very warm, loving family with traditional expectations. I didn't feel pressured by those expectations, and I don't feel that my life is a form of rebellion against or escape from how I grew up because I loved it. I just felt I would have a very stable life with a regular job, a PTA kind of life.

Then there's the me who traveled by

303

myself to gigs all over the country in my car for four years. It constantly amazes me how differently my life has turned out from what I thought it would be and how hard it is to find your way to the life you want, the kind of relationships you want to have, the songs you want to write, especially when those things are so different from what you knew growing up. It's even harder when your choices aren't fed by the energy that comes from anger or rebellion but just trying to discover what's right for you. I see the tension in my writing in those terms.

"You Can Always Be Gone," for example, is about joining with, not

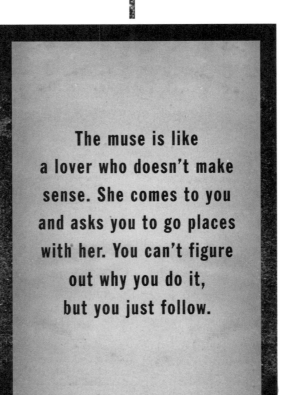

The muse is like a lover who doesn't make sense. She comes to you and asks you to go places with her. You can't figure out why you do it, but you just follow.

just escaping, something. I think of it as a song about being visited by the muse. The "she" in the song is whatever pulls you to art and makes you give up a traditional life to follow that path. The muse is like a lover who doesn't make sense. She comes to you and asks you to go places with her. You can't figure out why you do it, but you just follow.

Before I was hijacked by the muse, I was a well-adjusted, pretty normal kid. If anything, I erred on the side of trying to be good. I even won the DAR good citizen award. It's part of the irony that my life is so nontraditional now. But I also have a long history of being a bit of a square peg in a round hole. I was a tomboy growing up, the only girl on my Little League team, for example. I have a really close relationship with my dad, who taught me how to play all kinds of sports. Being a little different feels natural to me.

I was the youngest of three girls. It's certainly no coincidence that growing up as the youngest, I became a performer. A lot of youngest kids find ways to get attention; I always liked performing. My cousins would come over; we'd dress up in costumes and put on plays. We also did a lot of singing as a family. My mother taught us about harmony at a very young age. There was a lot of choral singing at church, which I

attended every Sunday from the time I could walk until I was eighteen.

I grew up in a small city of fifteen thousand people, one of many similar towns along the Maine coast. Our neighborhood was very much a warm and safe en-

vironment. There were a lot of houses up and down the street and lots of kids to play with. There was a Little League park across the street. We lived in an old house full of antiques. "Dad's Yard" describes my father exactly as he is. We had lots of old stuff, some of it really cool, some of it junky. We also spent a lot of time canoeing on the rivers in Maine. We were always outdoors.

I suspected I was different in high school, but it really hit me in college when I came out. That was the first major difference. I thought, *Wow, okay, I've got to make some serious adjustments and figure out how this is going to work.* It was pretty traumatic. I thought being gay would be the only thing different about my life, but then, little by little, I realized how big a role music was going to play—being on the road, traveling, not having a stable homelife.

Part of the transition was also the change from being a jock to becoming comfortable with the idea of being an artist. For a woman, I'm not sure if being a jock is more acceptable than being an artist, but I thought of myself as a jock for a long time. I played basketball in high school and for three years in college. I wasn't as devoted to basketball at Brown as I was during high school, and I quit my senior year. Then I went through a period of not thinking of myself as much of a jock. I've just recently become more comfortable with thinking of myself as an artist. I turned thirty last year and thought, *Okay, I'm thirty. Performing and writing songs is what I do now. I guess it's real. It's not just a phase.*

But even as recently as a year ago I was on a plane with a booking agent who told me how important it was for him to call everyone on his roster an artist, not an act. I thought, *I don't want to be called an artist.* Why not? It sounds so pretentious. I just write and sing; I'm just me. I didn't *feel* like an artist. In the last year, I must say, I've given up a lot for this life. I've really made a new level of commitment to it, knowing that it's such a part of me and I can't do anything else. I hit a point where I really had to make a decision. Am I really willing to live this way? Can I give myself over to this? I decided to do it. Since that decision it feels okay to be called an artist because it's a way of life now. I feel like an artist because of my commitment to observing, trying to take in what I experience in the world and putting it out in another form. That's a pretty big part now of who I am and what my life is like. So, I've started to become more comfortable with that label. It's a new commitment to my relationship with music, which I've had in some form for a very long time.

Early on my dad listened to Merle Haggard and Guy Clark. I eventually came around to the singer-songwriter thing by listening to Melanie, Karla Bonoff, and, like everybody else in my generation, Rickie Lee Jones. The first band I went to see in concert was Journey. All those years of bad

> I even won the DAR good citizen award. But I also have a long history of being a bit of a square peg in a round hole.

seventies arena rock! Actually I think it would be cool to draw on some of that material, play it acoustically at gigs. Although the songs might not all be particularly good, there's a lot to them because people who grew up when they were popular have a special place for that material even if they don't really respect it anymore. You can't divorce yourself from the place you were when you first heard it.

I was writing really awful songs in high school on the piano and guitar. Even before I started to write songs, I'd always loved to write. I have boxes full of the diaries and journals I've kept since I was eight. I still write poetry. Sometimes the poems turn into songs, but mostly they don't except for the occasional image that crosses from a poem into a song. When I write songs, I tend to sing nonsense until the words emerge organically from the music. I don't sit at a desk and write songs down. Once I have words on a page, I don't feel compelled to put them to music. For me, that's the difference between poems and songs. A written poem can wander a lot, be really playful on the page, and have a complex structure. A song's lyric, on the other hand, shouldn't be hard to memorize. There should be a geometric design, the use of repetition in a song so that unlike most poems, it comes back to you and is easy to remember. I like songs because they're part of an oral tradition.

After college I went out West not so much to become a singer-songwriter as because I was heartbroken. It was a very impulsive decision based on heartbreak. I used writing as a way to get through it—a function of writing that's served me well.

> There's truth and then there's *Truth*. The factual truth may not be as important in writing as the ability to reveal a greater truth through invention.

When I came back to the East, I was amazed by the folk scene in Boston. First of all, it was amazing to me that there was one. There aren't that many around the country with so much radio support, open mics, gigs to play, and other musicians. It's wonderful and outrageous how much music there is here and how much of it is acoustic.

I learned a lot when I moved to Boston.

I was in a songwriters' group. We critiqued each other's work and got really important feedback from one another. As I said, a lot of the music that influenced me growing up was really cheesy FM pop in the seventies and eighties. How do you recover from that? It was important for me to go through a period of having songs critiqued by people who could help me avoid some of the pitfalls I would have been subject to coming from that background.

As an artist who was on my own label for quite a while before I signed with Guardian, I was really nurtured and supported by the folk community, both in Boston and across the country. It's really important that I continue to acknowledge that support even as I gain exposure to a wider audience. It's a difficult thing politically because the label feels that every time I even talk about folk music, I categorize myself as a folksinger and turn off a lot of people who think that's not the kind of music they like. It's a tricky situa-

tion for me because not mentioning that part of me is failing to acknowledge all the support I've had from the folk community. So, I'm going to keep on mentioning it. At the same time I appreciate the label's concerns and feel it's important to get the music out there to a broader audience.

I also feel grateful for what I've learned from folk musicians. I really admire Cheryl Wheeler, Greg Brown, John Gorka, and Cliff Eberhardt. I have so much admiration for someone like Patty Larkin, who has been doing this a lot longer than I have. I admire how great she is, how she keeps growing and how long she's stuck with it. It makes me want to cry when I think about it. I know what she's gone through. I know what she's sacrificed and that she's worked her butt off playing all these gigs and trying to stretch as a musician. I also know she's put up with a lot of crap from people who don't appreciate all she's

> Lots of people tell me that they see themselves in "Radical" even if they aren't gay. We were thinking about doing a video with all kinds of interesting-looking couples. Mohawks, longhairs, nose rings, all genders, you name it.

done, people who write letters accusing her of selling out because she received an accolade from a source outside of the folk music world. Gimme a break. She's given so much, and all of a sudden someone wants to discount it. I admire and try to learn from the strength of someone like Patty.

Cosy Sheridan has talked to me at some critical moments. She's been instrumental in helping me accept the idea of being an artist by pointing beyond all the negative implications—the road, an unsettled life—and allowing me to trust that if you do what you feel you really need to do, things fall into place. There have been other musicians too who really *get it* like that. They struggle with issues of home versus the road and how much they have to give to each part of their lives. There's no one else who can really understand that other than the musicians who are out there. I feel a really strong bond with them.

It's a constant struggle to maintain the balance between your life and your work. Being on the road as much as I am now, things are definitely out of balance. I have a need to be with the people I care about and to be in a relationship. It's just so hard when you're away all the time. All I can say is that to handle this situation successfully, you have to have a creative, determined, and adventurous spirit. You need to find a way to make things work even if you don't have the amount of time together most people have with their friends and partners. I've seen it work for a lot of people. That's an area where I feel it's so important to hear other musicians' experiences. It can be depressing when we all sit around discussing how much of the time we're

> I can imagine going back to a small town, but this time going back as who I am. I would be different but it would be okay.

away from home, but usually there are one or two people in a relationship that's working out despite the road. I think it's one of the hardest things, trying to find that balance.

Part of achieving a balance in your life is about honesty. On *Truth from Lies*, I included a quotation from Emerson—"Truth is beautiful, without doubt: but so are lies"—because I was trying to understand why I allowed myself to believe things that later I don't feel to be true at all. There's a seductiveness, a kind of beauty, to some lies. In the process of writing songs, truths come out. While writing the songs for that album, I was trying really hard to get at some basic truths even though I continually felt the pull of what I wanted to believe rather than what was true. Depending on what kind of lie we're talking about, we might be tempted to believe it for safety's sake or for the security the myths that we grow up with provide. In "The Party's Over," for example, I used the Cinderella story to get at that idea. It's a pivotal song for me about deconstructing the myth and figuring out where we are without it. Coming out of the myth to reality is both positive and bittersweet.

Cutting through the expectations of what someone wants me to write is the most difficult thing about writing truthfully. When I think about what someone will think of a song, that really gets in the way of writing honestly. A lot of times, in order to write truthfully, I find it necessary to tell myself that a song isn't going to work for an audience. Sometimes that perception is true, and sometimes it's not. I find I have to make that pact with myself to push through and finish the song. Sometimes these songs end up being the strongest because I've let go of the desire to write for an audience. I think you can distinguish between different kinds of truth. There's truth and then there's *Truth*. The factual truth may not be as important in writing as the ability to reveal a greater truth through invention.

In "The Wolf," for example, I tried to get at a truth that isn't autobiographical. I haven't experienced any kind of domestic violence, but I could feel what it must be like from seeing its effects on people who have. I haven't done much acting, but I tried to use the method an actor might use to get at that emotion. By doing that, you can really become someone else in your head.

I was writing that song with a friend who worked with a boy whose mother's

boyfriend abused her. My friend told me so much about the child that I felt I knew him. We wrote out all these ideas about what he was thinking and feeling. It didn't come out to a song, though, because it sounded very clinical. I had to go by myself and sit by some railroad tracks with my guitar—we were in Maine camping—and just imagine being this little kid. It took me a long time to get into that frame of mind. Once I got there, I could speak in his voice, and the lyrics came out instantly.

I think about writing socially aware songs a lot more than I'm able to do it. It's really hard. The only way I can write them effectively is to get at an issue through a personal voice so the result feels almost like a love song. There's got to be some kind of emotional immediacy to it. I don't have an interest in laying out the clinical facts. I like to give a listener the effect of going somewhere. The song has to have enough direction and emotion that people don't feel they're being told how to look at the subject. I want listen-ers to be able to choose what they get from the song.

I did case management at social services, working with the elderly, visiting people at home. I didn't get into social work to make a career of it. I was involved with the Sarah Doyle Women's Center in college, where we discussed and worked on a lot of social issues. Volunteering there provided a great foundation for supporting the general idea of having a social conscience. The center also focused on practical aspects of what you can accomplish without being patronizing to people. Before joining social services, I'd waitressed for a year but didn't want to do that much longer. I wanted to do something that would make me feel that if I wasn't playing music full-time, at least I was contributing.

Even though I sometimes write a song with a socially conscious subject, I play music for purely selfish reasons. I love music. It's only a secondary discovery that it turns out you can do some good as a songwriter.

That's great, but it's not why I got into it. I just love to play.

I do try to integrate some of my social concerns with the music by helping with a benefit concert or doing whatever I can. There are opportunities as a performer either to provide a voice for people without one or to put some of your resources towards raising awareness about an issue. I want to bring more meaning to what I'm doing, and performing at a benefit makes me feel like this selfish career is not only about me. Performers sometimes have this crisis. We ask ourselves whether we've become totally self-centered because all we want to do is stand up in front of people and play.

So it's reassuring when people tell you that a song you wrote means something to them. Lots of people tell me that they see themselves in "Radical" even if they aren't gay. A twenty-eight-year-old woman who is involved with a fifty-five-year-old guy was saying that the song clicked with her.

Another person came up after a gig and told me she loved "that song about teenage angst." Other people think it's about interracial dating. Whatever. We were thinking about doing a video for the song with all kinds of interesting-looking couples. Mohawks, longhairs, nose rings, all genders, you name it.

I wrote the song back in '92 right after somebody I was involved with came out to her parents. It was really hard. So the song was very personal, a way to say, "You're going to be all right." I was frustrated with all the assumptions about why people get involved with one another, why we choose who we choose to be with. Writing that song provided a personal catharsis.

I think that song is particularly open to interpretation. If I'm playing a gig in a conservative town somewhere far from home, feeling a little vulnerable, I'm happy that a song like "Radical" can be interpreted on the level at which the listener is ready to hear it. I can sneak out of the hall on skates.

I feel mixed about being categorized as part of a particular group, and I like songs that move beyond categories. The fact that I'm a woman, for instance, doesn't seem at all important to my music. I don't particularly like the category of "women's music." Categories like that are not as much about the artists as they are about the audience that might appreciate them. Even then it can be a limiting category. I don't think you should suggest that a certain artist can only appeal, for instance, to women. The category of women's music is meant to suggest that this music might especially appeal to women. I can see the value in the heading, especially if you're an unknown artist with appeal for a certain audience. At least being filed in that bin might direct someone to your work who wouldn't find it otherwise. Still, I do think sometimes you end up limiting that artist's exposure to other audiences.

I think the sound of the voice or music alone—words and politics and meaning aside—cuts across all the categories. You don't need words a lot of the time. I don't know how to articulate this, but I know how I feel when I listen to someone really singing from the heart. It's a physical experience. It's less of an intellectual exercise and more of a sensory response comprised of passion and emotion. Words can do that too, but it's easier to hit people emotionally with the physical and visceral quality of the singing.

When I think about my own voice now, I believe that the voice just is. It exists. I haven't always felt that way about my singing. Sometimes I have to do some unlearning to get to the voice that is natural, not forced, not stylized.

I'm still learning how to stretch out as a singer and cover more ground emotionally, but I want to do it in my way and in my voice, so I'm not just trying to sound angry. I don't have that in me. That's kind of a cool thing to figure out: What's my angry song? I would be really bored as a writer if I only wrote songs with one kind of emotion. It's a

challenge to figure out what my take on a different emotion is, how do I get to that voice from where I am.

When I'm not singing and I have a day off, I sleep until I wake up, then boil water on *my own stove.* I have lunch with a friend, followed by an afternoon free to putter around the apartment. Just 'cause I feel like it. I make plans to meet friends for dinner, and in the meantime I have the chance to take care of things I can't do on the road—like laundry. Maybe I'll cook a chicken. I never used to be domestic, but now that I'm on the road I revel in things that take a long time like cooking a good dinner and being with friends.

My fantasy, apart from music, is doing what I grew up

thinking I would do. I imagine living in an old farmhouse, being home all the time, maybe having kids—not that that's out of the question in the fu-ture—and being part of the com-munity, coaching Little League. I'd like to be involved with people on a day-to-day basis. I can imag-ine going back to a small town, but this time going back as who I am rather than as someone who

fits right in. I would be different but it would be okay.

When I think of growing up in the South, I remember the flatland down in Mississippi around the small towns where my father preached. One of my earliest memories is standing by a field, too small to see anything but the cotton. On my first album, *Songs from the Levee,* there's a song called "A Cotton Field Away" which describes that early response to the place I called home. A lot of my songs attempt to connect my memories to the landscape and the culture I come from. That attachment to place is very important to me.

I'm still moved by the experience of looking over flat delta land from a levee or the feeling of familiar comfort I get when I'm in a church. I spent so much time in churches growing up I can walk into almost any one and find my way around; I know the sanctuary's going to be here and the bathroom's going to be over there. It's like being at home. Riding on an autumn night through Ken-

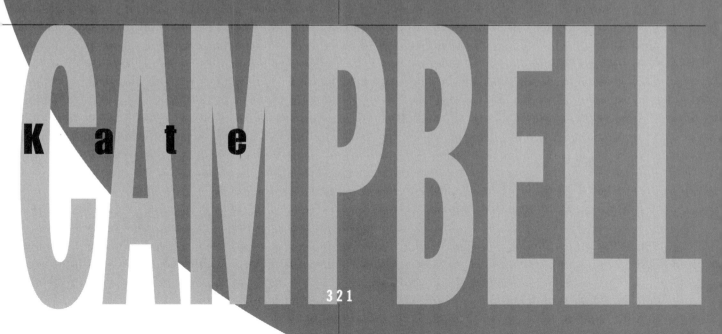

Kate CAMPBELL

tucky and seeing the tobacco-curing barns smoking like they are on fire brings me back to the times we made family trips to visit relatives there. My reference points as a writer go back to those places and experiences that are central to me and, in many ways, characteristic of the South.

To discuss the feeling you get when you're in those important places is hard to do. You just know it in your bones. That sense of being at home always hits me when I drive down to Mississippi from Memphis on Highway 61. I'm just cruising through the landscape, a flatness totally different from the hills of Middle Tennessee, when I see that old sign in serious need of a paint job sticking up out of the weeds: WELCOME TO MISSISSIPPI, THE MAGNOLIA STATE. Even though I'm only ten miles south of Memphis, wondering what it is that endears me to this place with its dilapidated sign and eerie flatness, that's when I get the indescribable feeling I'm home.

The minor-key strangeness of that landscape is a big part of me. I am an easygoing, happy person, but I'm also melancholy. A lot of that melancholy emerges in the songs. Anytime I'm in Mississippi or Louisiana I'm immediately struck by a sense of mystery. There's that quality of Gothic grayness. It can be a sunny day, one hundred degrees, but there are still these strange undercurrents. The idea of southern Gothic makes perfect sense to me though I'm inclined to call it southern noir. Religion and the supernatural are very intertwined here. I love walking in graveyards next to old churches. You know the people buried there are dead, but there's still something going on. All of us continue to pass things down even after we're gone. I understood that even when I was a child. I was fascinated by the portrait of my great-great-grandfather Bascom Gunn, which my parents hung over their bed. His eyes would follow you everywhere you went in the room. And, I have to tell y'all, my birthday *is* on Halloween, so why wouldn't I be tuned in to this stuff?

"Wrought Iron Fences" on the new album, *Moonpie Dreams,* tries to get at that noir quality. I carried around this image of the wrought-iron fences you see in front of broken-down houses in small towns for years before I put it in a song. Maybe there's a turned-over birdbath behind the fence, vines growing everywhere, and old furniture scattered around the yard. There are so many old southern towns that are slowly decaying—a state that's powerfully evoked in *To Kill a Mockingbird,* for example. "Wrought Iron Fences" didn't begin with a meaning or idea but with that image of decline, of rusting away, the small-town South that's represented by decaying buildings and old graveyards: "Tangled vines cover the lattice / They creep and crawl around the house / Nobody lives there / Only ghosts hang around / I've seen hope and glory fade away / I've heard old folks talk of better days / And all that's left to guard the remains / Are wrought iron fences." I was thrilled with how the song turned out, especially because the lyrics con-

trast with the upbeat, almost honky-tonk music. I think that combination reflects something about my identity.

I don't think you'd define southern music all that differently than you'd define the South as a region. It's related to the question I had to answer on the very first day of every southern history class I ever taught: What makes the South a distinctive part of

> The idea of southern Gothic makes perfect sense to me. I love walking in graveyards next to old churches.

the country? It's the same with southern music. The music, like the region, is made up of a singular blend of land, race, and religion. The music incorporates all of those things. When I hear the Allman Brothers Band or ture of musical idioms—white gospel, black gospel, rural blues, jazz—that defines southern music. Sometimes it's hard to find all those aspects in today's commercial country

some of the other southern rock groups I really love, I can hear all of those strains blending together, that mixture of music or modern forms of the blues, but for the most part the texture of the music is still a result of all those traditions.

On *Moonpie Dreams* I draw from those

influences more openly than I did on the first album. "Signs Following" has, on the one hand, a little bit of bluegrass in it because of the minor key while the chorus has the feel of a gospel hymn. "When Panthers Roamed in Arkansas" gives you more of the blues and the Muscle Shoals sound with all those horns. Musically the influences are more obvious than they were on the first album.

Those traditions, naturally enough, are all part of my musical upbringing. My mother is my central musical influence. She has a lovely alto voice and plays the St. Louis blues and swing that she loved as a teenager on the piano. I have her sheet music of Elvis's "Love Me Tender." Her name's on the front next to the price: fifty cents. She taught me to sing "The Tennessee Waltz," the number one pop song of 1951. You can trace my mother's interest in music back to her father, a Kentucky farmer who loved bluegrass and played a little mandolin, fiddle, and banjo.

She gave me a ukulele when I was four.

I don't know if I asked for one or not. Soon after, she told me that if I took piano lessons, she and my dad would get me any instrument I wanted. They stuck to their word. After learning to play the piano, I tried the clarinet and then the guitar. When I was in the third grade or so, Mom had this idea that my sister and I should learn a Dolly Parton song called "Daddy Was an Old Time Preacher Man." She bought the record, and I listened to it over and over, wrote down the words, and figured out how to play it. We sang it at a church event. That was a big deal to me.

Because my dad was a preacher, I heard a lot of hymn singing when I was growing up, but his role in the church also gave me the opportunity to hang out with teenagers when I was a child. Being with them exposed me to their music: protest songs, Peter, Paul, and Mary, "Galveston." I'd listen to what they played, then go home and try to figure out the songs. That's when I began to play the guitar. I loved the Carpenters. I remember being obsessed with a really gross song, "DOA" by Section Eight: "We were flying low and hit something in the air." It must have been 1970. My Brownie troop had a camp meeting, and some girl brought the forty-five, so we played "DOA" over and over again. Besides Dolly Parton, I loved James Taylor and early Dan Fogelberg. I had the forty-five of Janis Joplin singing "Me and Bobbie McGee," which I just couldn't play enough. I loved everything about her version of that song. I realized early on that Kris Kristofferson had written it, so I became familiar with him too.

On top of all that music, I was influenced by my dad's way with words. Even though he is not musically inclined at all, he's central to my songwriting. As the dreamer of the family, the word person, and the preacher, the storyteller, he's the most influential person in my life as far as communicating through words goes.

Those who hear him preach see some of his characteristics in me. So not only was I classically trained to read and play music, but I was influenced by church music and popular music, country and the Grand Old Opry, my father's preaching and storytelling.

Southern music sometimes seems like an inside joke to me. If you don't understand the context, you don't get it completely. Southern literature can be like that too: perfectly clear to southerners but not so obvious to people who aren't from here. At times music or words touch me in a way that I find hard to relate to a nonsoutherner. The song or sentence makes sense to me, but I know that not everyone is hearing it the same way.

The language I heard from the pulpit and in hymns are also going to show up in my work. Sometimes there's also a specific reference point. The most obvious one would be in the song "See Rock City." Rock City is a regional tourist destination, a reference you might not get if you live somewhere else. Once you know the character in the song is going to this tacky little tourist place called Rock City, you can think of the Wisconsin Dells or Coney Island, depending on where you're from, and the song will make sense. In "Galaxie 500" I mention Panama City Beach, which is also known as the Redneck Riviera although I didn't know that as a kid when we went there on vacation. If you haven't gone to Panama City or Rock City with your family, it may take you a little longer to get the point of those songs.

As I said before, most of my songs are an attempt to connect my own memories with the culture I come from. When I was taking southern history classes at college, I kept asking myself why I was so interested in delving into this past. For a while I was disconcerted to think that my interest was somehow connected to the idea that the South should rise again or to an unseemly pride about aspects of a heritage I'm not comfortable with.

That initial suspicion aside, something told me I had to make sense of how I was connected to the world I came from before I could go on to connect to the world at large. You have to start at home. I think place is very important to identity, maybe even more so for southerners and certainly for southern writers. There's something about the place where we grew up that gives us roots. Even if that place was a shack somewhere in northern Mississippi that you didn't own because you

> Mom had this idea that my sister and I should learn a Dolly Parton song called "Daddy Was an Old Time Preacher Man." We sang it at a church event. That was a big deal to me.

were sharecroppers, you still have that strong sense that this is our place, this is where we're from. The need to talk about that fact is obviously a major theme, in different ways, for writers like Faulkner and Eudora Welty. Even writers who don't specifically foreground it reveal a definite sense of place by the way they use language and how their characters relate to one another.

I'm interested in the fact that different places have their own unique traits and that the people who live there share them. There was a point when a lot of people seemed ready to concede that the South was just going to become another indistinguishable part of a homogenized nation flattened out by the reach of the media and the fact that McDonald's is everywhere you look. I don't believe that. I keep coming back to the idea that there's still something very different about this region. Again, it's tied to the status of land in our culture—there seems to be more of it here—the

place of religion, and the unique situation of race relations. The way those three things act on each other, how they're woven together, still has a great bearing on us. How those things act on us is a mystery that I think about a lot. I don't know if I'll ever figure it out, so I should have plenty to write about for a long time.

Even for people here who don't grow up on farms, the idea of land is important. Because I spent my earliest years in a rural Mississippi town and my grandfather was still a farmer, I've always had that connection to the agrarian South, so of course I write about it. Later, when we moved to Nashville, being in a city gave me a little perspective but only increased the way I felt drawn to the land. What is that strong feeling about? I've never farmed, for instance, so why do I feel like that? It goes back to that special role the land plays in determining how we define ourselves. My husband kids me about the way I'm obsessed with the weather as though I'm depending on crops for my livelihood.

"The Locust Years" and "Waiting for the Weather to Break" are songs that rely on the natural world for their imagery and speak about human emotion in terms that are tied to the land. "Waiting for the Weather to Break" is a regional poetic colloquialism, like so many phrases are if you take the time to listen, that uses the natural world as a metaphor. I was talking to a woman who had been caring for her elderly father in North Carolina. Every day he would sit on the porch for several hours without saying or doing anything. She'd ask, "What're you doing, Dad?" and he'd say, "Well, I'm waiting for the weather to break." I was just overcome by that phrase. It's a phrase I've heard all my life, but after I heard that story, I had to ask myself what it really meant. The phrase is extraordinary even though it's so commonly used. Language like that which is drawn from the natural world really speaks to me.

For all the beauty of the land and our feeling for it, the South has plenty of history that's ugly too. I think and write about that part of my culture as well. I keep trying to understand the dualistic aspect of race. On the one hand, there's a very close relationship between the races here. We've lived far more closely together than is the case in other parts of the country which seem much more segregated to me. It's easier to understand, if not forgive, the prejudices in a particular city or state where black and white neighborhoods are nowhere near one another. But because we've lived so closely together here, we have no excuse at all for what we've done. I just cannot reconcile the proximity of the races in the South with the violence between them.

When the Freedom Riders were about to come through Sledge, Mississippi, where my father was the pastor of a white Baptist church, he had to meet with the deacons to decide if the church would let them in. My father said, very strongly, "Yes, we will." He nearly lost his job at one of the churches he pastored over that decision. All of us don't like certain things about our parents— and there are certainly things I disagree with my father about—but if there's one thing my parents stuck to from the very beginning, it was the idea that they would not tolerate racism in our house.

From my earliest days we would talk about social issues, politics, or the war, so I was always aware of those things. I was deeply affected by desegregation and what was said about my father for having an open-church policy. None of his opponents said anything to me personally, but they said things to my father that I would never repeat. My father was also involved in expanding the church to include more young people by appealing to their interest in the youth culture of the sixties. He'd say, "Let's do a youth musical," and allow the band to have drums in the sanctuary. As you can imagine, at that time those kinds of changes weren't acceptable to all people.

My parents were still in their twenties during the social upheavals of the late sixties and early seventies. In the midst of Vietnam, the assassinations of the Kennedys and Martin Luther King, the rise of youth culture, and desegregation, they were quite progressive socially and politically. What a struggle that must have been. I'm grateful that they made the right decisions in the face of the very real repercussions that taking a stand could bring on. Even though my father knew the decisions he

> **Something told me I had to make sense of how I was connected to the world I came from before I could go on to connect to the world at large. You have to start at home.**

made could mean we'd lose our house the next day, he made the right choices.

My parents also made a conscious choice to send me to a newly desegregated public school at a time when many parents were starting private schools so their children wouldn't have to be with black children. Being bused to an integrated school was one of the most significant things that ever happened to me. It changed my life. I would not trade riding a school bus across town to the inner city of Nashville for anything.

The first thing I noticed when I went to my new school was that even though we were all southerners, we talked differently. I would come home and find myself using my black friends' lingo — much more so, I'm sure, than they picked up on mine. I also made a friend named Katrina who played on the basketball team with me. The team decided that Katrina was going to plat my hair for a basketball pep rally. I'm telling you, it was the funniest-looking thing, a white girl with little squares all over her head! Katrina kept saying, "Your hair is just like spaghetti. It looks awful. It just won't *do* anything." Those kinds of interactions are the ones I remember best. Even though both our cultures were so entwined in some ways, there were still many things to learn from

One of my favorite passages from Scripture is the beatitude "Blessed are the pure in heart: For they shall see God." I wish it were so simple.

one another. On a more abstract level, the experience of attending an integrated school made me understand later that even if you can change social laws, the economic differences that keep us apart are hard to eradicate. That's what I was trying to get through in "A Cotton Field Away."

I remember the powerful impact of hearing that Dr. King had been shot. Of course, I understood it from a child's perspective, but I was extremely sensitive to the importance of what had happened. I specifically remember sitting in the parking lot in our car and hearing the announcer on the radio say that Martin Luther King was dead and then advising everyone to go inside because there was the possibility of rioting. I remember feeling the tension. "Galaxie 500" has a verse about that moment: "Mama said kids I'll be right back / And left us in the Kmart parking lot / On the radio we heard the news / In Memphis Dr. King had just been shot / So late that night I sat alone / Feet propped up on the big dashboard / And

I cried myself to sleep again / Like every time before."

All the things that happened during those years have somehow encouraged the rest of the country to think that race is only a southern problem. The thing that's most disconcerting to me in the area of race relations is that American society as a whole has not been willing to deal with it. I do feel the great guilt and shame that southerners feel about the racist aspect of our region's history. Still, it's not just a southern thing. It's an American thing or, to think more universally, a worldwide thing. The race riots of the late eighties and early nineties are evidence that we're going to have to deal with our problems everywhere. We can't say that's just happening in Birmingham or Atlanta.

Along with the land and race, I don't think you can talk about the South without mentioning religion. I don't find faith all that easy. I wish I did. One of my favorite passages from Scripture is the beatitude "Blessed are the pure in heart: for they shall see God." I wish it were so simple. I write about faith in "Delmus Jackson," a song about the impressions I had of the black church custodian I knew growing up. He was a man who embodied that beatitude I love, but there's more to the song than the celebration of a pure heart. Faith is never that simple, and sometimes if it appears to be, we need to ask what we're giving up for its sake. Delmus Jackson didn't have a Martin Luther King in his generation to tell him he could want more than a heavenly reward. The song brings up the question of whether religious belief might not be a force that keeps us down in some cases.

A song like "Signs Following," which is based on a case involving a husband and wife who were members of a snake-handling congregation, also asks a question about the limits of faith. I was compelled to write that song after reading Dennis Covington's book *Salvation on Sand Mountain* in one night. As a Birmingham journalist he was assigned to research a case in northeast Alabama in which the husband apparently got drunk one night and forced his wife to put her hands in a rattlesnake cage. She was bitten twice but didn't die. She took her husband to court, where he was convicted of attempted murder and sentenced to ninety-nine years.

Dennis Covington went to the snake-handling services as part of his research and got to the point where he would handle the snakes himself. He also discovered that he had family roots in this religious tradition. He examines his background in the book while trying to determine what the line is between an act of faith and going too far. I hope that people who hear "Signs Following" realize that it's not my intention to put down in any way those people who handle snakes. The song is about how in religion, as in many other things, it can be really hard to tell when things get out of hand. I don't want the song to come off as a polemic; it's meant to ask a question rather than make a judgment.

"Jerusalem Inn" is also about questioning an aspect of religion that's always puzzled me. Having grown up in the church, I always found it inconceivable that a church might not be open to everyone. The church should be the most welcoming place, but often it wasn't accepting, and sometimes it was the most intolerant. If someone didn't dress as well as someone else, she would be made fun of in Sunday school. If someone was the "wrong" color or from a poorer family, he'd be treated differently. That kind of treatment didn't fit in with what my father preached and what the Gospel is about. When you think of southern Baptist preachers you do not necessarily think of people like my father, who are conservative theologically but progressive on social issues.

His views of race and class were nonnegotiable. "We're all equal in God's eyes"; he said that over and over and over again.

That idea of equality is also important

to me as a woman. My parents always said, "Kate, you can be whatever you want to be." They were very supportive, at least verbally, and always encouraged me. Within that context, however, I was still a member of a southern Bible Belt family and part of a culture that told me I shouldn't be too forceful as a girl. Fortunately my dad always said, "if you want to beat those boys in Ping-Pong or basketball, go right ahead." He never told me to hold back in any way.

I consider myself a kind of common, middle-class, regular southern woman. I'm not the made-up debutante or the syrupy "Haaiii, how are yooo?" type, but I'm afraid that all too often women from the South are still portrayed that way. We're still stereotyped as barefoot and pregnant more often than not. That's a very poor generalization. I get very tired of those stereotypes. It's not just southern women who are subject to them but people in all of our subcultures. The media presents the extremes rather than who we actually are. I take the mission to change preconceptions seriously because a lot of people's opinions are formed by *The Dukes of Hazard* or *Hee Haw*. That bugs me. We're not all walking

around barefoot and pregnant, saying "Haaay" while we bat our eyelashes.

That said, I don't set out to write songs from the perspective of a woman per se. I never sit down and say to myself that I want this song to get across a particular point about women. Obviously I'm going to bring the fact that I'm a woman to the table every time I write. "Signs Following" shouldn't be mistaken for a lecture, but it does talk about domestic violence from a religious perspective. I think it's important to bring that subject up. Most of the time car songs are associated with men, but "Galaxie 500" is from the perspective of a girl. I loved that car; it didn't matter that I was a little girl rather than a little boy. There's a lot that we share no matter what gender we are—or what race or where we're from, for that matter. A man could cover my songs in a lot of cases and, on the other side of that equation, I wrote "Tupelo's Too Far" as if Elvis were singing about his life: "I never dreamed I would be a king much less a star." It might seem kind of odd for a woman to be singing in Elvis's first person, but that's how the song worked for me. The point is not to compartmentalize what you do but try to make something that works, for yourself and for everyone else.

So even though a lot of my songs are about where I come from and what I think about my own experience of my culture, I write in order to find a way to connect with other people, whether they share my experience or not. There was one moment five years ago that made me understand that the goal of songwriting, like all art, is making what you know part of a much bigger picture. The way this realization came to me was strange. I was listening to the Chieftains' version of "Will the Circle Be Unbroken" (it seems I've

> I consider myself a regular southern woman. A lot of people's opinions are formed by *The Dukes of Hazard* or *Hee Haw*. That bugs me. We're not all walking around barefoot and pregnant, saying "Haaay" while we bat our eyelashes.

always known that song, first from the Carter family's recordings and later through versions by Emmylou Harris and Dolly Parton I heard at concerts) at the same time I was reading E. M. Forster's novel *Howards End* with its epigraph, "Only connect . . ."

At that moment, listening to Irish musicians (my family all came from the British Isles originally) really getting to the heart of a traditional American folk song, thinking about Forster's epigraph, I understood that we're all connected. Connecting is what I want to do through music: not just connecting my personal memories with my culture but also connecting my own experiences with everyone else's through the

songs. It doesn't matter whether or not the people who listen are from Mississippi or that they've even *seen* Mississippi. I've had letters from people in England who say, "I've never been to Mississippi, but I know what it's like from your songs." When I get that kind of response, I'm completely gratified. That's what art and humanity is all about: making that connection.

Rosanne RANERI

For a long time, I was afraid to have a voice. Just by being, I felt I'd committed some great sin that would be exposed if I revealed too much of who I was. I stayed silent rather than risk the possibility that what I said might show me to be incompetent or ignorant. I sabotaged myself and wouldn't allow my voice to come out.

Then, all of a sudden, I started to feel the absolute necessity of writing and playing music without all those conflicts. After all that self-defeating hesitation, I understood that songwriting is a medium through which I can speak truly. When I was growing up, my sister used to call me a fake because I was so worried about making waves that I buried the truth. Sometimes I still sidestep what's real in order not to be confrontational, but when I write, I *have* to say something that feels true. Writing allows and requires me to do that. When I ask myself

341

now who I am and what I do, I can answer, with a new confidence, "I write music; I'm a singer-songwriter."

There are still times when I may not like the sound of my own voice or wish I could play the guitar better, but I know this is what I want to do, what I love to do. I don't feel that strongly about anything else.

Many of my songs are about crossing boundaries because there are so many that we run up against. Some of them are created by what's expected of us, others define impasses in relationships, and still more are determined by etiquette and courteousness. The idea of breaking through those barriers is a powerful

As I stumble through life, I know with greater certainty that saying how I feel is more important than covering up to make everyone comfortable.

one for me. It's in the line "I ride across the narrow bridge feeling frantic and weightless" and in the chorus of "Unfinished": "There is no edge anymore." Taking a risk is about challenging boundaries, figuring out which ones I've invented that aren't really there or moving beyond the ones that others have set up. For a long time I defined myself through limitations. I'd say to myself, *I can't do that*. We all fall into that trap at some point. As I stumble through life, I know with greater certainty that saying how I feel is more important than covering up to make everyone comfortable. If we can see beyond the limitations we've made or been handed, there's so much more we can do. That's why I need to challenge myself when I write. I want the songs to admonish me, to call me out on something or help me come to a realization I hadn't understood before.

When I was growing up, and even into adulthood, I was obsessed with the fact that I was a big girl. That bothered me a lot even though I was lucky enough to have the support of my family and a lot of interests that I pursued with some success. Still, underlying everything, no matter how much I tried to ignore it, was this subtle and sometimes not so subtle feeling that I wasn't quite right. I tried to console myself by thinking I'd be okay when I changed and started to look different, that this was a "problem" I could "fix" someday. There were moments in adolescence when I saw friends going out with boys and thought, *I don't have that.* I never had a self-image so poor that I'd shut myself inside the house

and refuse to go out again, but I did obsess over how I looked. Much later—in my mid-twenties—I became really angry that the culture defines attractiveness for women in such a limited way. Why should I have to compare myself negatively to painfully thin models with "ideal" measurements that aren't a reality for most of us? Getting over the feeling that there was something wrong with me because

I didn't fit that picture was the best thing that ever happened to me.

When I was twenty-five, I was in a bookstore with some friends who were making fun of a book called *Real Women Don't Diet*. I waited until they walked away, and then I went right over, pulled that book off the shelf, and bought it. I'm ashamed now that I didn't buy it right in front of them. When I read that book, I felt grateful that there were other women out there who refused to feel bad because they didn't fit into society's preconceptions about how women should look. Since that time there hasn't been any question that it's okay to be who I am. Even the absolute anger I had back then when I felt like yelling to the world, "This is not right!" has abated. I haven't let the anger go entirely, and I'm still dedicated to changing attitudes about women's bodies, but now I try to "be" rather than looking to go to war over it. It shouldn't be a fight.

In a way I feel that I've come

back to the spontaneity and unselfconsciousness I felt as a child. Before I became self-conscious, my mom says I was a natural ham. She's got videotapes of me dancing around with this funny braided hairdo, high-kicking in the living room, just having a ball. I like having that spirit again. I want to reclaim all of it. My mom's main philosophy has always been to follow your spirit where it leads you. She made me feel beautiful, smart, and powerful, that I could do anything. The women in my family have always taken risks. They speak loudly and move grandly. They have been overwhelmingly generous and kind. They have handed down to me such a positive legacy as women who do nothing half-heartedly. So it's not surprising that my mother never tried to squelch my freedom. I did a lot of musical theater and drama when I was younger, and I was never afraid of performing back then. I loved being up there, interacting with people. I'm coming back to that simple, pleasurable feeling of performing that I had as a kid.

The first house that I lived in was a duplex, and behind it was an undeveloped area, just woods and water. I was fascinated by the bark that rolled off the birch trees like paper. Its surface was so smooth you could actually write on it. And there was a pond. I can't see the path to get there, but I can see the pond and around its edge, different kinds of moss. One kind was called "red soldiers" because it had little red caps. I took that magical place in the middle of nowhere for granted when I was a kid. In the yard there were swings, and I could look up while I swung and see unhindered sky, nothing in the way. My

> I became really angry that the culture defines attractiveness for women in such a limited way.

friend Josh and I would sit on the swings and name the clouds. "I see an angel"; "I see a pirate." I wrote about those memories in "Backyard": "Run to the forest / drop our secrets, light as feathers, in the pond / take the bark that's fallen from white birch trees / to carve our pictures on / race to the wooden swing / saw so many angels made of clouds / did you know / the dried up garden in the back yard was ours / so were the falling stars."

When I was very young, before the message that I was supposed to be a good girl got to me, I was the ringleader in my family. I made my brother and sister do artsy things with me. We formed bands, performed dances, made films—you name it. I was bursting with energy, and I wanted to pull them along. It was fun and chaotic all the time at home. At some point I started to feel very self-conscious and turned away from all that energy. Instead of inciting them to be wild, I became the policeman who kept my brother and sister

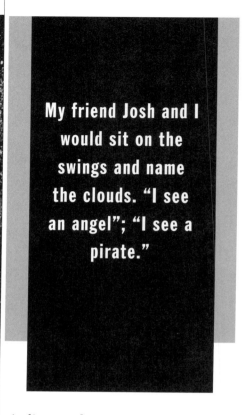

My friend Josh and I would sit on the swings and name the clouds. "I see an angel"; "I see a pirate."

in line, making sure they didn't get into trouble. My dad could be a little intimidating. We didn't see all that much of him, and when we did see him, he was a quiet presence. When he spoke, it was often in a "must have order" tone. I just picked right up on that. I lived by the rule that "Nothing bad must happen!" I became the peacemaker or, better yet, the diplomat. I wanted to see everything through rose-colored glasses and to make everyone feel okay about everything. My dad was the voice of reason, and I started listening to that voice, trying to be a good girl.

The thought that his children—and I was the first one to own up to it—wanted to go into the arts was a disturbing thing for my father at first. He used to leave brochures about careers in optometry, dentistry, or the law on the dining room table and mention, very subtly, that he'd left some information that we might want to check out. My beautiful, eccentric dad! I remember him touting careers in optometry, telling us, "People need their eyes"! I know he just wanted to just see us safe and able to take care of ourselves. He wanted me to go to col-

> In high school I got an electric guitar because I wanted to be cool and learn power chords. I learned a Duran Duran song or two and that was it.

lege, which I agreed was something I'd love to do, but he also wanted me to have a "real" career, if not as a lawyer or optometrist, then at least as an educator. When he realized I was going to major in theater, he didn't see why I couldn't get a teaching degree just to back it up. When I refused to have a backup, it was as if I had said to him, "I'm gonna be poor, and I'm okay with that." Now I feel a lump in my throat for what he was going through. My mother was saying to him, "Honey, she'll be fine," while he alone bore the burden of imagining a difficult future for me. Despite that burden, he said, "Here's the money for college. Be in theater." Once he saw that I was being given opportunities to perform and that people were acknowledging what I was doing, he felt reassured. Since I've been focusing on music, he's been incredibly responsive and will do just about anything to support me.

My mother always said that music was

and make up songs on the piano as a kid, I wanted to be an actress so I didn't pay much attention to her prophecy. In junior high I hadn't yet learned to play the guitar, but I'd taken piano lessons. In seventh grade I made some new friends through a musical and wrote a couple of songs for them. They were cute little blossoming-love songs and friendship songs. In high school I got an electric guitar because I wanted to be cool and learn power chords. I stuck with it for a cou-

going to make its way back to me. Even though I always liked to sing

ple of months, learned a Duran Duran song or two and that was it. I tried to play "De Do Do Do, De Da Da Da" by the Police but couldn't do it justice, so I put the electric down.

My mom had this old Stella that had been around the house forever. I'd always held it in high esteem and never touched it, but I finally took it to college with me and during my junior year started writing songs on it. I remembered a couple of chords from when I had the electric, and I began with those. Learning to write my own songs with that old guitar changed everything. Unlike performing in the theater, where the focus was on putting on a show, speaking someone else's words, and being part of a group, writing songs required me to be honest with myself.

When I picked up a guitar and wrote, all of a sudden there were my words and my voice alone echoing in the room. That allowed me not to feel strange about being by myself and representing in my own way whatever view I saw out of my window. College was a great time. We were all so productive and stimulated by everything that was going on. There was so much opportunity to do so many things with so many people. Then, all of a sudden, I was back in my room playing the guitar, writing songs. The solitude, and what it inspired in me, was incredibly empowering.

> You know how a snake uses its tongue to read its environment because its other senses are not as keen? In a similar way, playing music helps me sense where people are at emotionally.

A lot of songwriters I talk to agree that what we do is a selfish thing. You get to mouth off about how you feel and get a lot of attention for it. That's true enough. Writing and performing is also a way for me to gauge people. You know how a snake uses its tongue to read its environment because its other senses are not as keen? In a similar way, playing music helps me sense where people are at emotionally. When I couldn't express myself in everyday interactions for fear of revealing too much of myself, music was a way to be with people, no damage done. It's a way to communicate even when they're silently listening. You can see so much in people's faces, in

When I realize that I'm holding back, not taking any action at all, not taking a chance because of fear, that's when I become fierce about the need to take risks.

their eyes or in their gestures, how they move to the music. Sometimes it's less intuitive than that. People come right out and say, "Thank you for the music." But I'm the one that's thankful for the connection they make with me. I hesitated to treat music as a career for so long because being in a space with other people and the music was so gratifying in itself. It was hard for me to conceive of anything beyond that.

I played my first open mic night in college. I'd written all of three songs but decided I was going to sign up anyway. It was the theater person in me that made it possible to try it. I told myself, *I'm not just going to learn to swim, I'm gonna go dive into the ocean.* It wasn't too deep a plunge; most of the people in the audience were my very forgiving friends. It turned out to be a casual atmosphere; it felt like playing in a living room. Once I got my feet wet, I wanted to do it again. It was absolutely liberating.

The summer after college I began play-

ing at Caffe Lena, the coffeehouse in Saratoga Springs, New York, where Bob Dylan performed in 1963 and, legend has it, Don McLean premiered "American Pie" after writing it on napkins at a nearby bar. The first night I played there, I could feel my face burning. I thought, *Wow, I'm really casting off from shore, letting the boat go.* And then there was a moment when I could have wept. I know that sounds silly, but I felt that people were listening and, more than listening, *hearing* me. We all struggle a lot with that: "You didn't hear me right" or "Are you listening to me?" That night I was *heard.* I felt like George Emerson in the film of *A Room with a View* when he climbs up a tree and screams, "Yes! Yes! Yes!" because he feels a connection to Lucy Honeychurch, to the world. She doesn't understand what he's doing up there, but he feels at peace with the universe. That's what I felt. After that incredible experience I started playing every Thursday night at open mic and became a member of that community. I loved the feeling of being part of a group even while I was sharing the part of myself that came out of the solitude. Going the way of the coffeehouse and open mics not only affords you a testing ground where you can get honest feedback about your material but also lets you learn your craft at the perfect pace. I felt I was in a nest with a lot of time to grow. I never felt any pressure, and the most beautiful thing was the fact that I was *encouraged*. I was applauded for trying. There was no one saying, "Don't bother."

Of course, some people wanted to make sure I foresaw the difficulty of making music a career and others wanted to help by directing me. There were some uncomfortable moments when I had to navigate the waters stirred up by people who have experience and want you to acknowledge that. They say, in effect, "What you've done so far is great, but here's what you've got to do now." In the midst of all that, you need to remember that the path you take, whether in writing music or devel-

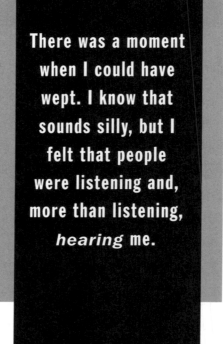

There was a moment when I could have wept. I know that sounds silly, but I felt that people were listening and, more than listening, *hearing* me.

oping a career, has to come from you. I was learning how to take information in and process it. If I'd tried to pursue music in another way—if I hadn't taken the time to work everything out for myself—I would have been lost and retreated. As it happened, I didn't retreat but just kept moving forward very slowly.

Part of that process involves learning

new things as a writer. After writing a lot in the first person, I'm trying now to use the voice of an outside narrator. That perspective lets me comment on what the character taches to the autobiographical first person. I'm experimenting with letting myself comment on the impact that

in the song sees and does with a different kind of clarity. Writing as an outsider lets me be grittier and takes away the fear that attaches a person or situation can have when I'm not the one who's experienced it firsthand. In those situations I don't have to feel any single way about what I'm describing. I can be

more objective, more various, free of sentiment. Instead of exploring a subject personally and holding something back, I can approach a situation with a certain harshness that I can't always summon when I'm writing from my own perspective. Joni Mitchell is a writer who makes astonishing songs out of what is uncomfortable. She finds beauty in what most of us overlook or take for granted. To write songs that do that is a goal worth pursuing.

The desire to get at other realities and other kinds of experience in my writing reflects where I'm trying to go in my life too. The harshest criticism I can level at myself is that I'm a coward. I'm much less susceptible to that criticism than I used to be. When I realize that

I'm holding back, not taking any action at all, not taking a chance because of fear, that's when I become fierce about the need to take risks. Even if the decision I make turns out to be the wrong one, I'm more than willing to take responsibility for it. When I read a book and confront a character who's really *living*, I ask myself why I'm not having those passionate and creative moments in my life. Being forced to consider that question pushes my buttons and makes me act more spontaneously. I'm pursuing more actively what I was too afraid to do in the past. I'm at a point in my life when I'm doing things I haven't done before. I want to take it all in.

Acknowledgments

Thanks and love to our parents—Peter, Susan, Bruce, Jenny and Steve—for everything. And to CB for her inspiration.

To all the artists in *Solo* who so generously gave us their time and words: we appreciate your kindness, energy and genius. We'd also like to thank the following people without whose assistance and interest we would have been unable to make our idea into a book: for Jonatha Brooke: Patrick Rains and Marion Wheeler-Henderson at PRA; for Mary Chapin Carpenter: Cal!, William Smithson at Borman Entertainment, Joni Foraker, Denise McIntosh at Loeb and Loeb, Myra Covington, Mary Ann McCready at FBS Financial, Seth Cohen at Shore Fire Media; for Kate Campbell: Kimberly Baum at Compass Records, and Ira Campbell; for Rosanne Cash: Danny Cahn, Merilee Heifetz; for Shawn Colvin: Lisa Arzt and Ron Fierstein at AGF, Kim Kaiman at Columbia; for Sheryl Crow: Pam Wertheimer (xo) at Weintraub Management—and Scout!; for Catie Curtis: Randy Haecker at Guardian; for Ani DiFranco: Joanna Gillespie, Scot Fisher and all the fine folks at Righteous Babe Records, Andy Stochansky, and Tracy Hill; for Dionne Farris: Miguel Bageur, Randy Jackson and company at Columbia, Wayne Rooks; for Jewel: Ken Weinstein, Patti Conte and Natalie Caplan at Atlantic, Bridget Hanley, and Nedra; for Lucy Kaplansky: Megan Zinn, David Tamulevich at Fleming, Tamulevich, and Ur Kell; for Mary Lou Lord: David Meinert at Curtis Management, Vickie Starr at Girlie Action Media, Maggie at Kill Rock Stars; for Sarah McLachlan: Terry McBride and Shauna Gold at Nettwerk Management; for Joan Osborne: Wendy Horowitz and Brett Raidon at DAS, Bruce Hartley at

Mercury; for Holly Palmer: Alexandra at Allies; for Rosanne Raneri: Tony Markellis, bassist, producer, artist nonpareil; for Suzanne Vega: Lisa Arzt at AGF, Steve Karras at A&M; for Lucinda Williams: Frank Collari at FCC Management, Heidi Ellen Robinson at American, and Richard Price; for Cassandra Wilson: Bruce Lundvall at Blue Note Records, Mark Satlof and Jordan Kessler at Shore Fire Media, Alex Hartnett, Ed Gerrard at Dream Street Management.

Thank you Jennifer Hengen, agent extraordinaire, at Sterling Lord Literistic for taking us and *Solo* on. Thanks also to Amy Yellin at SLL. Kudos and thanks to Jacob Hoye, supreme editor, whose sweetness and patience is matched only by his great taste in music. Thanks to Tia Williams at Dell. Best to Marc Smirnoff and all the gang at the *Oxford American*. Thanks to Natalie and Gary Waleik for good advice. Love to Rick Litvin for laughter, genius and company. Thanks Paul Safran for the FedEx Xpress. Thanks to Linda Steinman at Dell legal. Thank you Hillary Frey, the magnificent, for editorial help and general support. Thanks to Rachel Ehrlich for all-around brilliance. And to Bill Duffy, John Danison and Tom Travis for computer intelligence beyond the realm of mere mortals. A Druidic dance of gratitude inside a circle of standing stones for Linke. Thanks and love to Robert and Peg Boyers, and Tom Lewis, as always, for everything. Thanks and a toast to Michael Moore. To Wanda, Karen, Nancy and Carol for love and help on the homefront. Special-most nuzzlings and muzzlings to all those at Fluke Farm, Unincorporated, without whom we could not live: Kodah, Nick, Bela, Brayer, Shammi, Ming-Ming, TT, Gussie, Lamby, Kaboom, Vendela and Vidor plus Vega, the monkey-faced pansy-horse—and the king, Boch, son of God and cigar.

ABOUT
the authors

Emma Dodge Hanson and **Marc Wood-worth** live on a farm near Saratoga Springs, New York. Emma is a photographer whose portraits of artists and writers have appeared in *The New York Times*, *Poets and Writers*, *USA Today*, *The Oxford American*, and elsewhere. Marc is associate editor of *Salmagundi* and lectures in the Department of English at Skidmore College. His poems appear in *The Paris Review* and other magazines. This is their first book.

Artist Biographies

Jonatha Brooke's most recent album, *10¢ Wings*, was hailed by *Billboard* as "signaling the grand ascent of one of the most gifted and unique artists of the decade." After releasing two critically acclaimed albums, *Grace in Gravity* and *The Angel in the House*, with the Story in the early 1990s, Jonatha went solo. Her subsequent collections of songs, *Plumb* and *10¢ Wings*, are distinguished by her inimitable blend of poetically charged lyrics and a richly eclectic musical sensibility. Deeply imagined and unfailingly moving, Jonatha's music is distinguished by an "unfettered, expressive voice and intelligent lyrics that give these songs their wings" (*San Francisco Examiner & Chronicle*). Along with touring all over the country,

Jonatha has appeared on *In Concert on ABC, Mountain Stage, E-Town*, and *World Cafe*.

Kate Campbell's 1998 Compass Records release, *Visions of Plenty*, solidifies her reputation as one of the most engaging voices in the contemporary folk genre today. Campbell's music falls somewhere between Memphis and Muscle Shoals. *Billboard* lauded her as "one of the most innovative and fresh writers around . . . a songwriting dandy." Critics have praised Campbell's sweet, smoky vocals and her gifted ability to weave poetic images into a quilt of beautiful melodies. Her two previous critically acclaimed Compass albums, *Songs from the Levee* and *Moonpie Dreams*, earned her the *Farm Journal* Farm Song of the Year award for "Bury Me in Bluegrass" and a nomination for Folk Album of the Year from the Nashville Music Association. Campbell continues to impress audiences throughout the U.S. and abroad and has appeared on *Prime Time Country*, NPR's *All Things Considered*, and in the critically acclaimed southern music issue of *The Oxford American*.

Multiplatinum recording artist **Mary Chapin Carpenter** has received five Grammy Awards, two Country Music Association Awards, and a host of other honors since she released her debut album, *Hometown Girl*, in 1987. Her most recent albums, *Stones in the Road* and *A Place in the World*, reveal a maturation of her formidable gifts as a singer-songwriter, leading *The New York Times* to write that "the quality in Ms. Carpenter's music that bridges conventional categories is a down-to-earth directness and rock-bottom honesty." In addition to her six albums and a PBS concert film, *Jubilee,* she's written a children's book, *Dreamland*, and contributed an essay to *A Voice of Our Own*, a book commemorating the seventy-fifth anniversary of women's suffrage.

When **Rosanne Cash** released *Interiors* in 1990, she not only departed from the country music that had made her a star over the previous decade, but crafted a masterpiece. This harrowing chronicle of a breakup confirmed Rosanne's remarkable talents as a lyricist with songs that are intelligent and astonishingly frank. *The Wheel* was further evidence that she had turned her gifts into something extraordinary. As one of our most literate lyricists, Rosanne naturally began to turn to longer prose pieces, and in her first collection, *Bodies of Water*, her writing is "wise, funny, and eloquent . . . as deeply affecting as her songs" (*Booklist*). Her most recent album, *10 Song Demo*, released during the same season as *Bodies of Water*, proves an extraordinary companion piece to the stories. Rosanne's blend of emotional candor and artistic control, whether on the page or in a song, is unmistakably her own and deeply powerful.

Shawn Colvin was born in South Dakota, where she began teaching herself to play guitar at the age of ten. In 1983 she moved to New York City and launched a solo career, attracting loyal listeners in Boston and New York folk circles. Her Columbia debut, *Steady On*, won a Grammy, a feat twice repeated nine years later when "Sunny Came Home" from Shawn's 1997 breakthrough album, *A Few Small Repairs*, was named Record and Song of the Year. In the interim, Shawn released two critically acclaimed albums, *Fat City* and *Cover Girl*, a collection of favorite songs by other songwriters. Her work has not only been a success with critics and fans, but also with accomplished artists like Mary Chapin Carpenter, who praises her "extraordinarily original vision as a songwriter." The emergence of that originality is preserved on *Live '88* (Plump Records), a re-release on CD of the brilliant "live tape" Shawn made before she released her first studio album.

Born to musical parents in Missouri and trained as a classical pianist, **Sheryl Crow** released her first album after an apprenticeship as a backup singer for Rod Stewart and Michael Jackson, among others. *Tuesday Night Music Club* earned her a Grammy for best new artist and featured the enormously popular single "All I Wanna Do." Sheryl's eponymously titled second album yielded three major hits and won her many accolades and two Grammy awards. Her songs resonate with vivid characters and reveal the sensibility of an accomplished wordsmith. In addition to performing in Bosnia as part of a USO tour (an experience that was the catalyst for her song "Redemption Day"), Sheryl sang the title track for the latest James Bond film, *Tomorrow Never Dies*—two disparate items on her distinguished résumé that indicate the broad and eclectic nature of this singular artist.

Dubbed a "folk-rock goddess" by *The New Yorker*, **Catie Curtis** writes and performs songs that embody the lushness of pop and the storytelling of folk. By the time Catie signed with a major label in 1995, she had been touring nationally for five years, playing the grass-roots folk circuit on the strength of two independently produced recordings, *Dandelion* and *From Years to Hours*. Her Guardian debut, *Truth from Lies*, is "a remarkably self-assured and revealing collection of songs" (*Chicago Tribune*) that received enthusiastic reviews from hundreds of publications across the country. Her most recent, self-titled album features songs based on everything from bits of conversation overheard while on the road to the headlines of long-forgotten news stories, and the lives of people who populate small New England towns like the one in which she was raised. As *The New York Times* wrote, "In a folk-pop field awash with romantic self-dramatization and literary pretension, Ms. Curtis is a promising voice on behalf of truthful understatement."

Ani DiFranco began singing and playing acoustic guitar when she was nine, moved out of her parents' home in Buffalo, New York, at fifteen, started writing songs around the same time, and founded her own record company (the aptly named Righteous Babe Records) when she turned twenty. Eleven albums and well over a thousand concerts later, *The New York Times* now calls the twenty-seven-year old "one of the country's most successful completely independent musicians." That independence allows her to conduct her career completely on her own terms; she chooses the artists she wants to work with, produces her own releases, and sets her own touring and recording schedule. The same spirit can be felt in her music; her songs are political, poetic, and intensely personal—often all at the same time. Yet Ani's work is impossible to pigeonhole: In recent years she has toured with Bob Dylan, collaborated with storyteller Utah Phillips, recorded with the Buffalo Philharmonic Orchestra, covered a classic hymn and a Bacharach/David pop hit, and paid tribute in concert to both Woody Guthrie and Prince. As Robert Christgau has observed in *The Village Voice*,

"DiFranco opens up a secret subcultural life, in which folk and punk idealism enjoy genuine fusion."

After making her initial mark on the music scene as the voice of Arrested Development's "Tennessee," a Grammy-winning single, **Dionne Farris** released her first solo album, *Wild Seed — Wild Flower*, an eclectic collection of songs that testifies to this artist's wide-ranging talent. Dionne's music is an innovative collage, blending elements of funk, soul, jazz, rock, and blues and bringing it all together with a passionate, gutsy voice that weaves a message of hope and encouragement with "the gospel fire of Aretha, the easy wail and swoop of Chaka Khan, and the genial grit of Bonnie Raitt" (*San Francisco Chronicle*). On the heels of her Top Ten single, "I Know," Dionne shared the bill on a much-heralded summer tour with the Dave Matthews Band. Her success and creative achievement are just recompense for an artist who's willing to follow her muse in such a fresh and honest direction.

Jewel's music is defined by its ability to reach out and make an unfiltered and immediate connection with the listener. That connection has been responsible for making this charmingly idiosyncratic singer-songwriter from Homer, Alaska, one of contemporary music's most popular artists. Along with singing the national anthem at the 1998 Superbowl and appearing on the cover of *Time* magazine, Jewel's debut album, *Pieces of You*, has been certified five-times platinum in the U.S. alone, and her single "Foolish Games / You Were Meant for Me" set a record for longevity on the *Billboard* charts. But this imaginative and inspired artist's intelligence and sense of balance suggest that she's less impressed with the trappings of success than with the progress of her soul. Her first book of poems was published earlier this year and she will star in director Ang Lee's Civil War drama *To Live On*.

Lucy Kaplansky's two albums, *The Tide* and *Flesh and Bone* (Red House Records), are rich collections by a "penetratingly intelligent singer-songwriter" (*Boston Globe*) whose work is defined by what Greg Brown calls "the voice of an angel you find in an alley." After graduating from high school in Chicago, where she grew up, Lucy came to New York in the late 70's to join the resurgent Greenwich Village folk scene. As Shawn Colvin remembers: "I heard Lucy the first night I came to New York in the winter of 1980 at Gerdes Folk City. Then and thereafter," her former musical partner continues, "her singing has been a source of amazement, comfort, and inspiration to me." After leaving the folk scene to work as a psychologist during the latter half of the 80s, Lucy returned to music with a passion, writing (often with her husband, Rick Litvin) and recording the material for *Flesh and Bone*, an album that the Associated Press hailed as "an extraordinary, luminous collection of songs with lyrics that read like poetry . . . easily one of the best albums of the year."

Mary Lou Lord can still be found on occasion playing her favorite venue—the Park Street station T stop in Boston—even since the release of her major label debut, *Got No Shadow*, a recording of "refreshing originality" that contains "a cache of memorable songs" (*Billboard*). The album includes a few inspired covers as well as some true gems written with Nick Saloman of the Bevis Frond, but, as *Rolling Stone* noted, the album's "real story is the one Lord tells alone, about a woman settling into herself." The earlier portion of that process is in evidence on two Kill Rock Stars EPs, *Mary Lou Lord* and *Martian Saints*. Whether you're listening to Mary Lou's story on good speakers from the comfort of your couch or leaning against a girder in the subway, you know you're the recipient of a gift from a rare artist with an astonishingly intimate voice and a clear purchase on what it means to be real.

Sarah McLachlan was born in Halifax, Nova Scotia, in 1968 and has been on a musical path ever since. Following years spent studying classical piano, guitar, and voice, the singer was discovered fronting a new wave band in 1985 by the then-fledgling Vancouver-based company Nettwerk Records. Since that time she has released four albums of evocative and deeply emotional music, including *Touch*, *Solace*, and her U.S. breakthrough, *Fumbling Towards Ecstasy*. Her most recent recording—*Surfacing* (1997)—won four Juno awards and two Grammys, including one for Best Female Pop Vocal Performance for "Building a Mystery." During the past two summers, Lilith Fair, the traveling concert caravan conceived by Sarah and featuring a host of female-fronted acts, has been a resounding success.

Joan Osborne's songs are rich in visual wit and a filmmaker's eye for detail, while her voice, as *Billboard* observes, "manifests an almost mystical grasp of a culture in spiritual disarray." Joan's major label debut, *Relish*, went on to sell more than two million copies worldwide and was hailed by *Rolling Stone* as "riveting" and was named the number one album of the year by *Entertainment Weekly*, well-deserved praise after years of club gigs in New York and the release of two previous albums on her own Womanly Hips label, which are now available on the compilation *Early Recordings*. In addition to writing and recording her next album, Joan traveled to New Delhi, India, where she studied Qwaali singing, an ancient form of religious Indian music. She also performed at the VH1 Honors concert that paid tribute to the global human rights organization Witness. A former film student at New York University, Joan made her directorial debut with the video for her song "St. Teresa."

Holly Palmer was born in Santa Monica, California, but did most of her growing up in Redmond, Washington. Singing almost since the day she was born, she also played the flute and later the saxophone. She moved to Boston to study music at the urging of a trumpet-player friend and started writing songs around that same time. She moved to New York City in 1994 and signed a record deal with Reprise Records almost exactly a year later. Her debut album came out in the fall of 1996 and is filled with what Stephen Holden of *The New York Times* calls "sexy dream songs." *The London Sunday Times* calls the album "a sensual delight with a topping of intellectual chic," acknowledging her as their "Female Newcomer of the Year." Holly spent most of 1997 touring with k. d. Lang, Shawn Colvin, and Paula Cole, and is now hard at work on her second release.

A native of the Capital District in upstate New York, **Rosanne Raneri** is a young singer-songwriter whose emotionally stirring performances and deeply accomplished songwriting make her "one of the most powerful young voices in music" (Bruce Cockburn). Rosanne brings to her performances a presence that is

as moving as it is forceful and a voice that is by turns pure, impassioned, and haunting. Her self-released debut, *Frantic and Weightless* (Memory Red Records, P.O. Box 62, Troy, NY 12182), is not the work of a novice, but a fully realized collection of original songs that find the elusive balance between necessity and surprise and make a listener return again and again for solace and pleasure. The new songs Rosanne has been performing live for an avid and growing audience promise that her next album will place this extraordinary singer-songwriter in the first rank of her generation's essential artists.

Hailed by *The New York Times* for her 1985 debut as "the strongest, most decisively shaped songwriting personality to come along in years," **Suzanne Vega** has continued to develop as an artist whose intensely personal vision consistently lifts her songs into the realm of art. Her second release, *Solitude Standing*, yielded the haunting "Luka" and brought Suzanne's music to a worldwide audience. Since that commercial breakthrough, her subsequent work on *Days of Open Hand* and *99.9F°* has led critics to write that "she's now beyond borders, making an unaffected art music that's heady, heartfelt, very demanding . . . and very rewarding" (*Rolling Stone*). Suzanne's most recent album, *Nine Objects of Desire* (A&M), is a compelling song cycle by a masterful writer who displays a deep musical and emotional intelligence honed to a very fine edge.

Most country and pop music fans know **Lucinda Williams** for writing "Passionate Kisses," "The Night's Too Long," and "Changed the Locks," songs that became hits for Mary Chapin Carpenter, Patty Loveless, and Tom Petty. But no matter how convincingly these artists render her material, Williams's careworn drawl is still the best vehicle for her unflinching portrayals of longing and loss. Following the extraordinary recordings *Lucinda Williams* and *Passionate Kisses*, her latest album and her first with Mercury Records, *Car Wheels on a Gravel Road*, extends Lucinda's reputation as an uncompromising writer whose passion and force have drawn the attention not only of contemporary music's best songsmiths, but of a large and growing number of discerning listeners as well.

Contralto/composer **Cassandra Wilson** was born and raised in Jackson, Mississippi. Widely regarded as the top jazz singer of her generation, Ms. Wilson is praised as an innovator who has reinvented the art form and expanded its boundaries on such recent albums as *Blue Light 'til Dawn* and *New Moon Daughter*. In 1997 *The New York Times* wrote of her voice: "There's nothing like it in American music." A gifted songwriter as well as a unique interpreter, she has eleven albums as a leader to her credit, and more than thirty recorded collaborations with other artists and contributions to compilation albums. Ms. Wilson has lived in New York City's Harlem for over a decade.